Unlocking the Nature of Human Aggression

Unlocking the Nature of Human Aggression is a neuropsychoanalytic and scientific exploration of aggression and argues for its central role in psychopathology and the genesis of individual symptoms, as well as in broader systemic conflicts and violence.

Adrian Perkel creates a unique theoretical approach to the various manifestations we encounter of individual, group, and geopolitical aggression and destructiveness. Based on psychoanalytic investigations of this dynamic and Freud's incomplete exploration of this human drive, this book seeks to understand the science of aggression that Freud himself suggested would be possible with time and scientific development. Perkel investigates the commonplace inversion of the perpetrator and victim narratives, navigating through the complexity of how the aggressive drive, often driven by feelings aimed at homeostatic regulation, challenges the perception of any objective view of who is perpetrator and who victim. He includes his own personal experiences of South African Apartheid, as well as historical and contemporary data such as speeches from historical figures during times of war, including the Second World War and the Ukrainian/Russian conflict.

Offering a fresh and innovative insight into the nature of this paradoxical drive in humans, this book integrates the psychology, psychodynamics, and neuroscience of modern research into a coherent exposition of this key aspect of psychic functioning in humans. It is an essential read for analysts in practice and training, psychologists and other mental health professionals, and students looking for a modernised theoretical model of the destructive and aggressive drive of the psyche to facilitate better interventions for individual and couple patients and for interventions at systemic and organisational levels.

Dr. Adrian Perkel (M.A. Clin. Psych.; D.Phil.) is a registered practising clinical psychologist based in Cape Town. Since 1989, he has been lecturing, writing, supervising other professionals, and practising psychotherapy. His work is deeply informed by psychoanalysis and neuroscience.

Unlocking the Nature of Human Aggression

A Psychoanalytic and Neuroscientific Approach

Adrian Perkel

LONDON AND NEW YORK

Designed cover image: © Pobytov / Getty Images

First published 2024
by Routledge
4 Park Square, Milton Park, Abingdon, Oxon OX14 4RN

and by Routledge
605 Third Avenue, New York, NY 10158

Routledge is an imprint of the Taylor & Francis Group, an informa business

British Library Cataloguing-in-Publication Data
A catalogue record for this book is available from the British Library

Library of Congress Cataloging-in-Publication Data
Names: Perkel, Adrian Keith, author.
Title: Unlocking the nature of human aggression : a psychoanalytic
and neuroscientific approach / Adrian Perkel.
Description: Abingdon, Oxon ; New York, NY : Routledge, 2024. |
Includes bibliographical references and index. |
Identifiers: LCCN 2023034397 (print) | LCCN 2023034398 (ebook) |
ISBN 9781032590066 (hardback) | ISBN 9781032590059 (paperback) |
ISBN 9781003452522 (ebook)
Subjects: LCSH: Aggressiveness.
Classification: LCC BF175.5.A36 P47 2024 (print) |
LCC BF175.5.A36 (ebook) | DDC 155.2/32—dc23/eng/20230811
LC record available at https://lccn.loc.gov/2023034397
LC ebook record available at https://lccn.loc.gov/2023034398

ISBN: 978-1-032-59006-6 (hbk)
ISBN: 978-1-032-59005-9 (pbk)
ISBN: 978-1-003-45252-2 (ebk)

DOI: 10.4324/9781003452522

Typeset in Times New Roman
by codeMantra

To those who lit the spark
The Jester and the Butterfly
To those who keep the flame aflame
Jenny and Michaela

Contents

About the Author   *ix*
Preface   *xi*

Introduction   1

Chapter 1: Freud's Incomplete Theory   8

Chapter 2: The Development of Subject – "I"   21

Chapter 3: Beyond the Pleasure Principle   33

Chapter 4: Science and the Psyche   57

Chapter 5: Perversion of the Inner Guardian   86

Chapter 6: Geopolitics Meets Freud   121

Chapter 7: A Unifying Theory – Symptoms and Implications   150

Chapter 8: Concluding Comments   165

Appendices   *167*
Acknowledgements   *185*
Bibliography   *188*
Index   *193*

About the Author

Dr. Adrian Perkel (M.A. Clin. Psych.; D.Phil.) is a clinical psychologist and former senior lecturer in Psychology at the University of the Western Cape. He
has been immersed in psychoanalytic theory, writing, and clinical practice, specialising in individual adult and couple psychotherapy for over three decades.
He has been involved in numerous psychoanalytical, neuroscience, and editorial organisations both in South Africa and abroad, including the South African
Psychoanalytic Confederation and the South African Psychoanalytic Initiative
(SAPI) Psychotherapy College, and is a founding member of the Association
of Couple Psychoanalytic Psychotherapists (ACPP). He is also on the editorial
board of the professional journal *Psychoanalytic Practice* (formerly *Psychoanalytic Psychotherapy in South Africa*) and is a member of the International Ad-
visory Board of the *Couple and Family Psychoanalysis* journals. He has focused
his research over the past years on the aggressive drive in symptom formation
and couple conflict.

Preface

"We have decided to execute you straight away", he says to me as he briskly enters the room where I have been sitting since dawn, picking up an R4 rifle and pointing it at my chest. There is little emotion in his voice.

This member of the notorious Security Branch of the South African Police tells me this is their decision. His colleague has been guarding me all day since my detention before dawn that winter Monday morning. I am being held under the State of Emergency Security Laws which allow for indefinite and incommunicado detention. I find myself on the infamous 10th floor of John Vorster Square Police Headquarters, the notorious blue and white building in downtown Johannesburg.

It is 1986, still four years before the African National Congress is unbanned. Nelson Mandela is still in prison. I am quietly mulling my surroundings and the awareness that I am in the same office in which Dr. Neil Aggett, a medical doctor and activist, had been tortured to death four years previously. I had attended his funeral, alongside tens of thousands of others. The authorities said he committed suicide in his cell. It was to be many years before his death and the many deaths in this blue and white building would be reframed as murder.

Indefinite detention and solitary confinement are not easy. Stripped of all vestiges of control and human contact, the psyche quickly becomes vulnerable and distressed. Compounding this with hostile and often violent torture and interrogation, an uncertain future, and the constant challenges to normal defences and self-protection, the sense of dread and victimhood becomes a detainees' constant companion.[1] How you breathe, pee, and eat, what you say, do, or see is controlled by others. It is not a game, it is deadly serious, and for those who ended up dead through 'committing suicide', 'slipping on the soap', or 'falling out the window'[2] this experience of victimhood was hyperreal.[3] This was the height of Apartheid South Africa's civil war reaching its crescendo and spasms of violence and struggle.

Alone in the office on the tenth floor, the situation is intimate as the Security Policemen and I contemplate my impending execution. In those nanoseconds that the mind can process moments of crisis, I am not convinced such a noisy and messy method would be their choice. My guard has been telling me all day that what I represent is dangerous. I am struck by his perception that I am the threat in this equation. How could I possibly be the threat? Alone, vulnerable, and without any vestiges of control. I was, my interrogators would keep telling me, a perpetrator threatening their fabric of stability and civilisation, furthering the aims of powers arraigned like a total onslaught against the state and its people. It was indeed political, but it was also personal. Their lives, lifestyles, and security, and their families and futures were under attack. Who did I think I was, the one interrogator had repeatedly shouted at me in salty language, in my naive gullibility and martyred idealism to threaten them and contribute to this untenable situation? Did I really want to get slaughtered in my bed if the barricades came down and they were defeated?

There was a point at which the inversions of who was the victim and who was the perpetrator got weird and confusing. Alone and cold in my cell later that evening, I began to consider this inversion, and it gradually became clearer to me: first, it was a function of perspective and subjectivity; second, it was a function of who was preserving what interest and identity; and third, the greater the perception of threat, the greater the resort to the use of various forms of aggression. These inversions appeared in many places when I began to explore them, and as the science and psychology wrestled with these questions through my career, it became muddier and more vexing, riddled with paradox and counter-intuitive tensions that required answers.

The scourge of human aggression against other humans has plagued humanity since time immemorial, and as it turns out, probably originated before humanity even existed. In fact, the science has shown us that this aggressive drive probably had its roots as early as when molecular life stirred from its beginnings in the inorganic deep in the earth and oceans and became animate. Did electron gradients in hydrothermal vents billions of years ago have a link to the development of later human aggression?

In ways unique amongst the species, humans have the capacity to destroy each other at scale in endlessly macabre and inventive forms and to transgress against their own species in ways that seem to make little evolutionary sense. Often, individual squabbles, conflicts, and violence in the domestic space find parallels in group conflicts, geopolitical tensions, and wars. Too often, the drivers of destruction have underlying them only feelings of victimhood and threat. It is as if underneath so many acts of destructive aggression lies this *perception* of victimhood. This perception of being the victim facing threat often motivates an aggressive defence which can be rationalised as just cause, given the human minds' capacity to channel rage into ideological narratives. Such ideological justifications can hence suffer the mutilations of what is regarded as rational in the service of some deeper unresolved emotional perception.

Any organism must either resist impingement to maintain itself and its homeostasis or adapt to changing conditions in order to enable survival. In this sense, 'survival of the fittest' is about how any organism can adapt to new challenges and become 'compliant' to these demands in order to master challenges. Sometimes, as Freud noted in a letter to Einstein in 1933 addressing the question Einstein put to him about war,[4] that the "organism preserves its own life, so to say, by destroying an extraneous one". The drive of preservation turns to destructiveness but only, it seems, in an effort to better protect itself.

But is this true? So much human-on-human aggression ends up to be both self-defeating and often self-destructive, both to the individual and to the species. On the face of it, this does not seem to square with theories of evolution of adaptation. Whilst human aggression and destructiveness is all around us all of the time and seems ubiquitous to everyday existence throughout the ages of humanity, it also remains a mysterious and puzzling force the moment we probe deeper into it. Why on earth would humans be so destructive to other humans? It makes little sense in the context of science, evolution, and survival, let alone the psychology of well-being and actualisation. How can the human species thrive whilst simultaneously having the capacity to destroy itself and often seems intent on so doing? Closer to home, why do the majority of intimate relationship flame out in a tailspin of hurt and conflict, often leading to terrible costs to the children, mental health, and the purses of everyone involved? How do we explain road rage that leads to jail terms, violence against women that attacks the fabric of family and community, or sexual violence that tears apart societal cohesion? Or serial killers who relentlessly pursue their grim compulsion and invariably trigger their own eventual demise? Or suicide bombers that fly into buildings in pursuit of their cause in the full knowledge of ensuring their own premature entropy, hardly a natural course to end life as the theories would suggest? The list goes on, and none of these examples make much evolutionary or adaptive sense. Unlike other species, we kill ourselves and others with what to an outside species might appear to be with relentless and unfathomable gusto.

This book is not about philosophical speculation or ideological judgement about matters of aggression and destructiveness. I use ideological and theological references not as a religious or ideological plug but because human narratives are captured through history and this gives us useful data. Human history also has memory captured in the rich complexity of theological memory and its reflections on human nature, and I draw on some of these to provide deep and rich data on the universality and timelessness of the themes we explore in the science. There is no necessary contradiction between these narratives – even when they use different language to describe the same phenomena.

This book is about the science of aggression – delving deeper into the mysteries of this side of human nature. It is a psychological investigation that strives to draw upon and unify the good works of science and neuroscience with the less tangible or quantifiable qualities of feelings and consciousness. This may sound like an overly ambitious project requiring me to 'stay in my lane' of psychological expertise. However, even the great pioneer of the mind, the neurologist Sigmund Freud, who provided us with some groundbreaking, profound, and timeless insights into the mechanisms of the aggressive drive that we draw upon here, also lamented the limitations of his research works into aggression in his time. Struggling with the inadequacies of science and biology in his day over one hundred years ago, he nonetheless drew on the natural sciences to assist him in completing what he saw as his theoretical speculations around the mind and its aggressive drive. In fact, Freud made the point reflectively that "uncertainty of our speculation has been greatly increased by the necessity for borrowing from the science of biology", and that since biology is a land of unlimited possibilities, "we may expect it to give us the most surprising information and we cannot guess which answers it will return in a few dozen years to the questions we have put to it".[5] Freud's theory of aggression was incomplete as was his consideration of the implications of what he discovered. He noted how his theoretical observations raised a host of other questions "to which we can at present find no answer" – we must, he wrote, "be patient and await fresh methods and occasions of research".[6] This book aims to follow Freud's advice and take a small step forward, to complete our understanding of aggression, its origins in nature, and its mechanisms in human life. To do this, we will draw on the current knowledge of science and biology towards building a more unified theory of the psychology of human aggression and conflict.

So much of the psychological and biological evidence brings us to some strange and paradoxical conclusions: that inevitably, from a subjective point of view, aggressive enactments seem to derive from perceptions of injury and threat. Perpetrators invariably see themselves as the victims in their narratives. It is an uncomfortable correlation which raises issues of culpability to those who become victims or perpetrate enactments. The science of describing these mechanisms in no way serves to justify violence or destructive enactments at the personal or political level. Rather, science must be invoked to make sense of the often-unfathomable realities of complex life and the demands of living. Perhaps, by understanding why individuals or leaders of countries aggress in often vile and unfathomable ways we might better intervene to reduce such effects of what in essence, as we shall discover, aims to be a benign drive in the nature of living things.

For over three decades I have worked as a clinical psychologist specialising in individual and couple therapy. This work with couples in treatment has consistently demonstrated a correlation between perceptions of hurt and the activation of an aggressive response. The greater the perception of victimhood, the greater the aggressive mobilisation. What often appears to an outsider as a perpetrator, feels from the inside to be victimhood. It seems that those who aggress the most invariably feel the most hurt and aggrieved. The greater the aggressor response, the more likely they feel the victim. Whilst correlation is not causation, the deeper I have excavated this mechanism, the closer I have come to finding that perhaps, in fact, there is a causal link. This book aims to put that causal link into place and make sense of how a benign drive in nature with benign aims can become so malignant with such destructive effects. When one thinks about it, this ubiquitous aspect of humankind stops making sense the more one tries to understand its purpose in life. Marital conflict, group tensions, ethnic wars, violence on the street, and shootings in supermarkets or schools do not square with aggression serving any adaptive purpose.

A psychic drive, whether sexual or aggressive, can, it seems, become perverted and can develop a life of its own in split-off and separated ways. Unlike sexuality which impacts individuals, perversion of the aggressive drive can be scaled and this makes it so dangerous to both the individual human and humanity as a collective. Separated from its unconscious origins in memory, its immense power derives from the internal representation, often disproportionality perceived through old lenses in development. Accordingly, the tendency of a reactivation of old injuries will invariably be disproportionate to the trigger and only makes sense with the perspective of subjectivity in mind. Put in neuroscientific terms, aggression seems to serve the function of protecting a self-organising system from entropy. Or a little more strictly, aggression protects the self-organising system from their perception of threats to their subjective equilibrium. A guardian of equilibrium is essential to the mental apparatus' ability to safeguard and regulate both mind and body, but especially the mind's function in the service of the mind-body system.

Hence, under the strain of perversion when this mechanism develops a life of its own, separated from its original activations in life, this guardian of the peace becomes a weapon of war, the guardian of stasis becomes a tool of retaliation, trading outer destructiveness for inner peace of mind. As a former security policeman reflected on it after Apartheid ended:

> Fighting a revolutionary war is much more difficult than fighting ordinary criminals. You must remember that you are fighting the *crème de la crème*; the best brains available *in this onslaught* are your opponents. You must be one step ahead of these people.[7]

Aggression in the service of defence? This is a narrative you will see over and over as we explore the subject.

At least in theory, this would be its purpose but there is invariably a cost to the perversion of the aggressive drive – sometimes internal guilt and evacuation, like a bee that stings and in the process eviscerates itself. At other times, it contributes to the genesis of symptoms like anxiety, depression, or psychosomatic illnesses. Or on a grander scale, the loss of life that invariably leads to the aggressors' own geopolitical demise – a kind of geopolitical suicide by grand homicide. Such is nature's tendency to balance the books in the bigger picture of living life – but this may be little comfort to those who suffer at the hands of aggression whether in the domestic or social space. Understanding the aim of aggression, however, in both the clinical and social space may edge us closer to entering the unconscious motivators of those who aggress and decode and decipher the underlying unconscious triggers. As we will see, amidst the myriad of individual complexity and subjectivity, these links are not so mysterious after all, and we may be able to enable healthy aggression in the service of being the guardian of the mind's peace rather than its acceleration into scaled destruction, perverse in its effects, and unwanted at the end of the day, by everyone. This exquisite complexity of the mental apparatus is humbling, but like many phenomena in science and nature, paradoxes are often evident and counter-intuitive, like the concept of time being relative and space can curve. How strange to think of aggression and destructiveness as originating as the guardian of the peace?

What begins as a protective mechanism to maintain psychic homeostasis ends up in a perverse loop, aggression at others that is perceived through projection to be the source of risk to one's own subjectivity, the internal self-identity that creates a sense of cohesion in the world. The guardian of the self now becomes a perverted guardian, and in its wake, all manner of symptoms, psychopathology, and interpersonal strife can manifest. The costs of this drive unchecked can be high indeed.

This book aims to weave a tapestry of theory and science to form a picture of the nature of aggression, in both the most literal and abstract senses of the term nature. The journey takes us through various facets of evolution, biology, and neuroscience to build upon Freud's and psychoanalysis' deep insights into the processes of psychological functioning and the relationship of the human psyche to the energetics of biology and evolution. To accomplish this goal, we need to understand various aspects of the human psyche, its subjectivity, perceptions, and use of memory. We also need to make sense of the biological and evolutionary drivers of life and the mechanisms life uses to both survive and thrive whilst preserving itself against the constant threats of entropy. We need to investigate the pesky problems of consciousness and feelings, and the role these play in maintaining our inordinately complex functioning in a constantly changing and threatening world.

I have leant on great thinkers and scientists in this work, some of them are accomplished Nobel Prize winning experts in their fields that enable cross-links to be forged to weave the tapestry of a unifying theory of aggression. I hope these cross-overs will begin to make sense as we link the threads from various disciplines of biology, evolution, neuroscience, psychology, and psychoanalysis and place the real world and its examples under the feet of these theoretical giants. Some of these lateral and innovative thinkers are contemporary, like Kandel, Panksepp, and Solms. Others are the giants of our scientific foundations like Darwin and Freud, the conquistadors of new terrain, breaking new ground at a level that is permanently knowledge changing. These thinkers complement each other, because they describe different aspects of the same phenomenon from the vantage points of their respective disciplines. This complementarity allows progress and methods to complete aspects of theory and knowledge previously incomplete, for reasons of the limitations of technology and science in its day or because fresh methods emerge over time. This work is inspired by Freud's gigantic leaps and insights, some of which remain, by his own reckoning and acknowledgement, incomplete, awaiting fresh insights. To paraphrase Freud, what we don't achieve flying we can at least achieve limping. But sometimes, through the incisive thinking and dedicated footwork of others, we do take little quantum jumps forward.

In psychological work, there is nothing more sacrosanct than confidentiality, nothing more ethically compelling than complete respect for each and every patient's boundaries. As such, this book does not present clinical material from my consulting room. It does not need to – since there are ample case material and data in the public domain, geopolitical conflicts, historical figures, and public cases of violent offenders. In this work, I use that material because it captures so well the psychological processes that we explore, sometimes in its extreme forms, but often so much clearer as a result. The sacred space of the consulting room must remain inviolate, and I trust the reader will grasp the essence of the theory using the biological and psychological data at hand.

I hope by the end of it, you will make better sense of this strange human tendency to aggress and how it drives us in our relationships, cultures, countries, and wars. But also, as mental health issues foreground in the modern era, understanding the aggressive drive assists in making sense of individual symptoms, anxiety, depression, and maladies of the mind and body. It is this drive that holds the key to unlocking individual symptoms and why they occur the way they do. We may not be able to save the world, but we can reduce the struggles of living and the pain of life through insights such as these.

Notes

1 See Schlapobersky, J. (2021). *When They Came for Me: The Hidden Diary of an Apartheid Prisoner* for a powerful first-hand insight into the psychological effects on a detainee. As a practicing psychologist, his memoir provides unique insights into the experience.

2 In practice, argues Thomas Grant in his book on the trials and inquests during the Apartheid era, detention was not just used as a pretext for torture but also increasingly for state-orchestrated assassination. "At inquest after inquest police officers would straight-facedly explain that detainees had slipped on bars of soap, fallen downstairs, hanged themselves or engaged in acts of self-defenestration from high windows", he writes. In Grant, T. (2022). *The Mandela Brief: Sydney Kentridge and the Trials of Apartheid*, pp. 243–244.

3 See the poem 'In detention', written by Chris van Wyk, a writer and poet during the Apartheid era.

4 Freud, S. (1933). *Why War?*, p. 211.

5 Freud, S. (1920). *Beyond the Pleasure Principle*, p. 334.

6 Freud, S. (1920). *Beyond the Pleasure Principle*, p. 338.

7 "Fighting a revolutionary war is much more difficult than fighting ordinary criminals. You must remember that you are fighting sometimes against the crème de la crème; the best brains available in this onslaught are your opponents. You have to be one step ahead of these people.

In retrospect it's unfortunate that these things happened. If my opponents look back it's also unfortunate that certain policemen were killed in bomb explosions and in attacks on their houses. But both sides have to prove a point and you have to be result driven…We were there for the preservation of the internal security of the Republic. So sometimes it was very, very difficult."

Hennie Heymans, Former Security Policeman – https://artsandculture.google.com/story/detention-without-trial-in-john-vorster-square-south-african-history-archive/8AXhQ-3oNAMA8A?hl=en (italics mine)

Introduction

It is springtime in Berlin, but the songs of birds are drowned out by the relentless percussions of ordinance exploding near every junction of the city. The Red Army is closing in on the *Führerbunker*, containing in its bowels the chief architect of one of humankind's most catastrophic chapters. The blood of 50 million souls stains his hands, a human tragedy of such scale the mind can barely begin to comprehend it. When the concentration camps were liberated, the piles of shoes, monumental in their grotesque representation, tell the story of the scale of mass human loss. The mind can barely comprehend this. But nearby lies one little red dress-shoe, alone on its side in the mud. It tells the story of an individual, with her hopes and dreams and family and friends lost to the mists. This the mind can grasp. The loss of this one individual, a little life stolen.

As the era of the Third Reich reaches its eleventh hour, Hitler makes no attempt to wash his hands to clean the blood nor summons council to find exculpation. He is spewing vitriol at his generals who have failed him and grieving the cowardice of the German nation that has buckled in their weakness against their foes. They have coming to them what they deserve! "After all I have sacrificed for my people!", Hitler is yelling at the small crowd gathered around him in the stifling atmosphere of the bunker, "*this* is what it comes down to!" His capacity for theatre undiminished by the ravages of war, he declares, "The time has come", he tells his pilot. "My generals have betrayed me; my soldiers don't want to go on and I can't go on".

Hitler seemed to see himself as the victim in the story. This theme of Hitler-as-victim was not new. His rhetoric had been peppered with such perceptions of victimhood and oppression throughout his career. In his 1942 speech on the 19th Anniversary of the Beer Hall Putsch[1] he railed, "if this democratic Germany had not been plundered and oppressed in that way… both Germany and him personally would not have been victims…" Referring to England, he opined:

> They have destroyed idealism everywhere, and they have grabbed and taken possession of material worth and always grabbed and taken possession of it, too, by brutal force only. For in 300 years that nation has oppressed and yoked and subjected nation after nation, people after people, race after race … it was a

DOI: 10.4324/9781003452522-1

struggle for the preservation of Germany and, in the broadest sense of the word, for the preservation of Europe…

Annihilation, or at least Hitler's perceptions of it, appears as a constant theme. In the conclusion of his Stalingrad Speech of 1942 he said, "Think incessantly, men and women, only of the fact that this war will decide the 'To be or not to be' of our people".

It is not a particularly incisive observation to notice that throughout Hitler's life story he perceived himself, perhaps genuinely, to be the victim rather than the perpetrator. From his early beginnings in his family, through his rejection as an aspiring architect/artist, to the end of days in the *Führerbunker* as he dictated his last will and testament, we can observe the centrality of this victim-perpetrator narrative in his psychic experience. But how is this possible? How can it be that this vegetarian artist who loved opera and animals, and was presumably not short of intelligence, could in his mind switch the perpetrator and the victim with such conviction? Surely, even a cursory glance at the facts would be enough to persuade any intelligent person who the villain in the story was?

This puzzling phenomenon, of the villain obvious to the outside world experiencing themselves as the victim in the narrative, is a common one. Except in the comic books: "You are deluded, Captain", says Red Skull, the arch-enemy of Captain America and a personification of pure evil, "You pretend to be a simple soldier, but in reality, you are just afraid to admit that we have left humanity behind. *Unlike you, I embrace it proudly. Without fear!*"[2]

A lawyer whom I knew who was most familiar with adversarial discourse in his working life and who collected comic books since childhood confirmed this: "Unlike in the comic books", he perceptively observed, "where the villains take pride in *being* the villains, in *real life no-one* sees themselves as the villains in their story!" This off-hand comment struck a deep cord in my clinical experience. Working for over 30 years with individual adults and couples in the clinical setting, I had often noted how consistently and regularly that those who perpetrated even the most terrible cruelty, cold aggression, or hot explosive rage that rattled the windows of my consulting room never experienced themselves as being the villain in the story. In fact, the correlation invariably seemed inverse that those who *perpetrated* the most voluminously perceived themselves to be the most hurt, the real victims in the narrative. Usually, aggressive responses were justified as being *in response to* some or other perceived provocation or injury.

I noticed too, that those who perpetrate terrible crimes, serial killers for instance, would often notably see themselves as the injured party, hurt by circumstance or their attachments, for which a justifiable revenge was being enacted. When Mary Shelly's fictional Frankenstein's monster struggled with his own sense of victimhood, and as a *leitmotif* for the injuries of childhood and parenting, this icon of terror, deeply injured, reflected:

Inflamed by pain, I vowed eternal hatred and vengeance to all mankind… My sufferings were augmented also by the oppressive sense of the injustice and ingratitude of their infliction. My daily vows rose for revenge – a deep and deadly revenge, such as would alone compensate for the outrages and anguish I had endured.[3]

Wounded and rejected, the monster created by Frankenstein becomes increasingly enraged – his body injured and his pride wounded by rejection:

> I will revenge my injuries: if I cannot inspire love, I will cause fear; and chiefly towards you my arch-enemy, because my creator, do I swear inextinguishable hatred. Have a care: I will work at your destruction, nor finish until I desolate your heart, so that you shall curse the hour of your birth.[4]

To paraphrase Freud, neurotic acts of revenge often originate in hurts from those closest but can be directed at the wrong people. He noted, that "punishment must be exacted even if it does not fall upon the guilty".[5]

Shelly's fiction of the monster 'given birth' by Frankenstein has endured through the last century as a cultural icon because – like the timeless play of Oedipus Rex (which Freud referenced in his famous observation of the Oedipal complex of childhood) – it resonates so deeply with our unconscious experience of attachment, life and love, hate and hurt. It reminds us of the strange twist of fate that children experience the most injury, often, by their own parents who gave them the gift of life in the first place. Longing and its losses pepper intimate attachments from the outset, and the injuries from these experiences can endure into adulthood, sometimes in perverse ways. The woman bludgeoned to death by a real-life killer 'deserved it' because she was a woman – and since women have been his persecutor, so her gender in his mind might justify the exacting of punishment. Longing promoted by the sight or presence of someone simultaneously unobtainable itself becomes a source of frustration and potential mobilisation of an aggressive response.

Theodore Robert (Ted) Bundy was infamous for the predatory kidnapping, rape, and murders of more than 30 women during the 1970s.[6] Yet, of himself he said,

> I was essentially a normal person. I had good friends. I lived a normal life, except for this one small, but very potent, very destructive segment of it that I kept very secret, very close to myself, and didn't let anybody know about… And part of the shock and horror for my dear friends and family, years ago when I was first arrested, was that there was no clue. They looked at me, and they looked at the all-American boy.

He apparently blamed his violence on being the 'victim' of pornography, perhaps symbolic in his mind of women that entice and seduce and activate longings but are beyond reach – the source of his rage at them and need to feel omnipotence through his power over them. For the first three years of his life, Bundy lived in the Philadelphia home of his maternal grandparents who raised him as their son to avoid the social stigma that accompanied birth outside of wedlock at that time. Deceived into believing that his grandparents were his parents and that his mother was his older sister, Bundy eventually discovered these deceptions when a cousin showed him a copy of his birth certificate after calling him a "bastard". Bundy reportedly expressed a lifelong resentment towards his mother for never telling him about his real father, and for leaving him to discover his true parentage for himself. In addition, one can speculate about the psychological distortions of relating to what he believed was his sister but who was actually his mother. In some interviews, it was said that Bundy spoke warmly of his grandparents and even reported identifying and 'clinging' to his grandfather, who was later exposed to attorneys to have been a tyrannical bully and consumed by prejudices and hatred for blacks, Italians, Catholics, and Jews, amongst others. He also was reported to have beaten his wife and exhibited cruelty to animals, abusing the family dog and swinging neighbourhood cats by their tails. He also reportedly threw a family member down a flight of stairs for oversleeping in a fit of rage. His grandfather apparently also spoke aloud to unseen presences and apparently became violently enraged when the question of Bundy's paternity was raised. Bundy described his grandmother as a timid and obedient woman who periodically underwent electroconvulsive therapy for depression and feared to leave their house towards the end of her life. Not a happy mix for early life development.

There are many examples of violent offenders. For example, what about Pedro Rodrigues Filho, a Brazilian serial killer, also known as Pedrinho Matador or Killer Petey, who butchered a confirmed 71 people, while claiming his victim list was closer to 100.[7] How was this perpetrator a victim? The 63-year-old had been born with an injured skull because his father savagely beat his mother while he was still in her womb. He apparently nearly killed his cousin when he was just 13 when he first felt the urge to murder but it was a year later that he fully acted on his impulses, murdering the Vice-Mayor of Alfenas, because he fired his father on unsubstantiated claims he was stealing food from the school kitchen. He then went on to kill the person who he thought was actually taking food supplies, this perpetration at only 14 years of age. He then apparently moved towns to São Paulo, where he murdered a drug dealer and racked up a significant body count in the name of various associations to revenge perceived injuries. His girlfriend was killed by gang members, precipitating a rampage of torturing and killing people to uncover the culprit who killed her. Arguably, his most savage murder happened when he came face to face with his father. He reportedly executed him in a prison as he was serving time for killing his mother with a machete. Filho reportedly cut out his father's heart, cannibalised a piece of it, and then threw it away. But this was not isolated. The murders continued in prison, with Matador murdering four people while incarcerated, leading to his sentence being extended. In 2003, a court had sentenced him to 128 years – but since Brazilian law prevents any criminal from serving more than 30 years, he was eventually released in 2007. The question of what was going on in the mind of Filho as he murdered all those people remains vexing but he seemed to feel justified in so doing, exacting revenge for real and perceived injuries.

Was Filho, like Frankenstein's monster, the victim or perpetrator? In fiction and fact, we encounter this strange reversal of perspectives at times distorting our sense of normality and presenting paradoxes to our theoretical understanding of the mind. The uncomfortable reality is that it seems to depend on one's perspective, not in the sense of my opting out of an answer, but literally, it depends on one's perspective. From the perspective of his victims, he was the perpetrator, obviously. But from the perspective of the infant born with an injured skull because his dad savagely beat his mother while he was still in the womb and later murdered her, he may have answered that question differently. 'Born a victim' might be the internal reference point for launching into the world, one inherently aimed at persecuting him. Would it then make sense that anyone perceived as intent on hurting him, or at least representing such a thing, would be fair game for attack? Would the subjective representation of who is the villain and who the guardian of the persecuted not then take precedent over any objective representation of these positions?

These questions represent for us the conundrum of the human tendency to commit untold horrors on other humans, a tendency unique amongst the species, and invariably in the name of defending some perceived sleight, hurt, or threat. In the world of comic books and fiction, villains do not retract from their pride in being the villain. The fiction writer VE Schwab captured these tendencies in her novel about heroes and villains:

> But these words people threw around – humans, monsters, heroes, villains… it was all just a matter of semantics. Someone could call themselves a hero and still walk around killing dozens. Someone else could be labeled a villain for trying to stop them. Plenty of humans were monstrous, and plenty of monsters knew how to play at being human.[8]

In the media, we are exposed daily to the unthinkable atrocities that people commit against people. Some of these are individual against individual and some of these are nation states and their apparatus being used against their own people. Daily images of ISIS falling over themselves to find more grim and creative ways to kill and torture people in the name of God seem barely believable to an outsider watching from the sidelines. And these images one would hope are the works of madmen. But then we encounter something extraordinary and different. In this phenomenon, we see the intelligently, meticulously, and coldly planned attacks, over months and years, of the mass murder and atrocities of civilians, such as the attacks on the USA on 11 September 2001, committed not by psychotic inmates escaped from asylums, or even the works of psychopathic killers exacting some sexual or material benefit from their crimes. Here we have Mohamed Atta, with his bloodied hands at the controls of the newly hijacked aircraft, murdered pilot at his feet, calmly lying to the passengers whom he knows are all about to die, broadcast in error to Boston ARTCC. Air traffic control hears Atta announce, "We have some planes. Just stay quiet and you'll be O.K. We are returning to the airport". A little later he announces, "Nobody move. Everything will be okay. If you try to make any moves, you'll endanger yourself and the airplane. Just stay quiet". Atta speaks English fluently and likely makes the transmissions, but it is also possible that Atta's seatmate, al-Omari, accompanies him into the cockpit. Apparently, Atta tried to make an announcement to the passengers but keyed the wrong switch and instead his voice is picked up and recorded by air traffic controllers. In a third and final transmission, Atta announces: "Nobody move, please. We are going back to the airport. Don't try to make any stupid moves".

If we pause and consider this transcript, it is striking to note that here we have an intelligent, rational, considered, and carefully planned process in motion. Atta is about to knowingly commit not only mass homicide on innocent people but also certain suicide in the process, not due to some mental illness or despair – but because of some apparently internally logical and considered motive. This is not the usual stuff of combat and war where self-preservation takes precedence and survival at all costs necessitates the killing of others. Here, we have a planned attack guaranteed to lead to both other and self-destruction. These villains appear to consider themselves heroes, not just heroes but martyrs and have taken both individual and collective decisions to upend the usual mechanisms of the mind that strive for sustained survival and longevity. Whilst we may say, alongside Freud, that ultimately the "aim of all life is death", since everything organic becomes ultimately, for internal reasons, inorganic once again, we also note, as Freud also pointed out, that the pull towards renewed quiescence and rest is resisted through life by the fundamental and powerful life drive which tenaciously clings to the premise of self-preservatory instincts. As we shall discuss below in more detail, the function of these instincts is to assure that the organism shall follow its own path to death and to ward off any possible ways of returning to inorganic existence other than those which are immanent in the organism itself. It strives to find a long circuitous path 'from dust to dust' by resisting the pull of premature quiescence until the very last possible moment. Hence arises, says Freud, the paradoxical situation that a living organism struggles most energetically against events (dangers) which might help it to attain its life aim rapidly or via any short-circuit (of eventual quiescence or death). Yet here in the cockpit of a newly created weapon of mass destruction, instead, we find the calm deceit of men bent on the determined path to ultimate (self and other) destruction.

How do we explain such a paradoxical phenomenon as flies in the face of apparently natural instinct of self-preservation? Surely these paradoxes need some explanation. If the mechanisms that govern these headline-grabbing events are subject to the laws of nature, then surely they are not too different from the conflicts that contaminate every marital couple or every road rage incident? If our understanding of the laws of the mind suggests that the drive to life represents the most fundamental of organic drives then how do we explain these events that appear to defy such natural laws? It is self-evident that evolution built upon processes such as those represented by Atta and his co-conspirators would have achieved an abrupt halt to life's forward momentum. Yet here we have it, an apparent upending of the natural laws of preservation in the service of evolutionary reproduction – and as we examine this phenomenon, it takes us to some surprising insights about the nature of the mind, and in particular, of the nature of aggression and its purpose.

How does it make sense that an individual would choose his genetic end when the evolutionary imperative is to procreation of the self and the species? This is not suicidality for reasons of psychopathology. This is driven by some apparently noble and virtuous reason – perceived heroism of some considered magnitude. As Freud lamented in 1933 in his correspondence with Albert Einstein, entitled Why War?, in thinking about the destructive drive of the mental apparatus:

> On the other hand if these forces are turned to destruction in the external world, the organism will be relieved and the effect must be beneficial. This would serve as a biological justification for all the ugly and dangerous impulses against which we are struggling. It must be admitted that they stand nearer to Nature than does our resistance to them *for which an explanation also needs to be found.*

(italics mine)[9]

Notes

1 See for example, https://www.jewishvirtuallibrary.org/adolf-hitler-speech-on-the-19th-anniversary-of-the-ldquo-beer-hall-putsch-rdquo-november-1942; and Kershaw, I. (2001a). *Hitler: 1936–1945 Nemesis.*
2 Italics mine; Red Skull, 'Captain America: The First Avenger', (2011).
3 Shelly, M. (1918)/(1934). *Frankenstein*, p. 144.
4 Shelly, M. (1918)/(1934). *Frankenstein*, pp. 144–145.
5 Freud, S. (1923). *The Ego and the Id*, p. 386.
6 See https://en.wikipedia.org/wiki/Ted_Bundy for a more detailed description.
7 See https://en.wikipedia.org/wiki/Pedro_Rodrigues_Filho for a more detailed description.
8 Schwab, V.E. (2014). *Vicious*, p. 289.
9 Freud, S. (1933). *Civilisation, Society and Religion.*

Chapter 1

Freud's Incomplete Theory

Hate, it seems, predates love. The famous British paediatrician turned psychoanalyst, Donald Winnicott noted: "I suggest that the mother hates the baby before the baby hates the mother, and before the baby can know his mother hates him".[1] This statement may at first blush seem surprising. What, we may ask, has hate got to do with anything, and how can hate predate love? It may also be said that the first expression of an individual, the new born infant, is not one of love but of aggression as it *induces* a response in the environment. The first cry after birth may be regarded as a signal driven by the aggressive drive. This apparently wild assertion will make more sense as we explore the paradox of this mechanism in the human psyche. The solution to these paradoxes will prove helpful in making sense of the peculiar human propensity for intra-species violence and destructiveness, both physical and emotional, that plagues humanity at both geopolitical and domestic levels. It will, hopefully, also assist in understanding why we develop symptoms. For both these dimensions of being human, aggressive enactments and symptom-formation, appear to root themselves in the self-same mechanism.

The pioneering scientific work of the famed neurologist and founder of psychoanalysis Sigmund Freud is well known for his deep insights into the nature of the psyche. In particular, he emphasised the role of sexuality in the genesis of mind and its psychopathologies and brought into focus the major role this played in driving psychological development and its problems. Love and the libidinal drivers of life, the "breakers of the peace" as Freud called them,[2] seem easier to understand through Freud's significant insights and discoveries and intuitively the resonance of his formulations have continued to embed themselves in collective culture. The nature and science of aggression and its destructiveness, however, proved much more elusive scientifically and frustrating for the great pioneer of the mind. Since, why would any living organism have imbedded in its (psychic) make-up a powerful mechanism for destruction, one that so often turns against both self and others within the species? Surely this is counter to the evolutionary imperative? "It may be, however", lamented Freud in reflecting on his theories of aggression, "that I am overestimating their significance"[3] He conceded that "one may have made a lucky hit or one may have gone shamefully astray"[4] in trying to make sense of the aggressive drive in the human psyche. On the face of things, this destructiveness seems to

DOI: 10.4324/9781003452522-2

fly in the face of so much common sense and science. And yet, it is as if Freud did not fully appreciate his own discoveries nor recognise the implications they had in science. Many great theorists have suffered this self-doubt at their own discoveries, as the famous example of Einstein and his 'fudge factor' also testify, in which he introduced a 'cosmological constant' to fit the preconceived prevailing picture at the time that the universe was a stable entity. Apparently, he later lamented this theoretical footwork, regarding it as the "greatest blunder" of his scientific life. Sometimes the evidence overwhelms the familiar paradigms and great minds are not immune to this problem. In fact, Freud made the point reflectively, that "uncertainty of our speculation has been greatly increased by the necessity for borrowing from the science of biology".[5] Prophetically, he conceded that: "We may expect it to give us the most surprising information and we cannot guess which answers it will return in a few dozen years to the questions we have put to it".[6]

The science of aggression does not lend itself, it seems, to linear or easy intuitive insights, frustrating common sense and surprising us with strange paradoxes. And yet, Freud's wish to have future science corroborate his theoretical insights has proven just so. Apologetic for his "analogies, correlations and connections"[7] which accompanied his theoretical exploration of aggression, he was unapologetic for suggesting that the future test of his theory of aggression would rest in biology, "truly a land of unlimited possibilities",[8] as he put it, and I might add, from later developments in neuroscience too. Humbly, Freud conceded that we "must be patient and await fresh methods and occasions of research" to establish the voracity and truths of his work in this area. Fortunately, we now have the science and it indeed seems to corroborate so much of Freud's insights into aggression, his thinking and inking over one hundred years ago. This is the investigation we will be undertaking – making deeper sense of this strange characteristic of the human condition – aggression and its destructive *effects* – and integrating the science into the psychoanalysis to make better sense, hopefully, of this peculiar manifestation of daily human experience. Significant implications for understanding symptoms, psychopathology, and treatment flow from this integration. The theoretical tour below will hopefully take the next step in integrating psychological and modern scientific work towards understanding this deceptively paradoxical quality of aggression and its benign aims but destructive effects.

Proliferation and Preservation

At the extreme poles of aggression lie two familiar expressions: suicidality (and variations of self-harm) and homicidality (and variations of other harm), both of which are endemic to the human condition. But how can suicidality or homicidality, two opposing poles of the same aggressive spectrum, be at all adaptive to survival? Suicidality and homicidality appear on the same spectrum of destructiveness, neither manifestation appearing in the face of it to be helpful to human adaptation. Yet, Darwin observed, that "as natural selection works solely by and for the good of each being, all corporeal and mental endowments will tend to progress towards perfection".[9] How does self-induced individual or mass specicide square with this imperative? Aggress against the self in the form of suicide or other destructive self-harming tendencies or against others in the form of homicidal impulses or actions. Neither of these options strike as consistent with common sense or the evolutionary imperative. Darwin would claim that life and its forward drive places the interests of the species survival above that of the individual over time, but because the pursuance of life dominates above all else. But moreover, it places survival and *life*, underpinned by the drive to reproduce, as a guarantor of survival, which Darwin termed the "geometrical ratio of increase", a driving force that underpins the reproductive thrust of all life to try proliferate above the inertia of death. The drive to life strives to dominate over the tendency to entropy and inertia in life for if it did not, none of us would likely be here to navigate these questions.

In the processes of natural selection, Darwin argues, the species takes ultimate precedent over the individual for the greater good of the species, which appears to make some sense in the context of natural selection. Nature is not personal in its tendencies to adaptation for survival, and both individual organisms and whole species become extinct if they fail to adapt and proliferate. This is both intuitive and squares with the science, what Freud termed the life drive, sexuality being one expression of its push for survival. But how does aggression make sense, in which attacks on the individual or others within the species are *scalable*, beyond the striving to attain dominance within an intra-species hierarchy in which resources are in competition? The scale of human destructive capacity does not seem consistent with the theory of natural selection and the evolutionary imperative, at least not on the face of it.

In psychological terms, the libidinal drive prompts the organism from cellular level up to reproduce and strive to maintain the individual and the species. Darwin's observations elevate the reproductive tendency of species to the forefront of biological life, and of course it makes sense that this evolutionary imperative should forcefully imbed itself in all organic self-replicating life. Or, as Freud pointed out, "The hypothesis of self-preservative instincts, such as we attribute to all living beings, stands in marked opposition to the idea that instinctual life as a whole serves to bring about death".[10] Perhaps, it is true that the 'aim' of all life is *eventually* death, but the scale of human destructiveness appears to stand in stark contradiction of the evolutionary science of survival and its Eros-driven elongation at all costs. Often, it seems as if humans apply their intellectual prowess in the service of destroying ourselves, not prolonging life. So much of what we see in human intra-species violence seems to suggest that it appears as if the stronger thrust of instinctual life is to bring about premature demise of the species. But obviously, our survival on the planet indicates that we have not yet self-destructed as a species, though scalable aggression enabling that to happen is relatively recent in human history, particularly with the advent of nuclear weapons.

This issue Darwin partially addressed thinking about the role aggression and violence might play in the preservation of genetic reproducibility and the resource requirements for this imperative. Resources sustain an edge in competition for a mate as does the acquisition and preservation of a mate and her offspring. But then why in the modern era where resources are more abundant than ever in human history is the level of intra-species violence so marked? Equally important, why does so much of the violence we document appear to be driven not by an evolutionary imperative of resource acquisition and preservation and its scarcity but by ideology and ideas, and the perceived preservation of principles and morality?

Ideology and Ideas

Images of ISIS parading through conquered territories with blood dripping triumphantly from their fingers and conjuring ever more creative ways to torture people to death, in the name of some spiritual endeavour, appear to stand in sharp contrast to the Darwinian imperative. Darwin highlighted the role of aggression in competition for mate selection, and research is suggestive of size, innate weaponry, and brain structure as driving aggressive potential in species where competition for reproductive potential is high.[11] Or, as Evans & Cruse have argued, that Darwinian insights coincide with Freudian theories of identification and projection to show that aggression towards out-group members is a necessary concomitant of the development of 'conscientious' or moral emotions towards in-group members relating to blame, punishment, and guilt, which are essential to group cohesion and confer substantial selective advantages.[12]

These theories of innate aggression posit a necessary and, in a sense, positive function for intra-species aggression related to survival, competition for mate and resources, and insistent reproduction. In a sense, these theoretical trends help explain aggression and its end-point of death as a by-product of promoting life. Death, in this thread, serves the purpose of life. Death is the slave and life is its master. Without such an evolutionary imperative, would intra-species violence and death need to exist? Would there be a psychic imperative to aggress? In organised systems, humans pour a huge amount of resource into prolonging life and promoting it, raising the life drive to all-out importance. And yet, to personify Death, its relentless drive to outperform the life drive and take ultimate honours is common sense. We remain, no matter what, mortal beings. This obvious point is not to trivialise the complexity of these two fundamental drives of the human psyche, that of the life drive and the death drive, but to attempt to show that contained in these drives are strange paradoxes – for whilst the aim of all life may be death, as Freud pointed out, the aim of the death drive appears to be to preserve life, not subvert it. Aggression, like sexuality, can become perverse, but its aim is not always apparent from its effects. How, if this is true, do we square an image of ISIS beheading an innocent civilian with the *preservation* of life?

Aims of Aggression

The first port of call in this paradox is to separate two key elements in the nature of aggression. You may have noticed when reading above, that I have been guilty of a simple but problematic conflation of two aspects – namely, the aims and the effects of the aggressive drive. The terrible and ugly manifestations we witness daily in the media of heinous crimes against other humans, brings into focus the effects of aggression, often perverted for various reasons we will discuss later. To better understand this drive, we have to make sense of the aims of aggression, why it is baked into the nature of the human psyche. Why would Nature in her wisdom create such a fundamental drive that is so destructive if it did not serve some fundamental purpose?

I point out my own assumptions here that Nature has a distinct wisdom and that little if anything is superfluous in her design. Redundancies have a cost and any great complex design relies on any redundancies being written out of the design or the risk of some cost leaning it in the direction of poor competitiveness in a resource-sensitive world. Every neuron or cell in the human system has its purpose and function, despite the mildly disturbing reality, when you stop to think about it, that almost all bodily and mental functions go on unnoticed and in the background. The incredible and unfathomable complexity of both physiological and neuropsychic functions, billions of constant biological processes maintaining life, all continue in a near-perfect harmony through the diurnal cycle. Underneath the tip of the iceberg of conscious awareness lies a universe of invisible and fantastical complexity, mostly going on in the dark as it were. Such biological intelligence suggests that nothing in its function and design would be superfluous, since the sustainable equilibrium hangs in a delicate and fine balance. We need only think of relatively minor shifts in temperature, hydration, electrolyte balance, sleep, or even gravity to find that even minor tilts from homeostasis and equilibrium are met with significant threats to health and even life itself.

As embodied creatures, the same might be observed in the mental apparatus. The mind has a connection to the body and in many ways emerges from experiences of and through the body. This emergent mind evolved to become the structure and system that governs psychic and neurological function. Freud himself, a neurologist who started his research works into neuronal functioning and the nature of brain chemistry, was at pains to demonstrate the emergent nature of both the mental apparatus itself and its psychological processes that emerge through somatic and proprioceptive experience. Without the senses, and bodily sensating, the mind could not properly develop. With these conduits for the experiencing of an I or Self, particular exaggerations in the navigation of developmental challenges and those of life affect how defensive systems and perceptions evolve. This is a complex process to which I will return to later, but suffice to point out here that every biological and psychological process is designed for efficiency, survival, and purpose. Anything that is superfluous disappears once its function is fulfilled – like milk teeth, extra haemoglobin in infancy to protect against hypoxia, and the pruning of neural circuits that are no longer in use. Any intelligent engineer of a complex system will likely ensure that redundancies are minimised to avoid the drag of some cost.

Working from the observation that the neurobiological system is designed for its usefulness and efficiency in the homeostatic state leads to the obvious conclusion that any emergent system built on this would be governed by the same principle –

that if the psyche has systems or qualities, these are built in for good reason. The destructive effects of aggression that at times seem to ensure the destruction of the human species might seem to buck this trend, until we drill deeper into the aims of this system. Let us take the example of pain – which has two parallel processes – the electrochemical triggers and neural cascade of pain signals, measurable across the nerve system and into the brain, but accompanied also by the 'I', a subject having the *feeling* of pain. "I feel pain!", when the dentist pushes his needle into my gums is both a physiological process and a psychological one. Someone, in this case me on the dentist chair, is feeling the pain. If the pain signals cannot be subjectively registered, as in spinal cord injury or under anaesthesia, is there pain to speak of? Evidently, there are pain signals at the physiological level but these are not being registered at the subjective level. Psychic superfluousity maintains relevance in all its systems and processes in order to exert the pressure towards equilibrium and stasis, as Freud put it, to

> master stimuli that have broken in and binding them, in the psychical sense, so they can be disposed of … We may perhaps suspect that the 'binding' of the energy that streams into the mental apparatus consists in its change from a freely flowing into a quiescent state.[13]

This notion of energy being central to life is corroborated by modern science, which the biochemist Nick Lane argues, that "energy is central to evolution, that we can only understand the properties of life if we bring energy into the equation… this relationship between energy and life goes right back to the beginning"[14] and "emerged from the disequilibrium of a restless planet". The relevance of this latter point is essential and will become clearer as we traverse these relationships between disequilibrium and the mental apparatus, a system emergent from more humble origins but never free from the essential drivers of its early (evolutionary) roots.

Of course, internal and external pressures of life and living constantly challenge this homeostasis and as any parent knows, how rapidly internal developmental pressures create change and how external frustrations and limitations of the external world unsettle it – the mind treating internal or external pressures with no principle difference, as if from the vantage of the need to maintain stasis, or at least deviations that are close to it, internal or external exigencies will be responded to by a 'counter-cathexis' to bind the excess and reassert the dominance of a balanced or static state. There is always a mechanism in play that tries to maintain balance and homeostasis, physiologically and psychologically. Freud observed this principle over a century ago, noticing that the psyche strives to lower "excitation" in the face of impingements, and return the organism, biologically and mentally, to some level of comfort. It is obvious that any organism driven too far out of its ideal state of balance will suffer injury or death. The ecosystem itself, as we are witnessing with global warming and environmental challenge, precariously hangs onto a narrow idealised state of balance. Even a few degrees off the physical axis or on the temperature scale has the potential to lead to disaster over time. Nature premises itself on considerably fine balances in all spheres, from the micro to the macro.

Speaking Destruction

Whilst this point would not be original, it bears highlighting since the anomalous elements of an innate drive that has destructive potential must also have some inner purpose, a role in the service of survival and equilibrium. Let us also remember that whereas the violent potential of all other creatures remains limited by their natural constraints of energy, competition, and the complete reliance on their own natural tools (claws, teeth, mobility etc.), the damage they can do to life and ecology remains constrained. Humans are unconstrained in their capacity to aggress. Intellect enables the scalability of aggression – a feature unique to the human species. The ability to scale aggression equates with the capacity to annihilate a nation of tens of millions with a single instruction. Where the Bible reports The Creator 'speaking' the steps of evolution into existence, "And God *said*, let there be…", humans have the capacity to 'speak' the earth and its inhabitants into annihilation. The spectre of atomic armageddon represents, of course, the extreme of this scalable capacity. Often, the notion of "Sticks and stones may break my bones, but words will never break me. But names will never harm me"[15] seems so imbedded in our thoughts about personal injury that it presents as obvious. Yet, we may puzzle to notice in the data that the opposite is often true. Physical injuries heal and resolve unlike emotional ones that remain embedded so deeply in personal and cultural psychic memory. So often, hurt feelings underly many examples of extreme aggression. In March 1960, for example, 69 people were shot to death and 180 injured, including children, in a fusillade of bullets outside a police station in Sharpeville, Johannesburg.[16] A peaceful protest against Apartheid laws turned bloody when police opened fire with Sten Guns, handguns, and rifles, stopping to reload and continue the firing as the crown fled away. Most of the victims were shot in their backs. In the inquest into this massacre, it was interesting to note the sentiment from police involved that the crowd was threatening and as one key officer put it under cross examination, "I would say they wanted to assault and humiliate us. That is what their mission was". "Not to commit suicide?", the famous advocate Sydney Kentridge asked incredulous, considering the firepower arraigned against the unarmed crowd. "No", said Constable Saaiman, "to humiliate us…"[17]

This point centralising feelings of threat to person and mind was further highlighted by the revelation that Lieutenant Colonel Pienaar, a high-ranking officer in charge and involved in the massacre, had pointed out earlier in the day to a press reporter that his car had been slightly damaged, leaving "slight marks" as he put it. But he also had said that if "they do this sort of thing, they must learn the hard way". The enquiry's hearings had thus concluded with the implication that Advocate Kentridge had made that an angry police colonel ordered his officers to load their weapons and prepare to open fire because half an hour earlier, someone had scratched his car's paintwork. The author Thomas Grant asks rhetorically in reflecting on this transcript of the proceedings, "Could the genesis of this atrocity have really been that banal?"[18] Feelings of humiliation seemed to have served up at least part of the impetus for the attack. The trigger for this cascade was set. Feelings of humiliation and threat led to a massacre.

But noting the power of feelings and how words represent them in humans, does not mean that aggression is superfluous or anathema to natural laws. In fact, like all the laws of nature, this anomalous feature of destructiveness on a grand scale remains governed by the laws of nature and requires deconstruction through the same lens we might interrogate all laws of nature and science. Aggression must have a function that is purposeful. It is not an appendix dispensable to psychic function – rather, it seems to occupy pride of place in the overall significance of its role in the human mind.

The poets and philosophers through history have reminded us that aggression and hate are bad, traits to be conquered or mastered, ideally ablated from the mind and humanity. "Hate", wrote the poet Maya Angelou, "it has caused a lot of problems in this world, but it has not solved one yet." Nelson Mandela represented this position in his quest for justice and equality in South Africa, suggested,

> No one is born hating another person because of the colour of his skin, or his background, or his religion. People must learn to hate, and if they can learn to hate, they can be taught to love, for love comes more naturally to the human heart than its opposite.[19]

As lovely and endearing as these sentiments are, they are unfortunately not true scientifically. In fact, it appears that hate comes more naturally to the human heart than does love, since as we shall discuss later, hate *precedes* love and is activated in the primitive psyche of the infant from the moment the infant is subject to disequilibrium and impingements that unsettle – which is to say, from the moment the womb starts its process of expelling the infant from its perfect home into an imperfect and challenging world. The first cry of the infant represents the first expression of psychic aggression – a first attempt at throwing a punch in an attempt to induce in the environment a response that might restore a stable and comfortable state. The responsive breast and skin contact by the mother enables a return to balance, at least temporarily. And so the soft remedy of maternal bonding and love follows the unsettled state of a cold and hard world and helps restore it. Stasis to un-stasis to stasis is the natural order of things from the point of view of the infant. Aggression and its aim, to induce in the world a response toward a return to stasis, becomes in life the first psychical act of any newborn. This is an important point which bears repeating: the first psychical act of any newborn infant is an aggressive one! This counter-intuitive concept points us in the direction of the significance of the aggressive drive, and its function and purpose. Technically, hate comes before love and as naturally to the human heart than does love, if not more so. We can adapt to a world without sufficient love, albeit imperfectly, but we cannot survive in a world without sufficient hate, for without it psychic survival would not be possible.

This is quite a mouthful. And I do not refer to this idea because I like it or advocate aggression and its *effects*. I refer to it for technical reasons, to posit, as we shall see through the ideas below, that the *aim* of the aggressive drive, in its purest form, serves an adaptive purpose – the elongation of states of equilibrium in the service of prolonging life's journey towards a natural circuitous end – from dust to dust. As the biblical injunction reminds us: "For the fates of both men and beasts are the same: As one dies, so dies the other—they all have the same breath… All go to one place; all come from dust, and all return to dust." And again, "In the sweat of thy face shalt thou eat bread till thou return unto the ground for out of it wast thou taken for dust thou art and unto dust shalt thou return". Put in scientific language, life begins from a quiescent state (of non-being) and strives to return to a quiescent state ultimately, according to its own terms, and will resist at all costs in the normal state any premature diversion from this aim. The drive to live is powerful and resistance to any diversion from the natural aim of life to find quiescence is significant.

You may have noticed an apparent contradiction in this narrative: is it the life drive that pushes to prolong itself at all costs and strives to elongate and prolong life? Or is it the death drive that pushes towards this same end and also seeks to resist premature death?

Life and Death Drives

Freud's brilliant insight and theoretical leap in his book Beyond the Pleasure Principle, began to recognise a duality in the human condition, two forces of the psyche locked in an intimate but tensioned relationship – the life drive (libidinal) and the death (aggressive) drive. The life drive exerts a powerful force on both the conscious experience of a will to live, but also an unconscious one – at both the biological and by extension psychological levels, the 'Will to Live' exerts a profoundly forceful effect on living organisms. Our immune systems serve as the guardian of this force, since internal states of disequilibrium can be re-regulated by the body itself (e.g., shivering or sweating when out of the temperature range), but external impingements in the form of pathogens that unsettle stasis will trigger a violent and merciless response to annihilate the invading organisms. But in contrast to the invigoration of life instincts and needs, stands a drive whose task of the mental apparatus is mastering or binding excitations, not, said Freud "in *opposition* to the pleasure principle but independently of it and to some extend in disregard of it".[20]

What Freud had noticed in his research works was that a universal attribute of organic life in general and human instincts in particular is that it contains a mechanism for conservation and restoration, built in, as it were, from the ground up. This mechanism works with both short- and long-term agendas. In the first instance, the mechanism aims to keep homeostasis for the mind and body system and to resist impingements that unsettle homeostasis, such as reacting to hurts, threats, needs, and frustrations. But this drive also aims to direct an organism though the normal course of its lifespan to get to eventual death through timely and natural means. In his 1920 work, Freud wrote:

> At this point we cannot escape a suspicion that we may have come upon the track of a universal attribute of instincts and perhaps of organic life in general which has not hitherto been clearly recognised or at least not explicitly stressed. *It seems, then, that an instinct is an urge inherent in organic life to restore an*

earlier state of things which the living entity has been obliged to abandon under the pressure of external disturbing forces; that is, it is a kind of organic elasticity, or, to put it another way, the expression of the inertia inherent in organic life.[21]

Adding to this idea, he noted, that death is a natural state of an organism returning to ultimate inertia, or organismic homeostasis.

> … it must be an *old* state of things, an initial state from which the living entity has at one time or other departed and to which it is striving to return by the circuitous paths along which its development leads. If we are to take it as a truth that knows no exception that everything living dies for *internal* reasons—becomes inorganic once again—then we shall be compelled to say that 'the aim of all life is death' and, looking backwards, that 'inanimate things existed before living ones.'

From the earliest molecular matter that makes up the origins of life and which existed before organic life, so organic life returns to the organic matter, the 'dust' as life comes to its natural end. And hence:

> … arises the paradoxical situation that the living organism struggles most energetically against events (dangers, in fact) which might help it to attain its life's aim rapidly—by a kind of short-circuit. Such behaviour is, however, precisely what characterises purely instinctual as contrasted with intelligent efforts.[22]

This introduces a model of mind, and of life in general, that is dualistic, representing two complementary but competing drives. This *dualistic* view of the drives of mental life appear to share the same dynamics of all living matter, including the most primitive of self-replicating organisms. This continuity helps us to understand a fundamental premise, albeit on the face of it a contradictory one, of two drives in all living matter, emergent in the human psyche too: these drives Freud characterised as a drive pressing to life (and one which has greater contact with our internal perception, emerging as Freud put it, "as breakers of peace and constantly producing tensions whose release is felt as pleasure", and another, the death instincts which "seem to do their work unobtrusively".[23] The death instinct might be thought of as the guardian of stasis, its task to maintain life by restoring deviation from the natural state to the natural state and ensuring the organism arrives at ultimate stasis (or natural quiescence – death) by its own internal and natural rhythm. Any premature exigency that aims to divert the organism from this natural aim will be strongly resisted.

In this regard, Freud's observations that even at the molecular level these dual drives are present in living matter, concurs with subsequent observations in modern molecular science. Genetic variation, the ability for organisms to combine and better genetic coding, provides an evolutionary advantage to survival. For Freud, writing at the time it was hypothetical, prompting him to suggest that

> we might suppose that the life instincts or sexual instincts which are active in each cell take the other cells as their object, that they partly neutralise the death

instincts (that is, the process set up by them) in those cells and thus preserve their life; while the other cells do the same for *them*...[24]

All living matter thus behaves in what we might term a 'narcissistic' fashion (a topic I will return to later), prioritising their drive to life *from their own perspective* and resisting premature entropy through the mechanism of conservation, represented by what Freud termed the death drive. Some of these concepts may seem paradoxical, but as we shall explore below, coincides with modern biochemical science. There is evidence that primal forces of nature emerged from the earliest forms of life and perhaps drove the formation of primitive life, a form of "energy harvesting" that turns out, according to the biochemist Nick Lane, "to be conserved as universally across life as the genetic code itself".[25]

Freud alluded to the idea that through the sexual drive benefits accrue to life forms, including humans. Sex advances a major benefit to premature entropy of both individual and species in that it enables organisms to constantly adapt as environments change and challenge homeostasis, in this sense 'neutralising' the death drive, at least partially, and instead conferring a better opportunity for living matter to follow an optimum path to its natural end. The combining of genes through sex enables what Darwin termed 'variation', that is by preserving and accumulating variations in response to the conditions of life. This capacity confers upon each creature the ability to become more and more improved in relation to their conditions and hence also enables greater varieties of species over eons of time, in addition to improved variants of each species.[26]

The notion of 'variation' in evolution can be understood in two ways: random genetic variation coincides with environmental challenge and so that change by dumb-luck, as it were, proliferates – it is in this sense random since lucky genetic variants survive changing conditions and confer better adaptation by chance. There is another interpretation of the same data, suggesting that a *pressure* to survive *drives* variation in order to enable better adaptation to environmental challenge. It is interesting that Freud's use of the term 'drive', the dual energetic forces at play in all life, is used also by modern science. Lane makes the point that as he reflects on his depiction of the origins of life finds himself also using the term *drive*, since he says, "there isn't a better word" to capture the idea that it is not passive chemistry "but it is *forced*, pushed, driven by the continuous flux of carbon, energy, protons. These reactions *need* to happen...".[27] Libido in humans is not a passive energy – it *pushes* for expression, for the drive to pro-create in the service is not only self-survival but that of the species. In contrast, lies two billion years of stasis, in which primitive life clung to what it knew, sustaining itself only through conservation. As conditions changed in the geology of the environment, this became the only way of dissipating the unstable disequilibrium and of reaching what Lane jestingly describes as a new state of "blessed thermodynamic equilibrium".[28] At heart of the evolutionary dilemma is whether there is design or intelligence behind variation or it really is random and life emerged through simple luck. This debate is not central to what we come to observe in the mental apparatus much later in evolution where the life drive has through time certainly come to exhibit a quality of drive, a push, and a need-to-happen energy. Whatever its origins, these active qualities dictate the terms of the life force for adaptation.

Either way, we can see that the essential drives in the mental apparatus that Freud noted began their respective quests at the outset of living matter. Conserve, adapt through variation, and attempt to conserve again. More accurately, these energetic forces pit against each other through life – sparring as it were for the preservation of life through conservation or adaptation. In recognising these links through time, we have begun to lay the foundation for understanding the dual nature of both biological and emergent psychic systems – one pushing for life and its multiplication and one striving to guard against states of disequilibrium and as it were fighting to maintain the status quo, in order to ensure that the organism reaches ultimate quiescence through its own internal course.

In many old people, we hear the communication of a readiness to die, to leave this organic world, as the ageing body and mind gradually fail. Such is the natural course of dying according to the internal dictates of the body. You will notice that this ingenious set of observations by Freud carries another apparent contradiction. If as we explore the dynamics of aggression and the destructive elements of humans we seem to be suggesting that these violent drives are designed to maintain and restore homeostasis? Violence in the service of peace? How do we square such a paradox! How could a drive designed to maintain stasis initiate such intense violence and consciously wreak scalable destruction on other humans? How do we place this as Mohamed Atta took control of the hijacked aircraft and adjusted the course of Flight 11 into the Twin Tower in New York on that fateful day of 11 September 2001 that changed the course of history?

Notes

1 Winnicott, D.W. (1949). Hate in the Counter-Transference, pp. 69–74.
2 Freud, S. (1920). *Beyond the Pleasure Principle*, p. 337.
3 Freud, S. (1920). *Beyond the Pleasure Principle*, p.333.
4 Freud, S. (1920). *Beyond the Pleasure Principle*, p. 333.
5 Freud, S. (1920). *Beyond the Pleasure Principle*, p. 334.
6 Freud, S. (1920). *Beyond the Pleasure Principle*, p. 334.
7 *Freud, S. (1920). Beyond the Pleasure Principle, p. 334.*
8 *Freud, S. (1920). Beyond the Pleasure Principle, p. 334.*
9 *Darwin, C. (2003). The Origin of Species, p. 459.*
10 *Freud, S. (1920). Beyond the Pleasure Principle, p. 42.*
11 *Example: Evolutionary aspects of aggression the importance of sexual selection: Patrik Lindenfors & Birgitta Tuliberg.*
12 *Hopkins, J. (2004). Conscience and Conflict: Darwin, Freud, and the Origins of Human Aggression.*
13 Freud, S. (1920). *Beyond the Pleasure Principle.*
14 Lane, N. (2016). *The Vital Question: Why Is Life the Way It Is?*, p. 13.
15 It is reported to have appeared in The Christian Recorder of March 1862, a publication of the African Methodist Episcopal Church, where it is presented as an 'old adage' in this form: "Sticks and stones may break my bones, but words will never break me. But names will never harm me".

16 See Grant, T. (2022). *The Mandela Brief: Sydney Kentridge and the Trials of Apartheid*, p. 121.
17 Grant, T. (2022). *The Mandela Brief: Sydney Kentridge and the Trials of Apartheid*, p. 114.
18 Grant, T. (2022). *The Mandela Brief: Sydney Kentridge and the Trials of Apartheid*, p. 120.
19 Mandela, N.R. (1994). *Long Walk to Freedom: The Autobiography of Nelson Mandela*.
20 Freud, S. (1920). *Beyond the Pleasure Principle*, p. 307.
21 Freud, S. (1920). *Beyond the Pleasure Principle*, p. 308.
22 Freud, S. (1920). *Beyond the Pleasure Principle*, p. 312.
23 Freud, S. (1920). *Beyond the Pleasure Principle*, p. 337.
24 Freud, S. (1920). *Beyond the Pleasure Principle*, p. 323.
25 Lane, N. (2016). *The Vital Question: Why Is Life the Way It Is?*, p. 52.
26 Darwin, C. (2003). *The Origin of Species*, p. 124.
27 Lane, N. (2016). *The Vital Question: Why Is Life the Way It Is?*, p. 135.
28 Lane, N. (2016). *The Vital Question: Why Is Life the Way It Is?*, p. 135.

Chapter 2

The Development of
Subject – "I"

Do You Remember?

Human beings are blessed with higher order cerebral capacity that enables symbolic and abstract thinking and planning. But such is the nature of the human organism that its subjectivity and consciousness occupy a special and unique place amongst the biological species. Highly advanced forms of memory enable humans to store associations of personal history at a level of abstraction and subjectivity that supersedes any objective version of the same experiences and events. Memory, even in primitive organisms serves a highly adaptive function – to prevent exposure to toxic or noxious stimuli that might prematurely end the organism's life. In ground-breaking research, Eric Kandel (born in 1929 in Vienna), Austrian-born American neurobiologist and psychiatrist who, with Arvid Carlsson and Paul Greengard, was awarded the Nobel Prize for Physiology or Medicine in 2000 for discovering the central role synapses play in memory and learning. Studying the primitive but neurologically accessible sea slug the *Aplysia*, Kandel noticed that exposure to aversive stimuli led to neurochemical changes in the neurotransmission designed to temporarily store information that would 'remind' the organism that such exposure is noxious or potentially harmful and should next time be avoided. In Freudian terms, sources of unpleasure are best avoided because they create states of dis-ease or dis-equilibrium. These neurochemical changes tend to be temporary and the synaptic transmission returns to normal after a while, usually around 24 hours. But what Kandel also noticed was that prolonged exposure to noxious stimuli, such as the slug crossing a barrier that promoted a shock, would lead to neuroanatomical changes and the growth of neural circuits that embed as permanent features of the memory bank, in humans forming some of the substance of the vast reservoir of memory which Freud formulated as the Unconscious.

In the *Aplysia*, or other more primitive organisms, this permanent store of memory, hard-wired as it were into the structure of the organism, is adaptive but as you can infer, does not rely on a subjective evaluation of the source of injury, at least not is the sense of sentience we associate with human subjectivity. In other words, all the organism registers is something that every other organisms of the same ilk would also register, that is, 'out there' is an aversive stimulus that will cause harm to them. No sentient subjective element seems to be required and the organism

DOI: 10.4324/9781003452522-3

does not have any reflective agency in registering and evaluating the source of unpleasure. Humans benefit from these neural processes but their higher order neural capacity introduces a highly adaptive but complex emergent set of qualitative structure: that of sentient subjectivity. There is an 'I' perceiving and that 'I' can make evaluative choices about sources of unpleasure in its life field. In fact, more than that is the psychical requirement, not an optional one either, for humans to bring their subjectivity, based on experience, into their interpretation of what in their lives represent pleasure and unpleasure. Writes Kandel:

> For all of us explicit memory makes it possible to leap across space and time and conjure up events and emotional states that have vanished into the past yet somehow continue to live on in our minds. But recalling a memory episodically – no matter how important the memory – is not like simply turning to a photograph in an album. Recall of memory is a creative process. What the brain stores is thought to be only a core memory. Upon recall, this core memory is then elaborated upon and reconstructed with subtractions, additions, elaborations, and distortions. What biological processes enable me to review my own history with such emotional vividness?[1]

In other words, memory is subjective in a sentient conscious way but is also influenced extensively by unconscious associations governed by the principles of subjectivity. We have to *perceive* something as noxious, for example, for our neurobiological and emotional experience to react as such. Should we perceive an impingement as neutral or innocuous, no flight-fight response will be required.

The often sharp and polarised distinction between one person's perception of the same event and that of another can be striking. "But we only left you to cry for 5 minutes!", protests the mother to her 18-year-old daughter in psychotherapy. "That's not true!", says the daughter, "you were always leaving me! You were always abandoning me!" This unique human element of what I would term 'pure' subjectivity is not the same variability we might see in a dog who is more highly strung than another, albeit of the same species. This unique feature is also not one that emerges over a lifetime. Almost from the beginning, there appears to be an 'I' perceiving experience, storing such experience in memory even if it cannot at this early stage be 'declared' (it is 'non-declarative memory').[2] From this perception, primitive as it might be, templates of emotional learning are being developed, creating the lens through which the next experience may be filtered. Genes of the brain are not governors of behaviour or the absolute masters of our fate, Kandel argues, but are also guided by the events of the outside world and 'switched on and off' according to environmental challenges and influences.[3] Genes enable adaptation, and as the biochemist Lane notes, "genes are almost infinitely permissive: anything that can happen will happen".[4]

The Trauma of Being Born

An infant may be born through a relatively easy labour and without complications – it emerges into a shocking world of jarring lights, poking and prodding, cold, and startling conditions. It is no easy transition from the comfort and peace of the womb into the environment. The paediatrician on the medical team takes the infant to a nearby table, checks its APGAR scores,[5] suctions its mouth, checks hip flexor function, and generally intrudes into the peaceful slumber of the prenatal infant in-utero. The infant yelps, cries, and squirms helplessly. Although mentally still primitive and incapable of conscious or rational evaluation, we might imagine it asking itself if it could, whether perhaps it has just transitioned from heaven to hell. Hopefully, the infant is placed quickly on the mother's chest, latches, and begins to settle to her loving and warm skin embrace. Equilibrium is restored, at least relatively speaking, and the initial breaking of the trust is repaired, from the infant's point of view.

From the mother's point of view, or of everyone else in the room, no trust was broken at all! Everyone and everything was focused on the infant and its well-being. The infant's perspective on these events may have been somewhat at odds with this (adult) 'reality'. From the infant's perspective, life has dramatically changed from being perfectly balanced in every respect, including nutrition, temperature, and sound to one that has dramatically become cold, hard, and intrusive. Some authors in psychoanalysis, such as Otto Rank in his 1924 writing *The Trauma of Birth – Das Trauma der Geburt*,[6] (published in English in 1929) argued a case for birth *trauma*, in which he argued that the source of anxiety throughout all of life stems from the psychological trauma that one experiences during birth. *The Trauma of Birth* was an extension of Freud's idea that birth is the first experience of anxiety and therefore is the source and basis of anxiety. Throughout the book, Rank argued that birth is the ultimate biological basis of life and that the physical experience of passing from a state of contentedness and union with the mother in-utero to an environment of harsh separation creates a trauma that causes lasting anxiety. Relating feelings experienced during birth to feelings associated with anxiety, Rank argued that birth is the source of all anxiety by drawing parallels between the feelings of confusion, constriction, and confinement experienced during birth and other anxiety-related experiences.

Freud himself was not convinced about the theory and later suggested that no evidence existed that birth trauma had long-lasting residual effects in and of itself. Instead, Freud argued that the trauma of birth was not an adequate means of explaining anxiety, and that the foetus is not aware of its own existence and that it could not have the requisite sensory impressions during birth that would allow it to recall the trauma later in life. Freud refuted Rank's idea of a harsh separation between life in the uterus and being born into the world and argued that there is continuity between inter-uterine life and childhood. During and after the birthing process, the infant is activated into relating to the world, not strictly with its own mind untethered to the mind of the mother, but certainly emerging into a developmental space in which the mind of the infant is now unbuffered by the protective shell of the womb and is suddenly having to use its own mind and brain systems to regulate and register dysregulation.

However, to be fair to Rank there is a kernel of truth in his thinking. Much depends on the nuance of this transition from perfect environment to imperfect one and whilst Freud's refutation of Rank would bear the test of time, there also appears little doubt both clinically and theoretically that the process of birthing and impact of the environment on the individual infant can have neuropsychological effects that may last into later life but not in the universal sense that Rank suggested. Individual infants have different experiences of life from the outset and some of these can impact development. I should point out that not all of these impingements on the infant are external. Sometimes, the infant's own body produces intero-receptive impingements, such as blocked mucosa or mouth, temperature dysregu-lation, or acid reflux. An infant is unable to yet distinguish external from internal impingements – pain or discomfort are registered neurophysiologically as pain or discomfort. Distinguishing the one from the other takes time, months of develop-ment, to begin to recognise pain from inside or outside sources are different – that what is 'me' and 'not me' are different things from different sources. But for the early infant, disequilibrium is disequilibrium and these vary considerably from in-fant to infant, their health and birth experience, and own internal ability to regulate.

The question of whether an infant can tolerate their threshold being breached, where stimuli are overwhelming the infant's ability to process them, reregulate (usually through crying and inducing a response from the mother or environment), will also then influence psychic outcomes down the line of development. If the psychic threshold is breached, either because the parents cannot soothe the child and restore stasis, or because the environment is simply not responsive enough, or because medical intervention necessitated the infant being kept away from the mother (in an incubator for example), so the infant may have learned lessons of (its) life that the world is a harsh place, cruel and punitive, a source of pain and persecution, not to be trusted. This is part of the emerging 'I', a self who is already perceiving the world in particular ways, interpreting events though the lens of ini-tial experience. If the mother delays feeding, or the milk supply is short, the infant's perception of early experience may be reinforced, leading to temporary memory traces becoming permanent neuronal networks reminding the infant over and over that the world must be seen through this lens. Repetition becomes endemic, what Freud termed the repetition compulsion, a tendency in human organisms to repeat what becomes familiar and embedded in psychic experience. The mental apparatus becomes formed accordingly, sometimes with lifelong effects. Aversive events in particular form part of this template, useful in nature's tendency to triage survival – and so for an infant, abandonment may represent a life-threatening experience ren-dering the world an unsafe and persecutory place, even if such abandonment from the caregivers' perspective is in the interests of the infant's medical care, such as putting them in an incubator, or neonatal ICU, with its accompanying intrusions and insults to the infant.

This example brings to the fore a significant point about the human psyche – agency, perspective, and subjectivity. From the beginning, the post-partum infant is beginning to perceive events, experience them, and in a primitive fashion, interpret them. Whilst such memory circuits will not later be directly accessible to conscious retrieval (as mentioned, they remain in a memory form that neuropsychologists re-fer to as 'non-declarative' – cannot be declared consciously), they will nonetheless form memory imprints and neural circuits through which later experiences will be filtered. A later abandonment, such as the mother going off to the shops for a brief period, may initiate heightened anxiety about separation, even when the mother has been doting and attentive, because of the earlier insult to the infant's mental integrity. This also makes clear that there is often no fault in the maternal care or dynamics – sometimes, life introduces impingements that are simply beyond the psychic threshold to metabolise and hence *from the perspective of the infant and its subjectivity*, neural memory traces will form to programme the infant for later survival: As if given a voice, such neural circuits might say to the infant from their unconscious reservoir of memory: "do not trust your caregivers to be consistent! Hold onto them at all costs! Or if that does not work, shut off emotionally and become deadened to attachments needs!" What can be seen in these processes are the rudimentary foundations of subjectivity, development of the "I" that is perceiving and reacting *from its own perspective*. This notion that an infant has agency is not to suggest that it is fully conscious in these early days and months, but that templates of neural memory circuits are being laid, through which reality gets constructed by the infant itself. Laid strongly enough in the face of adversity that overwhelms the ability to re-regulate arousal following impingements that dysregulate it, these memory traces become like a lens through which reality is interpreted, not only as an external reality, but also as a Self, relating to that external reality and that external reality impacting on this Self.

Polymorphous Perversity

Freud recognised the embodied nature of the infant from the beginning, and what he termed their 'polymorphous perversity'. This means the world is experienced through the senses and the body and enters experience through every part of the sensory apparatus, including the skin. There is no a-priory 'mind' at the outset that drives development in a vacuum – there is a body interfacing with a developing and elastic mind whose senses enable the external environment to engage with its internal environment, the rudimentary ego being like the 'crust of the bread baked through', the outer layer of psychic skin enabling a differentiation of Self and Other, internal and external. The colloquial use of the term ego, meaning self-esteem or its over-inflation, is a technically incorrect use of the term. Rather, Freud noted that between the vast reservoir of memory traces making up the unconscious and the external world lies a thin layer of psychic skin, separating the internal and external worlds. The ego, or 'I', may be viewed as that thin layer of consciousness that optimises our ability to navigate a complex world. Solms has done pioneering work in this area, and the spectacularly efficient way the human psyche and consciousness is designed for efficient navigation and survival of incredible environmental complexity. "Consciousness emerges instead of a memory trace", Freud wrote, noting that consciousness represents the tip of the iceberg 'protruding' into awareness, but which hides beneath it a vast reservoir of unconscious memory traces and metabolic processes occurring constantly in the body and brain, and of course the psyche. The skin is to the human body a mere surface facing outwards into the environment but which represents a crucial layer separating the internal environment from the external environment – the 'me' from the 'not me'. This notion of a Self-organising itself somatically, neurologically, and psychically into a coherent self-functioning system differentiated from other external systems is perhaps premised on the self-organising tendency of all systems that exist in the cosmos, whether of matter, energetic, or biological. All systems become, Solms points out, self-organising according to Friston's Law (more on this later).

This propulsion towards internal coherence leads the organism to require mechanisms to preserve itself in this self-organised form, and to promote that coherence against the constant impingements and threats of the environment. In the human organism, the senses form part of this process but so too does consciousness and instinct. "Biological self-organising systems *must* test their models of the world, and if the world does not return the answers they expect they must urgently do something differently or they will die",[7] Solms points out. Referring to biological systems and biological system's capacity to use sensors and nerves to regulate the Self from the effects of internal or external impingements and resultant deviations from homeostasis leads to the direct sequence that emergent systems built upon these biological systems, the psychic systems of the mental apparatus which emerge from but are not reducible to the biological systems from which it emerges. This is an important point that more elementary systems give rise to more complex systems that emerge from them but cannot be reversed back into them or reduced to them. Simplicity can create complexity and in the case of the mental apparatus this complexity, driven by the capacity for consciousness and feelings (that is, subjectivity), becomes increasingly intangible and inaccessible to outsiders except through inference or as a result of self-report.

If an adult reports their sexual or aggressive fantasy, there is no way to objectively observe that report. Of course, we could measure changes to genital tumescence, pupil dilation, piloerection, blood pressure, or neurological changes to infer some internal mental process but the content of it would forever remain inaccessible. The same is true of feeling states – we can observe symptoms of depression for example, but the associated *feelings* of sadness or guilt cannot be known in any outside or objective sense. This point may seem self-evident but science has forever battled with the pesky and elusive question of the "hard problem", that of consciousness. How can a material world give rise to something apparently non-material and intangible, except to the individual subject who is doing the feeling or having the experience? And if consciousness which is intangible and non-material serves a purpose for the tangible material (biological) world, what is that purpose? We will return to these questions later, but what is relevant to this point of the self-governing system of the human body is also that the emergent properties of the psyche built on that system and in turn developing the capacity over time interpret and influence experience, can reciprocally influence this biological system through feelings being used to regulate deviations from stasis. This intimate connection between psyche and soma enables a subjectivity to become embedded in the navigation of the sensory world and *interpret* this world of present experience through psychic filters of past experience. Neural circuits that constitute memory and ideational traces (or ideas in their purest form – cognitive conclusions about the world) built an internal bank of experience that assists in interpreting and navigating an impossibly complex world and surviving it. Neurobiologically, Kandel points out,

> The ability to grow new synaptic connections as a result of experience appears to have been conserved through evolution. As an example, in people, as in simpler animals, the cortical maps of the body surface are subject to constant modification in response to changing input from sensory pathways.[8]

Synaptic Circuits versus Entropy

The absolute importance of memory to functionality and survival can be appreciated by thinking about what would happen if memory were to become impaired. We are all familiar with memory loss in old age or due to deterioration of the neural structure and process in dementias. But imagine if no new memories could be created, even in adulthood. If that part of the brain that is responsible for acquiring new memory traces becomes impaired, even basic functioning is seriously effected. You visit a place, let's say an airport, and are directed to the toilet. Relying on old memory and signage you can navigate the use of the toilet. Once there, however, you cannot remember how to find your way back. Or even, what you were doing at the airport in the first place. The ability to acquire new memory is critical to even basic functionality, even where such learning and memory has little emotional significance. Preservation of the mind-body system depends on the ability to acquire memory and store aversive threats as long-term memory. Being able to *efficiently* retrieve memories as necessary is essential to survival. Kandel's pioneering work on memory noted that memory is also not simply passive as if imprinted through a series of internal photographs. Instead, he points out that the fact that a gene must be switched on to form long-term memory shows clearly that "genes are not simply determinants of behaviour but also responsive to environmental stimulation, such as learning".[9] As mentioned, this capacity is embedded in life itself, noting that this ability to grow new synaptic connections as a result of experience has been conserved throughout evolution.[10]

As we shall see, memory has not only been conserved *through* evolution (because it is adaptive to survival) but represents the conservation *of* evolution itself. Without memory, there would be no mechanism to read the environment, retrieve information about what a stimulus represents, nor how to respond to it through approach or avoidance. In a world teeming with impingements and threats, without memory there would be no efficient system able to respond to what is required to quickly adapt to the environment and ensure survival. Some of these threats are inorganic and some organic, some animate and some inanimate. But they all represent challenges to homeostasis, which invariably require an evaluation and response. Efficient evaluation of the environment relies on a system of recording, storing information, and retrieving it rapidly. Long-term memory is a mechanism that seems to facilitate preservation of the organism and conservation of its requisite homeostatic state. Memory provides the data bank to which the organism can return repeatedly to reference current events.

Retrieval from memory that an impingement represents a threat to homeostasis is, however, not a sufficient response. In fact, it is not a response at all. A mechanism is required that facilitates action to address a disrupter. Libidinal energy tends to be a disrupter itself, a 'breaker of the peace', as Freud referred to it. But the aggressive drive provides an active response to threats, and it makes sense to link these two processes of memory and aggression. It could be said, therefore, that *memory is the registrar of states of disequilibrium and aggression its remediator.*

Long-term memory, the building blocks of the unconscious, requires more persistent synaptic changes that are based on alterations in gene expression, creating an objective rendering of what begins as subjective experience. It is only from the vantage point of the organism that something would be experienced as aversive and in this broad sense this places subjectivity in a central place, a topic to which we will return later. Only experiences that are based on an organism's subjective experience will require some form of encoding, which suggests that *subjective* interpretations and experience that a stimulus is aversive will require encoding into long-term memory for later access. This means that a bridge between the subjective and the objective is formed – not in the sense that one can ever access subjectivity through this mechanism since that would violate the notion of subjectivity (by definition what is subjective can never be accessed objectively) but that what begins as purely subjective becomes encoded into objective concrete neural pathways capable of both non-declarative and declarative access for later use. Memory can, in other words, be encoded even when some of it is too early in psychic development to be *cognitively* accessed. Other memory traces can be accessed, for example through psychotherapy, and which can later be 'declared' to consciousness.

When those traces are accessed through some associative process that triggers the pathway, psychic reactivity will be governed then as if the past were actually also in the present, a timeless quality to the unconscious that Freud noted in his work. Ideas, says Freud, are cathexes of memory traces – whilst the affects and emotions correspond to processes of discharge, "the final manifestation of which is perceived as feelings".[11] Freud distils the notion of the unconscious (and memory as an implication), as "*exemption from mutual contradiction, primary process* (mobility of cathexes), *timelessness*, and *replacement of external by psychical reality*".[12] As we begin to see, Freud's notion of the unconscious represents a mechanism of storage of ideation, memory traces that rapidly and efficiently capture and represent experience and can be later accessed and retrieved in order to facilitate a reaction aimed at remedy. This notion of memory as the storage of ideation for later retrieval and referencing dovetails with Kandel's later neuroscientific rendering of it.

Extermination in the Service of Preservation?

On 20 January 1942, senior Nazi and SS officials met at a Berlin villa to discuss the "Final Solution to the Jewish Question".[13] Deportations to ghettos and concentration camps had already begun, but the Wannsee Conference coordinated plans for the systematic mass deportation and murder of European Jews. The agenda was to ensure the co-operation of administrative leaders of various government departments in the implementation of this plan. The main and only item on the agenda of the Wannsee Conference was essentially the extermination of millions of Jews in Europe. Himmler had previously established a think-tank, comprised scholars and scientists from a broad range of academic disciplines, and this Ahnenerbe group was devoted to the task of promoting the racial doctrines espoused by Hitler and his governing Nazi Party, specifically by supporting the idea that the modern Germans descended from an ancient Aryan race seen as biologically superior to other racial groups.

The Wannsee conference, called together by *SS-Obergruppenführer* SS Reinhard Heydrich, director of the Reich security Main Office, included representatives from several government ministries, including state secretaries from the Foreign Office, the justice, interior, and state ministries, and representatives from the SS. In the course of the meeting, Heydrich outlined how European Jews would be rounded up and sent to extermination camps and the General Government (the occupied part of Poland) where they would be killed. The Nazi government used the Ahnenerbe's research to justify many of their policies and cited these in justifying the genocide of Jews and other groups – including homosexuals – through extermination camps and other methods. In 1937, the Ahnenerbe undertaking was renamed the Research and Teaching Community of the Ancestral Heritage (Forschungs- und Lehrgemeinschaft des Ahnenerbe), though some of the group's investigations were placed on hold at the outbreak of the War in 1939. Towards the end of the war, Ahnenerbe members destroyed much of the organisation's paperwork to avoid it incriminating them in forthcoming war-crime tribunals. This group and the Wannsee meeting and its 'matters' of business' was a cold, matter-of-fact discussion that might be familiar to any company or body corporate agenda.

Science in the service of ideology is not unique to the Nazis – what was unique to the Nazis was their total devotion to an apparently rational question, buoyed up by 'scientific' evidence, of finding a solution, from their perspective, of preservation of their race and culture. As unpalatable as it may be to suggest such an interpretation, the Nazi agenda from their own internal perspective, could be framed as 'extermination in the service of preservation'. Genocide was their avowed aim, not a by-product of any other ideological agenda or war, but a cold and calculated programme underpinned by intellectual thought and planning, design, methodology, the use of science, chemistry, engineering, architecture, medicine – that is to say, scientists, engineers, architects, doctors, highly educated and intelligent people acting together to create mass murder, not in a moment of impulse but with forethought and consideration. These people created a monster machinery designed for one of the most atrocious and incomprehensible chapters in the entire corpus of human history.

The ability to scale death becomes increasingly apparent and as mentioned before, entirely unique to all the species on earth. This scalability at once seems to place the instinct to violence in an entirely new category. Samuel von Pafendorf in 1673 wrote, "More inhumanity has been done by man himself than any other of nature's causes", possibly giving birth to the well-worn phrase of 'man's inhumanity to man', is used to try capture this programme of mass murder and genocide, and words like holocaust appear to distil a scale of violence and aggression usually incomprehensible to the normal mind. It is simply too difficult to both identify with each person's suffering, as we do when someone has an unfortunately accident, or is the victim of violence. At this level of scalable destruction and violence, it is as if the human mind struggles with personal identification and can only compute the magnitude of the atrocity from arms-length sympathy and horror. Empathy, in its more direct sense, becomes blurred when the scale overwhelms all emotional capacity. It begs the question as to whether this human capacity for scaling aggression therefore places it in a separate category from the *individual* drive to aggress and whether a new set of principles or laws of mind are required to make sense of such a destructive capacity. Whereas individual aggression in the service of preservation makes some sense, in that resources are invariably subject to competition and violence is often committed in the service of attaining and preserving resources, specicide from an evolutionary perspective makes little sense. How can it be evolutionary-adaptive for a species to develop the capacity to entirely destroy itself? Here we face a challenge to the entire notion of Darwinian adaptive evolution, which so skilfully explains intra-species variation and survival through inter-species competition for resources – to avoid being the food in the food chain.

As we make the quantum leap into specicide, the tendency of the human species to destroy itself on the grandest of scales, we appear to run into a violation of Darwinian theory. Evolutionary adaptation does not seem to be served by a species developing the capacity, and using it no less, to destroy itself. We are not even noting here a war of one group in the service of preserving itself over time through defence or conquest, arguably a form of 'survival of the fittest' through group identity. The Wannsee Conference serves up no resource advantage to the ingroup (of Germans), since Jews were a tiny proportion of the European population, represented no material threat, were powerless to in any way threaten non-Jewish German superiority and dominance in any shape or form. Intelligent people and scientists of the Nazi Reich knew this, or at least had to comprehend that in reality there was a sharp distinction between any objective reality of threat, and a subjective hatred for a relatively tiny group.

Why would any nation, particularly such a developed one, be in any way threatened by a tiny group of culturally distinct people whose cultural modus, unlike most other religious tendencies, strives to keep to itself and resists outsiders, except through onerous and determined conversion? Most other religions pros-elytise, some peacefully and some through violence, but Judaism is one religion that resists assimilation to the out-group and resists the out-group penetrating into the Jewish in-group. It is a people content to be left alone to follow their God with fervent obedience and celebration but with no desire of appetite to threaten any other culture of group. Proselytising is anathema to Judaism and so represents no threat to another's religious or cultural identity. And yet, the amount of intellectual and material resources ploughed into the programme of mass murder and genocide of this small group that posed no numerical or cul-tural threat to German culture, was uniquely scaled with deliberation and intent. How could 18 million Jews (pre-Holocaust – since one-third of world Jewry perished in the Holocaust) *in the entire world* possibly be a threat to anybody, numerically and culturally out-numbered by such a significant factor? According to the census of 16 June 1933, the Jewish population of Germany, including the Saar region (which at that time was still under the administration of the League of Nations), was approximately 505,000 people out of a total population of 67 million, or somewhat less than 0.75%. That number represented a reduction from the estimated 523,000 Jews living in Germany in January 1933; the decrease was due in part to emigration following the Nazi takeover in January (an estimated 37,000 Jews emigrated from Germany during 1933). How could half a million souls be any threat to 67 million? And yet, even in the face of the final fall of the Nazi regime towards the war end, the Nazis redoubled their efforts to murder innocents rather than put those resources into surviving their own defeat. Even this point seems counter-intuitive to Darwin's notions – how could this perver-sion of aggression, even when contributing to an effective suicidal outcome, be seen to promote survival of the fittest or be adaptive in any way from either the individual or species-level point of view?

Evolutionary explanations of aggression from a Darwinian perspective suggest that aggression serves an important function in terms of both individual survival as well as reproductive potential. This means that aggression has an adaptive pur-pose because it facilitates survival and adaptation to the environment. And sure, this makes sense to contemplate that the top-dog had better access to resources to perpetuate its life and genes and protect his progeny. At the level of the individ-ual, aggression is formulated to perpetuate survival through variation and adapt-ability, in Darwinian terms, and to ensure the continuation of genetic progeny, a virtuous cycle of survival for the species as a whole, since the strongest or most adaptive will survive the impingements of the environment. But this concept of aggression in the service of development which this formulation effectively pos-its does not seem to square up neatly with all the evidence that psychoanalytic investigation has produced. If the evolutionary imperative is driven by innate in-stinctual promptings, then how does scalable homicide and specicide in any way serve this imperative? To address this apparent anomaly, let us first return to one of the most profound intellectual leaps of the 20th century, at least in my view.

Notes

1 Kandel, E. (2006). *In Search of Memory: The Emergence of a New Science of Mind*, p. 281.
2 See for example, Solms, M. (2022). The Hidden Spring & Solms, M. (2013). The Conscious Id, pp. 5–19. It highlights that memory has different elements.
3 Kandel, E. (2006). *In Search of Memory: The Emergence of a New Science of Mind*, p. 264.
4 Lane, N. (2016). *The Vital Question: Why Is Life the Way It Is?*, p. 289.
5 The Apgar score is a quick way for doctors to evaluate the health of newborn infants. Originally developed by an anaesthesiologist Virginia Apgar to address the need for a standardised way to evaluate infants shortly after birth. The score is determined through the evaluation of the newborn using five criteria: heart rate, respiratory effort, muscle tone, response to stimulation, and skin colour; a score of ten represents the best possible condition.
6 Rank, O. (1929). *The Trauma of Birth*.
7 Solms, M. (2022). *The Hidden Spring*, p. 168.
8 Kandel, E. (2006). *In Search of Memory: The Emergence of a New Science of Mind*, p. 276.
9 Kandel, E. (2006). *In Search of Memory: The Emergence of a New Science of Mind*, p. 276.
10 Kandel, E. (2006). *In Search of Memory: The Emergence of a New Science of Mind*, p. 276.
11 Freud, S. (1915). *The Unconscious*, p. 181.
12 Freud, S. (1915). *The Unconscious*, p. 191.
13 Kershaw, I. (2000). *Hitler 1936-1945: Nemesis Volume 2*; also https://en.wikipedia.org/wiki/Wannsee_Conference.

Chapter 3

Beyond the Pleasure Principle

Beyond the Pleasure Principle

In his book *Beyond the Pleasure Principle*, written relatively late in his theoretical life, Freud in 1920 addressed the issue of two dialectical drivers of the human organism – the one striving for growth, proliferation, and change and the other silently aiming to maintain and preserve both the homeostasis of the organism and its various systems' integrity. Under the pressure of the life drive, or Eros, from simple cellular to complex systems, there is a striving for movement forward towards greater unities. These thrive on innervation and the challenge to stasis, since in the face of reality, no organism beyond the uterus can remain passive or unaffected by the impingements of reality. The life drive prompts preemptive redress and consolidation of life through what Panksepp calls 'seeking' behaviour and the procreative urges that flow from this part of the brain. But there is also in the organism a drive to resist impingements and to maintain the integrity of the organism, addressing the problem of "mastering the amounts of stimulus which have broken in and of binding them, in the psychical sense, so that they can be disposed of".[1] Cathexis, the urge to bond, versus 'anti-cathexis' is set up on a grand scale, a tension of excitation and quiescence locked in constant battle. "It is as though", argues Freud,

> the life of the organism moved with a vacillating rhythm. One group of instincts rushes forward so as to reach the final aim of life as swiftly as possible; but when a particular stage in the advance has been reached, the other group jerks back to a certain point to make a fresh start and so prolong the journey.[2]

The binding of excess energy and rendering it dormant becomes part of the task of this function. Where thermo-regulation, by way of analogy, is accomplished by shivering or sweating to maintain optimal steady state, mental energy requires a more complex system of regulation, factoring in one most significant factor: the *subjectivity* of the mental apparatus. It does not lend itself to any objective measures of deviations from an optimum. Resilience or sensitivity may be temperamental factors influencing subjectivity and its experiences, but nonetheless,

DOI: 10.4324/9781003452522-4

subjectivity forms a fundamental tenet of the way the life and death drives, the need for up-stimulation or down-regulation affecting the individual. But this also introduces the conundrum: since the mass murder of six million Jews by the Nazis is not really the murder of a singular entity, as this implies. It is the murder of six million individuals, each single one with their own subjectivities and life stories, by the many Germans who perpetrated or were complicit in these crimes, they themselves individuals, millions of individual subjectivities caught up in the Nazi machinery.

These life and death instincts do not suggest a tendency to self-destruct, as in the colloquial use of the term 'death wish', but a tension between psychic energy that drives forward, pushing development at both a personal and social level and a drive that counterbalances this arousing or seeking tendency by striving for quiescence and homeostasis – that is, the death drive is fundamentally a conservative drive aiming to achieve homoeostasis and preservation of the organism, including in its striving to reach ultimate quietude, to spring the mortal coil by its own natural route. The inanimate preceded the animate in life, and from dust to dust, from this inanimate a return to the inanimate appears to be an imperative of all life. But the astute reader will begin to ask themselves if it is my suggestion that a conservative, quiescence-inducing, peace-striving drive would be linked to genocide.

How do we square these apparently diametrically opposed concepts: the one suggestive of a conservative drive whose aim is homeostasis and quiescence, and whose modus operandi is to operate, as we shall discuss later, by stealth. Left unprovoked, this drive would remain latent and 'in hibernation', pending a change in the status of the organism; the other suggestive that aggression and violence are predatory, object-seeking, the initiator or destruction not the preserver of stability.

In order to make sense of this apparent contradiction, we need to examine two elements: first, the *aim* of the aggressive drive rather than its *effects* to fully understand why it operates and not just *how* it operates; and second, the nature of subjectivity in the mobilisation of this drive. So often, as we encounter 'senseless and random acts of violence', we fail to comprehend any objective sense or reason for it. At the level of scalable atrocity, we struggle with the meaning – like the Twin Tower attacks in the United States. But equally, when an individual is murdered for his cellphone or less, we scratch our heads at the terrible waste of human life so cheaply expended. "For *that*, he had to die?" There is often simply no objective sense we can make at the creative capacity humans have for hurting other humans. The reason for these anomalies lies in the answer to these two points – why aggress? And subjectivity.

Freud's brilliant theoretical development recognised a duality within the human psyche, in which an opposition between the life instincts (Eros) and the death instincts emerge, a characteristic of all organic material from the unicellular to the multicellular. There is a striving for multiplication and existence is balanced by an energy that predates the living matter, since the inorganic precedes the organic, and restitude precedes living energy. Before life there is non-life, merely a "twinkle in the eye" of a prospective union of male and female capacity to contemplate the idea of, or phantasy of having a child and reproducing; but a striking point is also that the life instincts "have so much more contact with our internal perception – emerging as breakers of the peace and constantly producing tensions whose release is felt as pleasure – while the death instincts seem to do their work unobtrusively".[3] It is this stealth-like quality of the aggressive drive that both obfuscates its function and role and makes it appear quite paradoxical. And yet, none of this is new. The biochemist Nick Lane laments these paradoxes in the very first flushes of life itself: "Since the first complex eukaryotic cells arose", he writes, "some 1.5 to 2 billion years ago, we have had warfare, terror, murder and bloodshed: nature, red in tooth and claw. But in the preceding aeons, we had 2 billion years of peace and symbiosis, bacterial love…".[4] In other words, Lane argues,

> only rarely is natural selection actually a force for change. Most commonly, it opposes change, purging variation from the peaks of an adaptive landscape. Only when that landscape undergoes some kind of seismic shift does selection promote change rather than stasis.[5]

Memory and Aggression

So far, we have made the case for three essential points: the aggressive drive in the human psyche has the aim of reducing stimuli and excitations brought on by internal and external impingements – it is not 'looking for a fight'; what constitutes a threat or impingement is not necessarily objective – in fact, it is always filtered through subjective experience and the unconscious associations that are revisited repeatedly giving rise to a lens through which experience is filtered; this is driven by memory traces of experience that embed themselves in the unconscious and are revisited and hence enacted in a repetitive manner.

This last point needs some elaboration since one of the core principles of psychic function is the tendency of the mind to repeat. Freud termed this the repetition compulsion, a compulsive tendency to return to the familiar and in the psyche to re-experience familiar patterning through creating relationships and feedback loops that are built on early memory. Traumatic processes and events will in particular have a tendency to 'hardwire' into the unconscious since memory has evolved to serve the function of registering and remembering those stimuli that offer potential harm. Let me use an example: if an infant has a troubled early few weeks in the post-partum period due to silent reflux, a condition in which the infant is experiencing pain and discomfort but which may be invisible to the mother. The infant is registering serious impingements on its primitive psyche which is no-one's fault. Nonetheless, the infant in the early days does not differentiate internal from external impingements – in its 'normal autistic' state (to use Margaret Mahler's developmental concept to describe the first month of the infant's mental life) these merge and all that is registered is an impingement unsettling stasis. Mahler notes: "I have applied to the first weeks of life the term *normal autism*; for in it, the infant seems to be in a state of primitive hallucinatory disorientation, in which need satisfaction belongs to his own omnipotent, *autistic* orbit".[6] The newborn's waking life centres around his continuous attempts to achieve homeostasis. The baby cries and the mother hopefully tries to soothe it. Mahler observes that:

> *Beyond a certain, but not yet defined degree, the immature organism cannot achieve homeostasis on its own.* Whenever during the autistic or symbiotic phase there occurs "organismic distress"—that forerunner of anxiety proper—the mothering partner is called upon, to contribute a particularly large portion of symbiotic help toward the maintenance of the infant's homeostasis. Otherwise, the neurobiological patterning processes are thrown out of kilter. Somatic memory traces are set at this time, which amalgamate with later experiences and may thereby increase later psychological pressures.[7]

Like Winnicott, Mahler recognised in the symbiosis of the infant and maternal carer, that the mother-infant dyad operates together – there is "no such thing as a baby" (on its own). The mother provides a metabolic function for the disequilibrium of the infant's mind-body state in the merged minds of the dyad. Thus, if the threshold of pain is breached and the infant cannot bring about relief through its crying, that is, inducing a response from the environment/mother to alleviate the impingement, then according the Kendal's research mentioned above, long-term neural pathways form as a memory trace, aimed at reminding the infant of potential threats to its well-being. It's a primitive version of you only eat a poison berry once to remember never to do it again. So adaptive is memory for survival and functioning, that impairments to memory functioning lead to a dramatic increase in risk for navigating a complex world. In fact, it might be safe to suggest that impairment in the encoding *or* retrieval of memory will seriously impair the capacity to function. You can find your way to the toilet in a restaurant by following the signs, but what then? How do you remember how to navigate your way back? Or operate that chainsaw? Which way is the right way round again? Or how about your many codes and pins that are standard fare these days? Even where long-term memory remains intact, clinical cases demonstrate how the inability to encode new data becomes a dramatic impairment not only for the quality of life but also for its quantity. Mortality and morbidity increase greatly when memory becomes impaired.

It may seem peculiar to link memory and aggression. However, memory forms part of the psyche's ability to preserve and protect itself and is fundamental to the aetiology of much psychopathology and its working through in psychotherapy. "It's the love that lasts forever is the love that has no past", sang the Beatles, inferring both the ambivalence inherent to bonding and attachment and the nature of past hurt that impacts future love. The content of individual memory is also dependent on experience – that is, *personal experience forms the basis of individual memory traces*. This is also then the basis for subjectivity – since memory cannot form traces except through the sensory apparatus of the individual. No-one else on earth can feel the feelings of someone nor have their experiences. Sensory inputs ingress into the psyche through that person's senses – and the memory traces of those inputs will form the basis of subjective experience, or subjectivity. In other words, there cannot be an objective version of memory for any individual. All memory is subjective, by definition, which makes any attempt to objectify experience as scientific a non-sequitur. The individual has sensations and experiences, through the sensory apparatus, which forms the basis of *feelings*, and feelings, as Solms has pointed out, form an adaptive layer of efficiency in the brain's ability to navigate a complex world. Feelings, or subjectivity, are the brain's most efficient and effective way of adaptation, survival, and navigation of a highly complex external and internal world. I say internal and external, because evidently the external world is a complex environment of constant threats to equilibrium and mortality. The internal world is equally a source of constant challenge, both in the microclimates that require constant maintenance from sleep to regulate brain function and its metabolic processes to drinking sufficient water to maintain hydration to the broader developmental changes that prompt disequilibrium from within as ageing instigates both mental and physical evolution of the individual. Subjectivity becomes the key source of this combination of complex impingements, a bank of memory traces through which these challenges can be navigated.

The idea of objectivity of experience becomes from this point of view an oxymoron, which cannot exist. We can observe certain objective criteria that would indicate internal states (of mind) but these are invariably correlative observations, which would always require confirmation from the subject. For example, if someone seems slowed and stooped, an experienced psychologist would infer that the person is likely depressed and the slowing and loss of vitality appears to be suggestive of a vegetative symptom of a depressive episode. But this objective indicator is only valid if it can be confirmed not just against other objective symptom clusters for depression but also if confirmed by the person's subjective experience, that they *feel* depressed. Otherwise, these symptoms could indicate anything from a poor posture to fatigue-related anaemia, a spectrum personality, or someone with a sore back. Subjectivity is key to confirmation of any mental state for by definition a subjective mental state is not open to direct observation. It is this element of the human mind, subjectivity, that makes memory such a vital component and which defines the nature of experience. Experience defines memory traces. Memory in turn defines experience. It is this dialectical process that enables individual subjectivity to emerge and forge a role in defining reality, *for that person.* This creates a strange view of reality – which is to suggest that from a psychological point of view, there is no objective reality as it applies to an individual interpretation of the world through experience.

The Unconscious

This concept of subjective interpretation of reality determining reality rests on one of the most profound discoveries of science, the presence of a vast reservoir of memory traces, residing entirely beneath the surface of awareness. Consciousness is but the tip of the iceberg, the visible elements available to retrieval and awareness – but which hides beneath its surface a vast mental structure which Freud termed the Unconscious. This concept has become intuitively embedded in modern culture, but its structure is a recent discovery. Consciousness is but the surface of the skin, so to speak, of the mental apparatus much like the surface of the skin of the body and those sensations we consciously register through the senses represent a tiny fraction of the millions of metabolic, nerve, organ, neurological, and hormonal process occurring constantly without any conscious awareness or control. In fact, most of what occurs in the body never makes it into conscious awareness and does so only occasionally when something goes wrong and homeostasis is threatened. In other words, in the normal course of biological functioning, we only *feel* thirsty when we are thirsty, a representation of homeostasis becoming unbalanced. The psyche too holds within its folds enormous amounts of neurological and psychological data, mostly traces of experience and memory encoded through interpretation to create the building blocks of personality and its relationship to the world and the attachments of the world. Kandel makes this point neuroscientifically that the brain "does not simply take the raw data that it receives through the senses and reproduce it faithfully. Instead, each sensory system first analyses and deconstructs, then restructures the raw, incoming information according to its own built-in connections and rules…".[8] This suggests that subjectivity is baked into sensory perception and neurobiological *experience*, even when such experience is occurring in the dark, so to speak, beneath conscious awareness.

This also suggests that external objects in the world can *represent* internal objects. Memory has an associative quality, in that internal representations are triggered by external stimuli or symbols which are associated with these previous memories or are reminders of them. Internal representations can therefore also be understood to be capable of being projected onto external objects that are associated with them. So too, this particularly applies to internal representations of previous (and significant) attachments that directly influenced how memory traces formed. In infancy and early childhood, invariably, for obvious reasons, the mother and (later) the father will hold a grand quota of the energy invested in, or cathected to these representations. But let us not forget that often the source of these encoded memory traces that come to represent the world derives from within the infant's own body. Colic or reflux, for example, originated within but is experienced as an impingement that unsettles equilibrium – and which often becomes associated with food and eating – obviously the representative of this being the breast and the mother. So the pain from within may become associated with the breast and its caregiving function, leading to a memory trace forming of an association of the maternal caregiver with toxicity and discomfort. The world becomes an unsafe place and persecutory anxieties of a primitive sort can form; that the love object that is supposedly keeping the infant alive is simultaneously trying to hurt or even kill it. This conundrum is navigated through the use of various defensive manoeuvres that are available at that primitive stage, but which if too prolonged will become stuck in place, forming a layer of perception through which future experience may be interpreted. A more sensitive infant may experience this in an amplified form but the principle of encoding experience through the filters of subjectivity and its defensive organisations becomes the bedrock of that person's mind into the future. Unconscious influences of experience and perception will forever remain present so long as it remains unconscious, or if not modified through psychotherapy or analysis, which seeks to make these memories conscious and hence modify them.

I will say more about these defensive organisations and mechanisms later, but for now note that different defensive systems are available according to the developmental phase in which they are brought into service. This notion of returning to an earlier stage of development psychically refers to 'regression' to earlier unconscious stages, even when they occur in adulthood. Since the unconscious has no reference to time, the most primitive memory traces can influence later adult personality as if they were current. *Regression is current.* Experience through a regressive filter is experienced as if it were in the present, no matter how much time has elapsed since the original fixation driven by the perceived injury or trauma. The oft-repeated social cliché that you 'can't change the past' becomes nonsense in this technical context – because the past is only as good as the internal representation of it, through memory traces, that endure into the present. This suggests that fixation and regression are interlinked – that the psyche regresses to earlier development points in life, to those layers of fixation in which noxious impingements that have stirred disequilibrium are encoded as memory. The aim of this psychically is paradoxically to protect and preserve. Regression is therefore aimed at protecting the psyche from future noxious stimuli through representation – symbolically associating external objects with those internal ones. This also suggests that earlier stages of development *repeat* constantly – in fact, repeat constantly *compulsively* because repeat they must, if they are to fulfil the protective function that has devolved to them. Early defensive organisations compulsively repeat through later development, for that individual psyche. This idea of the repetition compulsion, as Freud termed it, suggests that we cannot consciously escape or shed our defensive systems and filters by simply deciding to do so.

Aggression Is Immunity

No conscious decision or cognitive manoeuvring can simply undo the embedded layers of subjectivity that compulsively press into present life any more than we can make a cognitive decision to switch our somatic immune systems on or off at a biological level, the bits of proteins that are recombined in what Lane calls "marvellous ways" to form billions of antibodies, thereby "setting in motion the killing machine of the immune system".[9] Note that this biological function is violent and merciless but launched from the innate imperative to fulfil its mandate of remaining dormant until stasis comes under threat. The emergent mental process of this immune function, this "killing machine" of the mental apparatus, is not one that looks for the fight either. It is happily latent, resting in the background until some provocation or impingement emerges that threatens this state. Then this merciless and 'destructive' (to the 'other') process gears up rapidly, relying on biological or psychological memory, to guide its attacks on the (perceived) source of this disequilibrium.

Our immune system has memory, and after exposure to a pathogen will create biological memory of that pathogen in order to be able to neutralise it at any later stage. Somatic immunity, like psychic immunity, operates by stealth and remains out of awareness unless prompted into action by a pathogen threatening the body. We can try influence these responses as much as we like, but they will continue to operate according to their own dictates and according to their own designation. Psychic memory is no different, since the function of this response is the same. Memory is part of the psychic immune system. But the fixation of defensive organisations at particular developmental stages is often triggered by an impingement that threatens equilibrium, and evokes an aggressive response that exceeds capacity to metabolise and restore the state of disequilibrium. Aggression is triggered by impingements, like it or not, and this drive must find a mechanism or channel. When aggression is activated, it is the mind's way of mobilising a response whose aim is the restoration of an earlier state (of equilibrium). It may seem strange to suggest but we arrive at a point in which we can posit the idea: *Aggression is psychic immunity.*

This claim needs considerable justification. The elusive quality of the aggressive drive and its latent or stealth-like quality make it difficult to access by investigation, since all we can observe are the effects of externalised aggression through words or actions or somatic symptoms such as tics or flushing of the skin. But unlike the sexual drive which is much more felt and experienced through the sensations of pleasure and arousal in the body and its surfaces, the aggressive drive operates silently, maintaining a latent state except under the pressure of some impingement that mobilises it. The apparent contradiction of this observation is how does a predator like Ted Bundy, who goes out seeking a target for his violent intent, be said to have mobilised under a condition of impingement? These women were not seeking him out – he hunted them! The fusion of sexual and aggressive elements is one element of this contradiction – a powerful seeking drive mixed up with a violent one. But this explanation does not always square with many examples of sexual preferences, such as BDSM (BDSM stands for 'bondage and discipline, dominance and submission, sadism and masochism', and the acronym has largely replaced the earlier term 'sado-masochism'). Here these elements fuse without any predatory development in people practicing various forms of BDSM. We must look deeper into such a mind to realise that the aggressive component is met internally by a representation of an object, and it is this internal representation to which the person is mobilising a violent response. "You remind me of…", is often accompanied by unconscious internal representations that can trigger affects that are consciously 'felt', but also affects that surprisingly are not consciously felt, at least not directly in a conscious connection to the internal representation. The problem here is becoming apparent – how can unconscious affects not be felt as feelings if by definition they must be consciously felt to serve a purpose?

This was part of Freud's dilemma too – drives trigger affects which can operate at two levels – one felt as pleasure and unpleasure through the sensory apparatus and registered consciously – the other maintained unconsciously, or at least finding a path through channels that are not fully registered consciously. This compromise formation of the inner tensions of the mind both wanting and not wanting to know at the same time evolved to maintain equilibrium at the source of the intra-psychic conflict. But the compromise formation, whilst resolving the conflict at the time, creates a developmental fixation point in the psyche, to which the person returns again and again. Regression to old reference points operates in the service of psychic integrity, meeting the pressing need for the psyche to store threatening data points along life's journey for future use. But reacting to these data points as if they were present tense creates a new set of problems for adults reacting to the world and its attachments as if they were current, since as I mentioned above, memory and the unconscious have no reference to time. This notion is well accepted in psychoanalysis and psychology and its penetration into the cultural consciousness reflects its relevance that we all experience – both knowing and not knowing at the same time. Being aware of reacting in the present to the present but sometimes under the influence of something past is something we can all relate to at some level, even if one's emotional reaction cannot be helped.

Profile of an Artistic Villain

The villain in our next story is a vegetarian, dog-friendly, opera-loving weedy young man with ambitions to become a great artist.[10] Apparently, sensitive in nature, this aspirant creative struggled to find recognition for his greatest ambitions – entrance to the Art Academy in his city. Hardly the profile of a villain. Allow me to repeat: vegetarian, artist, opera-loving, animal lover. Not exactly Attila the Hun.

His early years were spent under the smothering protectiveness of an over-anxious mother, to whom he was exceptionally close and bonded. His home was dominated by his father, a threatening presence of a disciplinarian, against whose wrath the submissive mother was helpless to protect her offspring. The mother was described by his sister as a

> very soft and tender person, a compensatory element between an almost too harsh father and the very lively children. Parents quarrelled mainly about the children, and he in particular challenged his father to extreme harshness and who got his sound thrashing every day. His mother, however, caressed him, trying to obtain with her kindness what his father could not with his harshness.

His father was prone to sudden bursts of temper and would then immediately hit out. He did not love his father but in fact feared him all the more. His poor beloved mother, he used to remark, to whom he was so attached, lived in constant concern about the beatings he had to take, sometimes waiting outside the door as he was thrashed.

Later in life, this seemed to be associated with a rather patronising contempt for the submissiveness of women, and perhaps also his feelings of betrayal by those weak and ineffectual, those who 'betrayed him', something he felt later in life about his people and nation. He developed as a result his own thirst for success and dominance. He seemed to struggle forming deep personal relationships as a result and battled with alternating between self-hatred and marked narcissism. His adolescence was 'very painful', and marked by increasing tension with his father, who died suddenly when he was about 13 years, leaving him to step into the shoes of the 'man of the house', and perhaps increasing the closeness with his mother. After school, he was cosseted and looked after by his doting mother, her sister (his aunt), and his own little sister, who washed cleaned and cooked for him. He spent his time on the piano they had bought for him, drawing, painting, reading and writing poetry, and in the evening going to the opera or theatre, fantasising most of the time about himself and his future as a great artist.

A friendship he developed became part of his evening routine of theatre and opera, and this friendship helped this weedy young man to navigate his life, albeit a rather aimless one at this point, and perhaps gain some self-confidence. He became passionate about classical music, describing listening to Wagner as an almost religious experience, an example of supreme artistic genius that this (we might infer sensitive) young man wanted to emulate. This was affected later when his mother became ill with incurable cancer, and he became distracted by tending her during her illness and was anguished at the pain she suffered. This perhaps added to his resolve to become an artist and he made plans to apply and enter the Academy of Fine Arts. Armed with a thick pile of drawings he sat various entrance exams but did not succeed. His test drawings were described as "unsatisfactory". He had been convinced he said, that passing the entrance exam would be 'child's play'. "I was so convinced that I would be successful that when I received my rejection, it struck me as a bolt from the blue". A double blow came in the form of his (young, at mid-forties) mother's death, leaving the young man 'prostrate with grief' (according to his General Practitioner) and a "dreadful blow" (as he himself put it), leaving him feeling alone and bereft. The double loss in a four-month period was a crushing blow to his already fragile sense of self and his fantasies of effortless path to success as an artist.

Nonetheless, he decided to try again and enter the academy but again admitted angrily, "they rejected me, they threw me out, they turned me down". The blow to his self-esteem was profound and the bitterness showed, often through flaring up in an instant into boundless anger and violent denunciation of all he thought were persecuting him, including mankind in general who did not understand him, or appreciate him, and who left him feeling persecuted and cheated. These tirades of hate directed at everything and everybody were those of an apparently outsized ego desperately wanting acceptance and unable to come to terms with his personal insignificance with failure and mediocrity. This seemed to affect his sexuality too, in which he avoided contact with women, apparently repelled by homosexuality, and refrained from masturbation, although apparently was both horrified and fascinated by prostitution. During this period, he did not drink or smoke, preferring milk or fruit juice, became vegetarian, and in his struggle to survive economically, spend his small amount of money on opera or classical concerts. This second failure a year later to get into the Arts Academy left him bereft, his hopes of an artistic career now lying totally in ruins. He felt like a confirmed failure. Incidentally, these experiences also sensitised him to prejudice, which worried him and encountering it left him unsettled, perhaps understanding the experience of being marginalised. Once he came across an anti-Semitic pamphlet which disturbed him and left him saying: "it seemed to me so monstrous, the accusations so boundless, that tormented by the fear of doing injustice, I again became anxious and uncertain".

Here we have the story of an apparently sensitive and wounded young man, suffering physical and narcissistic injuries from his father, narcissistic gratification from his mother, and later rejection of his dreams of great art – pained, anxious, feeble, but as a young man, facing these failures and rejections, finding himself also increasingly enraged, aimless, angry, and emotionally isolated. We don't normally associate sensitivity, anxiety, artistic passion, love of music, love of animals, vegetarianism, with merciless cruelty. Yet presumably, the narcissistic injury underlying this personality lent itself to human devastation unparalleled in the history of humankind.

This man became directly and indirectly responsible for more deaths in human history than any other person. Fifty million people lost their lives in the Second World War, one key factor in this human catastrophe being the personality of Adolf Hitler, a 'sensitive' would-be artist with aspirations for greatness that had so eluded him in his youth. This case is useful in assisting to demonstrate the link between underlying injury and aggression, forming itself into a perverse loop separated from its original traumas and links. Nonetheless, the aggression served to constantly expunge the defeated, undignified, humiliated person and nation that was Germany in the years between the Wars.

A reading of this case suggests that the inner world of Hitler was contorted by narcissistic injury and humiliation, betrayal and deflation. Beginning in his early parental relationships, his rage response to perceived injury created a volatile and thin-skinned character, becoming increasingly embittered at the perceived injustices of the world. Himself as victim of these, he found a scaffolding on which to enact these bitter internal representations, finding, perhaps opportunistically in the political climate of the day, scapegoats upon which his projections could be manifest.

Whilst psycho-biographies are invariably imperfect representations and can be ridiculed as being void for vagueness, this extreme personification of pure evil must also follow the laws of nature – like any psychic entity or mental apparatus. Hitler was human and his brain and psyche were governed by the regular laws of nature that applies to all human psyches. As an interesting case of juxtapositions, this case does not conform to the normal profile of the psychopathic killer, the predatory sociopath that pulled the wings off butterflies and tortured little kittens in childhood. How does the one representation become the other? How does this mental apparatus morph from enfeebled creative to genocidal mastermind?

This material touches the elements we have explored earlier – the encoding into memory of injury and threat, states of disequilibrium, and manoeuvres to manage these threats and restore stasis. Fantasies of aggrandisement, initially to be a great artist and later the conquistador of Europe, the saviour of a nation and their indignities at the hands of malevolent patriarchal power-mongers, and those Western leaders who 'robbed' Germany not only of their material foundation but also of her dignity and pride, pepper the discourse of Hitler's later life. We also witness the repetition of these compensations in his life, symbols of grandeur and greatness, unlimited power, symbolised through representations of phallic prowess, despite the observation that the man himself was limited sexually and appeared to demonstrate little sexual prowess or phallic presence at all. Prone to rages under the threat or experience of humiliation, the material, limited as it is, also demonstrated the power of regression, returning to the origin and source of earlier fixation points. Developmentally, these points are 'floors' to which the individual returns repeatedly under threat of association to re-experience some earlier insult or injury. However, a psychoanalytic psycho-biography, such as the one I am attempting here, is by definition wholly flawed: since psychoanalytic insight can never be fully achieved without subjective report and association. We have none of that here – and so these links are at best likely interpretations of links that could only really be verified under the pressure test of self-report and free association. As I mentioned before, the individual mind emerges into 'being' through experience, through *feeling* feelings, through innate drives being affected by the complex mix of external and internal impingements, filtered through the lens of subjectivity. We have no access in this case to that subjectivity – nonetheless, the case is extreme and compelling and enough data exists for some links to be considered in illuminating the paradox of the complex drive that triggers aggression.

The Three Faces of Aggression

The Nazi regime was not an individual nor was driven by spams of impulsive rage. In fact, the most heinous of its crimes were committed in the coldest and most calculated of fashions. Professionals designed the ideology, mechanisms, and architecture required to create the machinery for mass murder – no small undertaking. Cold and calculated appears on the face of it to bear little resemblance to the phenomenon we usually associate with aggression – fists flying, knives flashing, voices raised. Here, at the Wannsee Conference in Berlin on 20 January 1942, we have a calm business meeting discussing matters of business, its problems, goals, and implementation across Europe. They could have been discussing the construction of a railway line or the timetable for garbage collection in a city. Instead, the single agenda relates to the mass extermination of a people. The Final Solution to the Jewish Question is not a document of rage and bellicosity, but of cold hard business-like discussion pertaining to a task to be accomplished.

The minutes from the Wannsee Conference, and various other speeches we will discuss later, represent some of the data for our discussion. Accordingly, I include the full minutes in the Appendix A to capture for the interested reader the cold, intellectual business meeting whose sole agenda was genocide, mass murder of an entire cultural people. The meeting and its minutes discuss mass deportations and mass murder, allocation of responsibilities for the tasks at hand, lines of account-ability, who is in charge of what by name, numbers of people to be dealt with, and the usual items required in any business. It begins with the statement:

> Under proper guidance the Jews are now to be allocated for labor to the East in the course of the final solution. Able-bodied Jews will be taken in large labor columns to these districts for work on roads, separated according to sexes, in the course of which action a great part will undoubtedly be eliminated by natural causes. The possible final remnant will, as it must undoubtedly consist of the toughest, have to be treated accordingly, as it is the product of natural selection, and would, if liberated, act as a bud cell of a Jewish reconstruction (see histori-cal experience).

At first blush, we detect no aggression in the conventional sense in the tone or con-tent of this document, and even statements such as "In the course of the practical execution of this final settlement of the problem, Europe will be cleaned up from the West to the East", if we were not pondering with hindsight the historical implica-tions of these statements, we might have wondered if this was a document put out by an environmental organisation. Terms are technical, procedural, statistical – 30% of..., 280,000 of... "(r)egarding the handling of the final solution in the European territories occupied and influenced by us...". Foreign countries are referred to as simple extensions to be influenced and controlled. Rumania, Hungary, France, Slo-vakia, and Croatia, the Scandinavian states are all referred to as areas through which some policy and control can be implemented. The 'science' of how the entity in question is defined, the blood composition of what defines a Jew in the first and sec-ond degrees and the degree of 'mixed blood' which defines who shall be deported for destruction and who not. Those of mixed blood exempted from the evacuation "will be sterilised – in order to eliminate the possibility of offspring and to secure a final solution of the problem presented by the persons of mixed blood". Opinions are proffered, such as "SS-Gruppenfuehrer HOFMANN advocates the opinion that sterilisation must be applied on a large scale..." but because of the "endless admin-istrative work" that would be required by the problems of 'mixed blood' cases, "it was suggested by Dr. STUCKART to proceed to forced sterilisation...". Forced removal of Jews from Germany was suggested because "Jews represented an im-mense danger as a carrier of epidemics, and on the other hand were permanently contributing to the disorganisation of the economic system of the country through black market operations". Mindful of the challenges of this task, it was noted:

> Towards the end of the conference the various types of possible solutions were discussed; in the course of this discussion Gauleiter Dr. MEYER as well as

Under Secretary of State Dr. BUEHLER advocated the view that certain preparatory measures incidental to the carrying out of the final solution ought to be
initiated immediately in the very territories under discussion, in which process,
however, alarming the population must be avoided.

Following a request from the Chief of the Security Police and the SD for assistance in carrying out the tasks involved in the 'final solution, the conference was
adjourned'.

I include some of this detail to bring to the fore the extent of intellectual cal-
culation and forethought, business-like in its entirety. This extract requires some
distantiation to begin to comprehend the scale of this blueprint, as well as the implications of its suggestions. These are well known – one of the most heinous crimes
against humanity ever conceived and executed. The ruthless efficiency, as well
as the collusion of ordinary German citizens and soldiers in both the ideological
underpinnings and its implementation, was unparalleled. This historical chapter
seems to represent intra-species violence scaled to the nth degree. The Wannsee
Protocol of 1942 represents to us the capacity for the human mind to harness a
form of aggression we might term cold, impersonal, and unprovoked. It is in many
senses a form of aggression we might characterise as predatory, like a Great White
shark attacking a surfer. No feeling involved, nothing personal, just the appearance
of a meal. Hot anger, on the other hand, is much more personal, a response to an
attachment that has triggered hurt, much more individually based, and invariably
recruiting a greater amount of personal projection to its triggering and expression.
The neuroscience assists in this differentiation of different forms of aggression,
which as we shall see helps to make sense of this particular conservative drive in
humans, which Freud identified as the Death Drive, and which the neuroscientist
Panksepp differentiated into different neuropsychological systems.

Rage and Predation

Jaak Panksepp, the celebrated neuroscientist, makes the important distinction between different forms of the rage response, and the fact that predatory aggression
can be differentiated neurologically from other forms of aggression more commonly associated with *felt* anger. He puts these terms in capitals to make clear that
these are neurological systems he is describing. Ironically, cold predatory aggression may appear on the surface to be void of feelings of anger, as the Wannsee
document demonstrates – extreme human destruction with no feelings as such.
"Indeed", says Panksepp,

neuroscientists have had a difficult time accepting that the 'quiet-biting' predatory attack of animals, just like our human urge for hunting, emerges more from
the psychic energies of the SEEKING system than from the RAGE system.
In a sense, the SEEKING system is always searching for satisfying endpoints,

whether it is a predator chasing down a meal-on-the-hoof, or humans aspiring to win a contentious argument.

Aggression comes in different forms, and the point that there is not a singular representation of aggression enhances the distinction that aggression underlies different responses in humans, and as Panksepp reminds us, "demonstrate decisive differences between RAGE and predatory aggression".[11] In fact, of interest is that research indicates that the rage system requires living objects on which to vent the rage for any cathartic process to be achieved. Punching a pillow in a fit of rage to try vent it, may have little benefit, unless fantasy of a hated object is projected onto the inanimate object.[12]

Much neuroscientific research is based on animals, rats, and so on, which whilst enabling some extrapolation to the brains of humans also limits the parallels we can make. It is like trying to understand the human hand by analysing the "four-rayed hand" of the frog. Some extrapolations are helpful but you would not want your hand surgeon relying solely on this study. Animals, as best we can tell, do not have the capacity to filter instinct through higher level cerebral mechanisms and hence also lack the capacity for symbolisation, fantasy, self-reflection, and the diversion of innate drives along other paths of defence or displacement. Animals also do not seem to fuse drives in the manner humans can, since symbolisation and diversion of instincts onto different internal and external representations enable drives to fuse. The seeking system Panksepp denotes can, in humans, fuse with aggression in various ways to blur the pain-pleasure distinction and like with BDSM[13] create the capacity for aggression and sexuality to heighten erotic experience, rather than cancel it. But with these provisos in mind, neuroscientists such as Panksepp point out that put together, experimental findings do suggest that "RAGE and predatory aggression produce different physiological responses, behaviours, and affects".[14] In humans, the fusion of libidinal and aggressive drives might enable more complex drivers to emerge based on individual experience, a subjectivity that lower animals do not necessarily enjoy.

Added to this complexity, Panksepp notes the neuroscience behind the drive for social dominance, particularly in men, and the distinction between the three forms of aggression – hot or rage-driven aggression, cold predatory aggression, and aggression in the service of social dominance and hierarchy. We might for the sake of convenience think of these forms as hot, cold, and hierarchical aggressions. Despite the dangers of theoretical reductionism, this neuroscience assists in understanding some of the biological underpinnings for aggression but does not adequately satisfy the complexity of the psychical fusions that occur in real time in humans, as opposed to laboratory rats, where single variable dimensions can be mapped more effectively. As useful as the empirical research is in uncovering the neural pathways and mechanisms, *subjective* experience and psychical representations of aggression in all these forms are more often than not connected to intra-psychic symbolic representations rather than simple concrete triggers. A patron kept waiting in a busy restaurant for his food does not usually bit the hand that feeds him, so to speak, which an animal might do if frustrated in its quest to reach a desired morsel. A huffy or uptick in irritation might of course emerge and that would be normal frustration. But a patron with a history of being kept waiting by their mother for a feed, perhaps amplified by a higher-than-normal metabolism amplifying feelings of hunger and discomfort, might regress to this early stage of psychic life and connect with the emotional response of the time. An explosive rage and storming out, or worse, could result in the person "creating a scene" for reasons that appear to an outside observer disproportionate. Or, if that same aggressive energy is turned in (introjected) or in some way defended against, an implosive result might follow, associated with anxiety or feeling down and defeated. "I'm such a loser! – even the waiter forgets I am here!"

The human psyche does not bend to simplicity or linearity in its reactions – concrete triggers interface with memory, symbolic representations, associations in the individual response and subjectivity. Intuitively, the rage response, or what we think of as hot rage, is a response to provocation and frustration. Triggered, anyone can react. It is felt and obvious, a lot like lust is felt and obvious to the person experiencing it. But the cold predatory aggression may not be felt at all, may remain elusive, operating by stealth, unknown until some sort of symptom appears in its wake. This function is like the immune system of the body and the automatic activation of aggression in the face of subjectively experienced impingements that threaten equilibrium. This again makes sense in the individual level. A mechanism exists which is activated to protect the individual mental apparatus from states of (negative) disequilibrium. It bears mentioning that such a scenario can occur for entirely internal reasons – a young person sexually charged from within cannot easily find a release for his or her lust and becomes irritable or even aggressive because the desired object is not attainable. Hence, the frustrations of the loss of the desired object may give rise to aggressive impulses, protecting the person from the shame, humiliations, and frustrations of their plight. This too makes sense, since aggression is activated in response to any state of experienced disequilibrium, including frustration.

Genocide and Its Anomaly

We can understand the neurology behind the various forms of aggression and its evolutionary benefits that enable competition for resources, enhancement of survival, and adaptive advantage. It makes sense also that pleasure from seeking behaviours could be associated with predatory and hunting behaviours, fusing seeking (associated with libidinal impulses in which the life drive is met) by aggression in the hunt. We can also see the adaptive merits of hot rage in which threats to the self-organising system require a defence to a perceived threat or frustration, where snarling, baring of teeth, chest thumping, or throwing fists protects the animal from direct threat. These represent different evolutionary systems – and in animals at least this makes sense as it does for humans, but only to a degree. But on the other hand, these responses do not square neatly with the counter-benefits from intra-species violence in which neither threat nor conquest is present nor invites any benefit at all, beyond pure perception and projection. Reflecting on the Wannsee Conference and its agenda as an extreme example of the data, brings this anomaly into better focus. It is, of course, only one representation of aggression in humans but one in which the clarity of the data makes for useful pickings for our discussion.

Murder, particularly on scale, is a messy and resource-consumptive process. The massive consumption of resources for mass murder would have to compute to fit the evolutionary theory, particularly when its implementation would *enhance* the threat to the organism in question (the Nazi State) rather than protect it or add any evolutionary advantage. Put differently, how can a group of Jews in the 1930s, a tiny sub-section of German and European societies, making up 0.2% of the world's population, without recourse to any physical or military capacity at that time be a threat? Moreover, being culturally non-proselytising (in fact discourage conversion to Judaism) even in the most abstract sense how could this tiny section of the populous be in any conceivable way a threat to anyone, least of all a militarily and cultural powerful and cohesion society? And yet, this relatively tiny cultural group (even today, nearly 80 years after the Holocaust constitute only approximately 13 million people in a world of approximately eight billion) became the central and complete obsession of the mighty German war machine, sacrificing its own military resources in the pursuit of genocide and mass murder. Germany was an organised and intelligent society, developed culturally, technologically, and militarily, but ploughed endless resources into a programme of mass murder. This makes little sense from any theoretical or scientific point of view. None of the evolutionary imperatives – hot aggression as protective, or even cold predatory drivers that might bear some fruit in the end-game of the hunt – bear little resemblance to the systematic genocide of a tiny, unarmed, people with no imperialist intent, and no cultural stomach for incorporating any other culture. If anything, the opposite was true with hindsight and perhaps even with foresight at the time the outcomes could have been predictable by this intelligent community. Such hubris invariably ends in self-annihilation since both history, science, and theology have demonstrated such through eons of time.

The Wannsee Conference of 1942 represents for us this anomaly. If science is to be consistent, and that predictability is the hallmark of a scientific theory, then we are faced in this example with an anomaly for which a scientific explanation is required. Is Wannsee an anomaly? Is anything in our theoretical toolkit able to account for this level of human barbarism and intra-species violence? And further, does an understanding of individual intra-psychic dynamics enable an understanding of group dynamics of this sort, particularly, to state the obvious, groups emerge from a self-organising collection of individuals, and individuals emerge from a collection of self-organising cells?

Embodiment and the Emergent Mind

One of the groundbreaking observations Freud made from early on in his discoveries was the notion of the embodied psyche. This link is not reductionistic in the sense that mind can be reduced to brain function but as we now know from neuroscience, there is an intimate and mutually influencing relationship between these two inter-related entities. As Barnaby Barratt, a deep-thinking psychoanalytic theorist[15] reminds us in his writings, the human psyche in psychoanalytic terms is a mind rooted in both neurological function but most importantly in somatic experience. The body is the initial conduit through which experience is forged and these somatic impressions influence the emergent properties of the mind, the sensuality of our embodied experience "constitutes a wellspring of energy that animates every moment of the life of the psyche",[16] and embodied experience is the foundation of our psychic realities. Freud noted: "The ego is first and foremost a bodily ego; it is not merely a surface entity, but is itself the projection of a surface".[17] The ego, he said, is

> ultimately derived from bodily sensations, chiefly those springing from the surface of the body. It may thus be regarded as a mental projection of the surface of the body, besides, as we have seen above, representing the superficies of the mental apparatus.[18]

Somatic, neurological, and emergent psychological work in a unifying system.

Barratt's reminder is an important one, easily lost in the ideological transformations of society that can fall prey to cherry picking the data or theories that are preferred to suit a particular position. Although Freud stands at the head of *somatic* psychology, as Barratt reminds us, and his theorising is inescapably and ingeniously a body-mind approach, "the discipline that bears his name has all to frequently become the "science" of the disembodied subject".[19] Equally true, we might assert that the centrality of the aggressive drive in the genesis of symptoms and psychopathology in post-Freudian analytical circles and in psychology in general is to relegate it to the margins, often due to its association with a characteristic of ideological distaste. Of course, destructiveness is not desirable, but failure to understand this prevalent dimension of human functioning is to neglect its fundamental role in both individual and collective dynamics.

In reality, a dialectic is created through which emergent mental properties built upon the foundational drivers of somatic experience, can in turn exert an influence on the brain and body. Defence mechanisms become representations of somatic experience at particular phases of development, the mental apparatus forming according to the conduits through which experience is enabled. An infant cannot drive a truck or control when it defecates. So, these capabilities have no impact on mental defences in the earliest stages of life. However, oral determinants place the mouth and the gastro-intestinal system central to the infant's somatic focus. The sucking reflex dominates the early days and weeks of life, creating a focus around the muscles and sensations of the mouth. An infant cannot do much, but it can close its mouth, it can incorporate elements from the environment in the form of milk, and it can eject those contents. These represent early capabilities of the infant, over which some agency is possible. The infant can quickly learn to suck and ingest, or eject, or deny access to its inner world though refusal and closing the mouth. These primitive capabilities form the first building blocks of psychic capability – the prototypes for mental representations of agency over the world. If I close my mouth, the world no longer exists, it cannot penetrate, denial as an early but primitive mechanism. Denial of reality, if it persists, can of course be seen in later development in the form of psychosis and other psychopathology.

It bears repeating that in the early days of development an infant cannot distinguish internal from external impingements and so sources of unsettlement from their own bodies (such as reflux, cold or heat) or from the external environment (a pin prick or scratchy beard of their father hugging them) are treated and reacted to in similar ways. The key question the infant's psyche will ask itself is, is this impingement a source of pleasure or unpleasure. In the early undifferentiated state, there is no capacity to isolate sources of impingement or in any way regulate them effectively without environmental support, primarily maternal. This strange challenge, where an infant is required to regulate and re-regulate itself from states of disequilibrium whilst simultaneously being utterly helpless to do so, creates a neuropsychological challenge. How does nature meet this challenge? It enables the mechanisms of crying and the variants thereof, such as niggling or fussing. Where initial vocalisations do not induce from the environment a satisfactory response, the crying will invariably escalate. In the normal course of things, an increase in pitch and intensity. As anyone exposed to a crying infant will testify, especially when there is no escaping it, such as on a long-haul flight, the effect on surrounding adults is compelling – it leaves people feeling 'frazzled', edgy, sometimes even hostile – "can't that mother do something?!" – is an often-heard grumble in such circumstances, as if the mother isn't usually trying. Put differently, the infant's crying *induces* a response in nearby adults, and obviously especially the mother.

Inducement is a forceful process, since it has penetrative qualities which are psychically irresistible and which create states of disequilibrium in the surrounding adults so that they will action a response to remedy the state of discord in the infant, in any way possible, often by trial and error. The astute reader will notice that this infantile mechanism of remedy, the baby's ability to cry, which we associate with distress, is driven by a mechanism of inducement, by definition an aggressive concept. The drive that triggers crying in response to states of disequilibrium is driven by the aggressive drive which induces or forces a response from the environment in order to activate a way to restore homeostasis. It may seem strange to connect crying with aggression in infancy, but if we deconstruct the aim and the effects of this mechanism of crying, we quickly see that in both aim and effects forceful inducement in a penetrating way shares its raison d'être with the aggressive drive of the later developed psyche. It is, ultimately, the young infant's sole mechanism of psychic protection and restoration, its internal mental immune system operating in the service of returning the infant to homeostasis, a key focus and challenge for the young infant, as Mahler observed.

The First Drive

As many authors have noted, such as Barnaby Barratt,[20] Freud stands at the head of a somatic psychology, and he offered a profound rendering of the nature of emergent systems that in turn interface with, but cannot be reduced to their somatic origins. Mental representations emerge from somatic experiences and biological mechanisms, but in time develop a 'life of their own quality', no longer reducible to its origins but always maintaining some connection to it. The sperm and ovum give rise to an exceedingly complex living body with highly differentiated organs and systems, but we can never reduce life back into the sperm and ovum, even though life will always carry the residues, the genetic influences of these simple cells. Billions of cellular processes in later life carry the residues of these two simple originating cells. Physics might lend a hand in recognising the teleological quality of all systems in biology, the movement-forward into greater but irreducible complexity whilst at the same time grappling with the trend towards entropy. Left alone, all systems appear to decay back to a natural state. In nature, we may therefore also observe that two dynamic forces coexist – the one driving towards greater unities and order, like energy coalescing into galaxies with its own governing systems and order, and the tendency in nature towards entropy and decay. I use the word decay ill-advisedly since decay represents from nature's own point of view, a return. Not a backwards step, but a forward step towards restoration of the homeostatic quietude that existed prior to the energetic drive towards order and creative change. The universe itself, appears to mirror the human life cycle that Freud so insightfully understood, that before the thrust of the Big Bang towards a living universe of exceedingly complex order and energy, was a universe of non-being, quiet and inert but with potential for intense life and energy. Freud's recognition of the biblical narrative of "from dust to dust" captures the notion that before life and the thrust of the life force was a state of quietude and non-being, a state to which the human being, in any case, strives to return ultimately through its own circuitous path. Freud wrote:

> On the contrary, it must be an *old* state of things, an initial state from which the living entity has at one time or other departed and to which it is striving to return by the circuitous paths along which its development leads. If we are to take it as a truth that knows no exception that everything living dies for *internal* reasons—becomes inorganic once again—then we shall be compelled to say that 'the aim of all life is death' and, looking backwards, that 'inanimate things existed before living ones.'

The death drive is, ultimately, according to Freud (1920) the 'first drive',[21] since, although it appears to be a logical contradiction, the inanimate predates the animate, the quiescent state of non-being precedes being, and hence contains within it 'a compulsion to return to an original inanimate state' (p. 38). In fact, Mills reminds us that Freud (1933a) makes the point that the death drive 'cannot fail to be present in every vital process',[22] since it is there from, and perhaps before, the beginning of life. As life emerges from the inanimate, it therefore carries with it the essence of a pull to stasis and restoration that acts in contest with the life drive.

A Dualistic View

This dualistic view of both inorganic matter and organic matter, and by extension the mind, is recognised by Freud and becomes part of his later formulations of psychic life. The complexity of human functioning and the human psyche, does not separate us entirely from lower animate or for that matter inanimate systems, even though we may enjoy dominion over them. The theoretical development into this *dualistic* view of psychic functioning is reflected in life's tensions more generally, not between ego-instincts and sexual instincts as Freud initially thought, "but between life instincts and death instincts". This development in Freud's theoretical insights pertaining to the highest and most complex of organisms in the known universe, the human brain and mind, evolved to come full circle back to the origins of life, and as time marched on through the researches of scientists in other disciplines, such as neuroscience and biochemistry, his lamenting of the limitations of his theories were met with verification. The point Freud had made back in 1920, that the "uncertainty of our speculation has been greatly increased by the necessity for borrowing from the science of biology",[23] and I might add physics, appears prophetic with hindsight, cementing the progression of the innate tensions that drive all systems in our known cosmos. Freud added, that

> one of the earliest and most important functions of the mental apparatus is to bind the instinctual impulses which impinge on it, to replace the primary process prevailing in them by the secondary process and convert their freely mobile cathectic energy into a mainly quiescent (tonic) cathexis.

That is, a drive that prompts life forward is also met with a drive that strives to bind mental energy and return it to a state of stasis.[24]

The idea that the infant is *pushed* into life and along life's paths of greater development, greater unities at both cellular and social levels, concurs with what we see and intuit in life. But what remains less visible is the equally powerful drive to maintain stasis and guide the organism towards a state of renewed quiescence once the waning of the life drive settles. This is also a dynamic we witness in greater systems, such as couples where the ascendance of the life forces and libidinal elements dominates in the early stages, a gradual return to a more quiescent state occurs, leading to conflict and disillusionment which requires management. These broad processes do not do justice to the exquisite variability of individuality in all these spheres but do provide the framework for making sense of the processes that emerge in anomalous ways, such as the propensity humans have for inter-species violence and destruction.

Left in a state of imaginary homeostasis, would an infant have any need to aggress by inducing environmental response? Unfortunately, it would appear intrinsic to the human condition since under the pressures of the life drive, what Freud calls the internal "breakers of the peace", development pushes states of constant deviations from equilibrium towards developmental change. And unfortunately, change brings its stresses and challenges, the bitter-sweet of growth. Under the pressures of the life drive, or Eros, libidinal pressures push humans via what Panksepp terms neurologically the SEEKING system to strive for connection to objects and attachments; the aim of libidinal pressure is cathexis with the object, human or other, foraging, looking for, finding, bonding, attaching, possessing, and creating – the stuff of evolutionary advantage and survival. These strivings operating at the complex human level seem to have precursors in the primitive organic level, operating and originating at the level of physics and inorganic matter. The precursor to complex human strivings, or drives, can be found therefore also in the properties of primitive matter down to the level of particles. Mark Solms, in his pioneering work on the neuroscience of consciousness points out that all systems are invariably governed by the tendency to self-organise and once organised attempt to maintain stasis to preserve itself as a system. He writes that the

> rule that govern these particles are of the same broad character as those governing the behaviour of real atoms and molecules: mindless (but not indiscriminate) propensities to attract and repel one another. Such interactions evidently produce *order from chaos. Spontaneous ordering of this kind is thought to have occurred when life emerged from the primal soup.*[25]

Solms links the concept of homeostasis, or what I would want to call *emergent* homeostasis, to Friston's Free Energy Principle. This principle suggests that all energy systems begin to self-organise into some form of identity. I add the term *emergent* since nature has a tendency to form order from chaos and only once formed does a resistance to entropy begin to embed itself in the now organised system. This principle appears to govern all matter and life in the universe and suggests that energy at all emerging levels of complexity trend towards becoming self-organising. That is, they move from chaos to order and once ordered strive to maintain that order and their now-formed identity. This applies whether you are an atom or a galaxy, an amoeba, or an elephant. This notion of the self-organising nature of all living matter assists in building a bridge between the principles governing the inorganic and the organic. The laws of nature govern the laws of nature, it might be said. As Solms explains this basic fabric of life: "billions of little homeostats wrapped in their Markov blankets".[26] A Markov blanket, he explains, represents a statistical concept which separates two sets of states from each other, a partitioning of states into internal and external. Without such partitioning, entropy would prevail over any living system. In organic matter, the cell membrane comes to represent this 'envelope', the skin around the body, and the ego of the mind. Michael Kirchhoff (2018) in his paper[27] corroborates these points, suggesting that "autonomous systems are hierarchically composed of Markov blankets — all the way down to individual cells, all the way up to you and me, and all the way out to include elements of the local environment". Systems must self-organise to form an 'identity' that defines it as separate from the 'other', in order to facilitate survival.

Notes

1   Freud, S. (1920). *Beyond the Pleasure Principle*, p. 301.
2   Freud, S. (1920). *Beyond the Pleasure Principle*, p. 313.
3   Freud, S. (1920). *Beyond the Pleasure Principle*, p. 337.
4   Lane, N. (2016). *The Vital Question: Why is Life the Way it Is?*, p. 157.
5   Lane, N. (2016). *The Vital Question: Why is Life the Way it Is?*, p. 196.
6   Mahler, M.S. (1967), On Human Symbiosis and the Vicissitudes of Individuation, *Journal of the American Psychoanalytic Association* 15:740–763, p. 741.
7   Mahler, M.S. (1967), On Human Symbiosis and the Vicissitudes of Individuation, Journal of the American Psychoanalytic Association 15:740–763, p. 745.
8   Kandel, E. (2006). *In Search of Memory: The Emergence of a New Science of Mind*, p. 302.
9   Lane, N. (2016). *The Vital Question: Why Is Life the Way It Is?*, p. 200.
10 See the superb and definitive double volume by Kershaw, I. (2000). Hitler 1889–1936: *Hubris Volume 1*.
11 Panksepp, J. & Biven, L. (2012). *The Archaeology of Mind: Neuroevolutionary Origins of Human Emotions*, p. 165.
12 "This indicates that animals *like* the affective feelings generated by SEEKING arousal that pro-motes predation. But if one stimulates the brain sites that induce pure RAGE, animals will invariably exhibit escape behaviours. Thus, RAGE generates an unpleasant affect while SEEKING feels good. So, predatory animals enjoy going in for the kill. But they don't enjoy feelings brought on by excessive arousal of the RAGE system".
13 Abbreviation for bondage, discipline (or domination), sadism (or submission), masochism – types of sexual practices.
14 Panksepp adds: "It is important to re-emphasise that abundant evidence about differences in behaviour, neuroanatomy, brain chemistry, psychopharmacology, and affective experience has indicated that predatory aggression is a function of the SEEKING system rather than being an expression of RAGE (Panksepp, 1971)".
15 Barratt, B. (2013). *What Is Psychoanalysis: 100 Years after Freud's 'Secret Committee'*.
16 Barratt, B. (2013). *What Is Psychoanalysis: 100 Years after Freud's 'Secret Committee'*, p. 67.
17 Freud, S. (1923). *The Ego and the Id*, p. 364.
18 Freud, S. (1923). *The Ego and the Id*, pp. 364–365.
19 Barratt, B. (2013). *What Is Psychoanalysis: 100 Years after Freud's 'Secret Committee'*, p. 87.
20 Barratt, B. (2013). *What Is Psychoanalysis: 100 Years after Freud's 'Secret Committee'*.
21 Freud, S. (1920). *Beyond the Pleasure Principle*, p. 38.
22 Freud, S. (1933a), as cited in Mills, 2006, p. 376: Mills, J. (2006). *Reflections on the Death Drive*, pp. 373–382.
23 Freud, S. (1920). *Beyond the Pleasure Principle*, p. 334.
24 "Our views have from the very first been *dualistic*, and to-day they are even more definitely dualistic than before—now that we describe the opposition as being, not between ego instincts and sexual instincts but between life instincts and death instincts" (Freud). He follows: "We have found that one of the earliest and most important functions of the mental apparatus is to bind the instinctual impulses which impinge on it, to replace the

primary process prevailing in them by the secondary process and convert their freely mobile cathectic energy into a mainly quiescent (tonic) cathexis. While this transformation is taking place no attention can be paid to the development of unpleasure; but this does not imply the suspension of the pleasure principle. On the contrary, the transformation occurs on *behalf* of the pleasure principle; the binding is a preparatory act which introduces and assures the dominance of the pleasure principle".

25 Solms, M. (2022). *The Hidden Spring*, p. 149.
26 Solms, M. (2022). *The Hidden Spring*, p. 165.
27 Michael Kirchhoff *et al.* (2018) in their paper 'The Markov blankets of life: autonomy, active inference and the free energy principle', defines the Markov blanket as follows: "A Markov blanket, originally coined by Judea Pearl in 1988, defines the boundaries of a system in a statistical sense. Here we consider how a collective of Markov blankets can self-assemble into a global system that itself has a Markov blanket; thereby providing an illustration of how autonomous systems can be understood as having layers of nested and self-sustaining boundaries. This allows us to show that: (i) any living system is a Markov blanketed system and (ii) the boundaries of such systems need not be co-extensive with the biophysical boundaries of a living organism. In other words, autonomous systems are hierarchically composed of Markov blankets — all the way down to individual cells, all the way up to you and me, and all the way out to include elements of the local environment."

Chapter 4

Science and the Psyche

Impingements

We can begin to see the overlap of contemporary physics and biochemistry with Freud's formulation of the human psyche. The differentiation of 'me' from 'not-me' becomes a fundamental emergent quality of the psyche itself in relation to impingements from the world that it perceives to be external. As I mentioned, internal and external states are not distinguishable in the early days and weeks of infancy and so impingements will unsettle homeostasis whether from internal or external sources. The infant's recourse is still the same – cry and cry some more until a response is *induced* to restore equilibrium. Homeostasis is a key principle governing survival and well-being. The ego, as Freud formulated it, is like the surface of the skin of the body, separating internal from external, and as the ego evolves provides a thin layer of conscious awareness through which the internal system of the self can navigate the complex demands of the world around it.

One can see that the self-organising principle is governed by an energetic drive *towards* something, that is, a self-organising entity that can differentiate itself from other entities, and certainly from the external environment. Failure to do so and maintain the self-organised state (once it exists) leads to the risk of "entropic chaos", or death of the self-organising entity. Once an entity is formed and has a life-of-its-own quality, it must strive to maintain itself and develop systems towards this end. Homeostatic mechanisms, in other words, are required to sustain and maintain the self-organising entity. As Solms connects these two concepts, we have in physics a quantifiable driving force using Friston's Free Energy Law which we can also connect to the functioning of the mind. It relates to Freud's definition of a Drive, which he defined as "a measure of the demand made upon the mind for work in consequence of its connection to the body". The mind has to register the state of the body in all its needs, both conscious and unconscious, in order to trend towards a broad state of homeostasis and prevent entropy. The mind therefore has a job to do, it performs 'work' on behalf of its relation to the body and as part of the self-organising system that is the individual.

This tallies with the Free Energy concept that all systems have to perform work to this end. Solms writes that "the fundamental driving force behind the volitional

DOI: 10.4324/9781003452522-5

behaviour of all life forms is that they are obliged to minimise their own free energy. This principle governs everything they do".[1] So here we have a step in the direction of unifying the human mind with the principles of all matter. All matter, including living organisms, are driven by two fundamental drives: one which presses towards coalescing into organised (life) forms that become self-organising and can differentiate themselves from the external environment of other systems (that is a 'me' from the 'not-me'); the other is a more conservative drive that strives to return this entity back to states of equilibrium when deviations threaten to unsettle it or even destroy the system, a potential for the 'entropic chaos' that could lead to the system dissipating. In psychodynamic terms, the constant tension between the life and death drives governs the psychic apparatus, these drives being mental representations of the fundamental principle governing energy and life forms. Freud's formulation represents the emergence of these more primary and primitive tensions between adaptation (or variation) and preservation (or homeostasis).

Psychic Immunity

This latter drive, the conservative one that aims to preserve the organism, is one that interests us most in making sense of our key inquiry about aggression. As we can see, homeostasis represents one key dynamic of all systems in the universe, including organic ones, somatic ones, and by extension, emergent psychic ones. Feelings are, as Solms points out, the most effective complex mechanisms we have to register and respond to states of non-homeostasis. *Feelings* make a demand upon the mind for work, as Freud noted, a mechanism to enable response to states of change that in any way threaten the organism. Consciousness itself, says Solms, "Is homeostatic",[2] a revolutionary idea powerful in its role. In order to remain within one's biological parameters for survival, and I might add for *optimal* survival, we are required by nature to use biological feedback, through neurological filters that process this feedback and generate feelings about how to best respond. Feelings, for humans at least, represent the most efficient and advanced complex system to enable information to be interpreted by the individual and best responded to in the circumstances in which the individuals find themselves.

Choking under a rolling wave represents a different action requirement for a surfer than does choking on a sip of water at the dinner table, even if the sensation being registered by the brain is similar or even the same. The idea that we are required by nature to maintain homeostasis might seem obvious, since if we deviate even a few degrees from normal body temperature, we become hyperthermic or hypothermic and die fairly quickly. The same is true of most biological parameters, some requiring very rapid remedy for any deviation, such as facing poor oxygenation through disease as in Covid or asphyxiation of some sort. Some deviations require a more measured response, perhaps less dramatic but equally compelling in the requirement for remedy over time, such as poor nutritional intake that eventually leads to symptoms.

Either way, morbidity and mortality are dramatically increased when we deviate even marginally from normal homeostasis. This might be said for psychological parameters too, with one simple qualifier: that psychological parameters for homeostasis cannot be defined by any objective criteria – except in the broadest-brushstroke terms. Subjectivity and its representation through consciousness, that pesky 'hard' problem of neuroscience, dominates where the homeostatic settling point rests for any emotional need. We cannot measure that in any real objective sense since if you *feel* like an ice-cream, nothing in any objective measure would enable us to find that fantasy in your brain. Or if you feel sad because of some perceived loss, no one can experience that on your behalf. These are manifestations of your specific individuality and subjectivity. According to the Free Energy Principle, every system requires a drive or mechanism that resists entropy by maintaining as best approximation of homeostasis as it can. Shivering or sweating are obvious examples of this for thermo-regulation in humans but drives and their conscious representation through feelings bring into awareness states of dysregulation that are building or being triggered in the self.

As we can see, there seems to be a dovetailing of the laws of physics and the Free Energy Principle and Freud's formulation of the mental apparatus. In Free Energy a system coalesces to form a self-governing entity that requires the Markov blanket to separate the self from the other. This separation requires a skin, sometimes an invisible or conceptual skin that provides a mechanism to ward off threats to the integrity of the entity. The human body relies on the surface of the entity, that is skin, for example, to act as a separation barrier distinguishing self from other. But this is of course insufficient to do the job of protection on its own. Via mucous membranes, air-born toxins, ingestion through the mouth, or pathogens that threaten the body float abundantly in the environment. There are also concrete threats that puncture the skin and gain entry to the body. Without a supplementary mechanism to protect the body, life would be short and brutal. An immune system, in its complexity, provides us with a magnificent mechanism for recognising hostile pathogens, fighting them off, and storing their biological molecular signature in memory. This memory, stored at the molecular level, enables immunity to be created which makes future responses more efficient. This is immunity and its biological 'memory' in the somatic realm. The psyche is an emergent entity, and as such carries elements of these foundational characteristics of the body. The mind requires its own mechanisms to maintain its own integrity and its own memory to serve an 'immune' function for the mind. In this psychic realm, this mechanism presents in less tangible or measurable ways than the mechanisms of the body. But nonetheless, such representation must be and is present. We may posit the claim in this context of emergence, that the aggressive defence of the body through the immune system has a representation in the mental realm also, and it appears that aggression plays the role of the immune system for the mind. It also uses memory to register threats by referencing impingement and perceived hurts against past memory, especially that memory that has encoded previous injuries and hurts, prior threats to the system. These memories held in the unconscious act as trigger mechanisms for a defensive response, manifesting through feelings. So, we arrive at the claim: *Aggression is to the mind what the immune system is to the body.*

Freud and Beyond

Freud wrestled with this function and indeed late in his writing and career came to the conclusion that aggression serves the function of regulating Eros and libidinal pressures. As mentioned at the beginning of this book, it is probably fair to suggest that Freud never quite completed his theory of the function of the death drive and its aggressive derivatives, a point he lamented himself, noting at the end of his brilliant work on Beyond the Pleasure Principle, that "Was man nicht erfliegen kann, muss man erhinken" ("what we cannot reach flying, we must reach limping").[3] It is time and the painstaking endeavours of science that will ultimately clarify his theoretical insights, with fresh methods of data and enquiry to guide our thinking. Recent decades' research into the links between mind and body seems to have corroborated much of Freud's thinking but also, in my view, assisted in completing what felt for him a theory without enough evidence. For how can the paradox be resolved of trying to establish a proof for a drive that by definition 'presents' in a latent form. This point is how he ends his work, noting that, "the life instincts have so much more contact with our internal perception – emerging as breakers of the peace and constantly producing tensions whose release is felt as pleasure – while the death instincts seem to do their work unobtrusively".[4]

The death drive is such a central and significant drive carrying profound importance to the manifestation of both mental health and psychopathology that the resistance to this concept in both professional and lay worlds is surprising. Authors such as Mills have lamented the resistance within psychoanalysis to a proper engagement with this central and, in his view, indispensable tenet of the mental anatomy, the "dialectical tension" between Eros and death, these drives remaining, he argues, "ontologically inseparable".[5] In fact, the downplaying of this theoretical tenet of the dual model of mind is to leave exposed without the explanation of the purpose and its manifestations of aggression, and the most prevalent of this is the world of hate in its many forms. Our exposure via the media to the vast and macabre forms of prejudice, violence, and 'othering' finds little respite if our theoretical and clinical models are unable to map meaningfully the drivers of these potential perversions.

I am not alone in linking the aggressive drive to psychic immunity. Other authors have touched on this function of aggression-as-immunity, such as Solan. The notion that aggression preserves a system psychically also then suggests that such preservation must be driven by the triggering of mental memory, and memory in the psychic realm is invariably encoded through the perceptions of the person, from their subjective experience. This brings us to think about what defines a person's subjectivity, or in a sense their narcissism and its role in marking the self-organising system of the individual.

Alongside Solan I propose to consider narcissism and its preservation through aggression "as one of the psychic envelopes that function as the 'immune system' of our familiar sense of self while being permeable to excitations with the nonfamiliar other".[6] 'Death-work for Freud was ultimately in the service of restoring or reinstating a previous state of undifferentiated internal being',[7] that being a state in which tension is reduced or eliminated. The death drive, in this reading, is not merely a force acting against arousal or pleasure but one which aims to restore quiescence when internal equilibrium is disturbed. As Mills writes,

> Freud did not argue that death was the only aim of life, only that it maintained a dialectical tension in juxtaposition to a life principle under the ancient command of Eros, yet the two forces of mind remained ontologically inseparable.[8]

Mills captures the broader notion of the death drive as restorative, arguing that the organism must have, as Freud conjectures, an intrinsic capacity to protect itself from powerful stimuli that create disequilibrium. This is done through a resistive process that operates internally and which is sensitive to intrusive encroachments from the outside, especially those that threaten it with potential destruction. As mentioned, in the body the immune system appears to fulfil this function. The implication, as will be discussed below, is that the human mind requires such a capacity and itself has a mechanism to restore equilibrium through a restorative process. Mills makes the point that Freud's entire discourse is an economy of energetics designed to transform stimuli *in the service of self-preservation*, thus defending from both external and internal stimuli that create states of unpleasure. Mills therefore concludes that the aim of this mechanism is ultimately restorative, as Freud extends his hypothesis, 'that all drives aim toward a restoration of earlier events or modes of being, namely unmodified quiescence' (p. 378).

Before exploring further what constitutes the self, the subjectivity of the subject being preserved, it is helpful to revisit some of the fundamental drivers in evolutionary theory, most eloquently put by its founding master.

Variation and the Life Drive

Darwin made the point in his book *The Origin of Species* that in our ignorance of the mutual relations of all organic beings, we can observe certain truisms. He writes:

> All that we can do is to keep steadily in mind that each organic being is striving to increase in geometric ratio; that each in some period of its life, during some season of the year, during each generation or at intervals, has to struggle for life and to suffer great destruction. When we reflect on this struggle, we may console ourselves with the full belief, that the war of nature is not incessant, that no fear is felt, that death is generally prompt, and that the vigorous, the healthy, and the happy survive and multiply.[9]

Natural selection suggests that organisms strive to reproduce themselves in order to act in the service of improving their chances of survival. There is a self-reflective capacity in and by Nature to trend towards evolving by adaptation to new conditions. But it also trends towards the preservation of the self and self-species in relation to threats and impingements of change. This suggestion that even primitive organisms somehow intelligently reflect on their position in the universe is not, of course, what Darwin was suggesting in observing the principal drivers in all living matter. Rather, Darwin is observing in organic matter two developing trends, one favouring reproduction and one favouring conservation, and these 'intelligent' trends tension against each other constantly.

> It may metaphorically be said that natural selection is daily and hourly scrutinising, throughout the world, the slightest variations; rejecting those that are bad, preserving and adding up all that are good; silently and insensibly working, *whenever and wherever opportunity offers*, at the improvement of each organic being in relation to its organic and inorganic conditions of life.[10]

Darwin's observations point to the notion that life forms follow the same principle seen everywhere in nature: one force or energy prompts and pushes adaptation and 'variation' (facing the imposition of inorganic and organic impingements) in order to trend towards survival and thereby prolong the natural course of life; but in dialectic with this force, what Freud would later term the death drive, runs a counter drive that seeks to *preserve*, to maintain a defined self and character in relation to the pressures for change and variability. Put differently, the conflict between adaptation (and growth through variability) and the *energy of stasis* (the drive towards remaining intact and protected) is a feature embedded in all facets of life. Given organic life's ability to adapt and evolve, it demonstrates an ongoing tension between the life drive and the preservation drive, or in Freudian terms, the life and death drives which stand in simultaneous dialectical juxtaposition both conflictual and complementary. This latter principle of preservation, what Darwin calls natural selection, leads to the improvement of each creature in relation to its organic and inorganic conditions of life "and consequently, in most cases, to what must be regarded as an advance in organisation", or the improvement in survival through adaptation.[11] But in contradistinction to this tendency lies a drive to maintain the Markov blanket and try maintain the constancy of the self-organising system. Darwin too, was observing this tension of two drives in his biological researches.

On the face of it, however, there appears to be an apparent contradiction. It might seem to suggest that species are driven by one thing – the need to survive and hence constantly adapt through change. But implicit in this narrative is also that in order to preserve their character species must resist impingements and push back against them. The natural selection imperative suggests that enabling adaptation can only be on the terms of the organism or species itself. From the vantage point of any species, there may be the advanced idea that the subject in the species asks itself constantly, can I resist this impingement through some already present mechanism and preserve myself without change? Or, if this mechanism is proving insufficient must I develop and alter my strategies in order to meet the challenge and survive? In other words, can we argue that every living organism has individual and species-driven 'subjectivity' in which these two forces are in tension?

Of course, such individual subjectivity does not exist in lower organisms in the *sentient* sense, but we could say it is as-if such subjectivity did exist since decisions for sameness and preservations are constantly being tested against the need to alter, change, or modify the biological or psychological strategy for surviving, even if you happen to be a bacterium or virus or single cell organism. Solms' point about the Markov blanket is relevant here, that there is a constant need to keep the self defined, preserved, and a need to sustain a natural course towards the end of the (individual) life cycle. As quoted above, in Darwinian terms, faced with ongoing existential choices, all living organisms maintain an evaluation process, rejecting the bad, preserving the good; working at every opportunity for their improvement in relation to its organic and inorganic conditions of life.[12]

From each organism's and species' point of view, there is therefore a form of *implicit subjectivity*. Each organism must decide, from its point of view, how to preserve or adapt to the conditions and challenges of life. This is not to suggest, of course, that simple organic or even complex organisms have conscious subjectivity as we do in the human mind, but nonetheless, all creatures are governed by the need for making 'decisions' as to how to meet a challenge, *from its point of view*, and this may represent the basic underpinnings of a greater subjectivity in the complexity of humankind. The manner in which a threat or challenge is represented psychically must be governed by the pressure of their own point of view. This *pressure of subjectivity* underpins all organic adaptation (or life drive pressures) which tensions internally against preservation and stasis. Only when the mechanisms for stasis that already exist fail will new methods require development or the organism will perish prematurely. I mentioned previously that the laws of nature must represent themselves universally, and in all facets of nature we see the struggles for survival and adaptation – but let us not forget that the decision to adapt and change or preserve and retain is always driven from the point of view of the organism, that is, from their subjective point of view, their own internal locus of perspective. There is a subjective relativity, a *perspective*, always in play, as Bob Dylan penned the line, "Steal a little and they throw you in jail. Steal a lot and they make you king". *Perspective* in the human condition is central.

It may seem obvious that I am conflating two related but different levels of this 'subjectivity' – one that is species-general and one that reflects the individual within a species. How a species can be said to have subjectivity and adapt over time to their environmental impingements and challenges remains for the minds of experts like Darwin to point the way. But to note that the same pressures of conflict, change versus stasis, seem to apply to the human psyche too. Whether this links to the scalability of aggression in humans we will address later but the link does seem compelling to make. Where I can make a greater claim at this point is to understanding how the individual psyche within a species wrestle with the tensions between adaptation and preservation, and how these mechanisms in turn give rise to group trends of adaptation versus preservation, again, invariably from their own point of view, from their own subjectivity. If an individual within a species, or perhaps a species itself, represents threat to their own integrity, a response will be required, a decision governed by all the complexity of the data available to it – some of which are obvious and conscious and some of which remain embedded in memory (both personal memory and species memory, contained in the genetic code which is really an extremely complex form of biological memory) and are unconscious but exert an influence in this 'decision-making' through *association*.

First Conserve Then Adapt

Unconscious determinants that Freud discovered play a critical and outsized role in human subjectivity. Not all subjectivity is conscious, or can be consciously controlled, even when such subjectivity exerts a significant effect on consciousness and how one feels in the world. One may, for example, suffer depression with all its associated effects, even when there is no obvious or conscious reason to be depressed. Patients will often report that their lives are, on the face of it, successful, abundant, and free. And yet, this persistent depression deprives them of any hedonistic rewards from it – they are anhedonic, a classic symptom of depression. Unconscious factors, associated with previous experiences in life *filtered through the lens of subjectivity*, are exerting an influence on current experience and perception. Put the other way round, Freud noted that under the pressure of impingements that trigger associations, people *regress* to earlier stages of development, go backwards in time, as it were, via memory traces that activate feelings or affects, which in turn create in the present subjective experience that is as if it were real in the now.

This peculiar quality of human consciousness to regress under the pressure of any violation of homeostasis means that reactivity in the present can recur as it was alive in the past. The unconscious, in other words, has no reference to time, and associative activations through embedded memory, whether that memory can be declared (is 'declarative' according to neuroscience) or not, can exert a powerful influence on behaviour and feelings no matter how many years have passed. A war veteran, diving to the floor at the sounds of a car backfiring, may seem utterly counterproductive to an observer of the objective facts. Behaving in such an impulsive or even self-harming way makes little sense given the facts as they present – a car backfiring in the distance represents no threat. But from the vantage of subjectivity, of that individual's experience, associating a bang with gunfire makes diving to the floor infinitely adaptive and sensible. Once such an association has been rendered, traumatically endowed as such an experience would be, a bang is a real threat to the integrity of the organism, and survival depends on reacting instantly and without thought to such a stimulus. We call the feeling of jumpiness that accompanies Post-Traumatic Stress Disorder (PTSD) an 'exaggerated startle response', but that exaggeration is only true for the objective outside observer – not from the vantage of the person's own internal Unconscious, which is decoding current reality through the emotional filters of the past. It is probably fair to suggest that there is no psychological present without the past, and that those who dismiss the past as being in the past do not adequately account for the quantitative and qualitative effects that memory plays in interpreting current experience.

Memory is both species-general and individual. Through epigenetic plasticity a species can adapt and modify their genetic coding, in that genes can be switched on or off in response to the environment. Genes are not a static blueprint but a fluid mechanism through which an organism can engage with and respond to the environment. Genes represent species memory, those traits and attributes that facilitate survival and adaptation – not really those of the 'fittest' per se, but those organisms best able to adapt to the challenges of reality. But an individual within a species still requires mechanisms to facilitate individual survival, such as a skin that separates self from other, and an immune system that can recognise a hostile pathogen from a friendly or symbiotic one. The psyche requires such a mechanism also, one that can facilitate adaptation to impingements. You will recall that I mentioned that the first order of business in managing an impingement and a challenge to stasis is in an 'immune' response that strives to maintain stasis. If that fails, if the threshold for restoration is breached, only then does adaptation emerge as a second-order necessity to facilitate survival – and therein the tension between the life and death drives. *First conserve, then adapt.* If the temperature drops and you get cold, your first order of business will be to shiver to attempt to restore optimal temperature for your body. If that fails, you may reach for a blanket or jersey. Adaptation requires a drive to enable it, energy that pushes towards change through subjective creative problem solving. Those that achieve this, says Darwin, are more likely to survive, procreate, and pass on their more adaptive genes. But it also comes at a high cost – energy expenditure and consumption, initiative, and flexibility. Conservation of existing parameters requires less cost to the organism, and so the drive that existed before life, the inanimate that preceded the animate, represents as Freud noted, the "first drive".

The Death Drive

The Death Drive is poorly understood by many, perhaps because of the implications of the term Freud gave to this mechanism. Freud observed that there is "an urge in organic life to restore an earlier state of things" – the inorganic state from which life originally emerged. From the conservative, restorative character of instinctual life, Freud derived his death drive, with its "pressure towards death", and the resulting "separation of the death instincts from the life instincts" seen in Eros. The death drive then manifested itself in the individual creature as a force "whose function is to assure that the organism shall follow its own path to death". Put differently, Solms makes the case that minimising free energy becomes the task of all homeostatic systems, and that according to Friston's Law, systems will minimise expenditure of energy, the work required to maintain homeostasis, or what we might refer to as a preservatory function. As mentioned, the Markov blanket represents a self-organising system that is capable of self-other differentiation.

Whilst the notions of the Markov blanket can be applied in an abstract sense, in biological terms the cell's outer membrane represents this capacity to differentiate self from other. Although just two molecules thick, the Nobel Prize winning biologist Paul Nurse points out that the outer membrane forms a flexible 'wall' or barrier that separates each cell from its environment, defining what is 'in' and what is 'out'. He writes: "Both philosophically and practically, this barrier is crucial. Ultimately, it explains why life forms can successfully resist the overall drive of the universe towards disorder and chaos".[13] Energetically, the system will strive to first preserve through conservation since preservation is far more energy-efficient than is change, then adapt to form new methods to manage survival if required, doing all they can to "display a sense of purpose: an imperative to persist, to stay alive and to reproduce, come what may".[14]

The first strategy failing, would be the subjective experience of the system, so must form new variations on any existing systems to manage this impingement that threatens homeostasis. Nurse argues that life is constantly experimenting, innovating, and adapting as it changes the world and the world changes around it. Nurse concurs with this notion that genes must balance the need to preserve information by staying constant with the ability to change, at times substantially. Freud identified these forces in the psychological realm as a

> free flowing cathexis that presses on towards discharge and a quiescent cathexis. We may perhaps suspect that the 'binding' of the energy that streams into the mental apparatus consists of a change from a freely flowing into a quiescent state.[15]

When the "protective shield against stimuli" that the psyche uses is breached, says Freud, for example in trauma, then the psyche will employ mechanisms to manage these breaches but invariably with some symptoms or consequences. PTSD, for example, represents the experience of trauma breaching the threshold of the ego or the psyche's shield, which then creates enormous disequilibrium. But states of severe and often sudden threat, whilst breaching the threshold to manage disequilibrium, suggest that the restorative drive, that being aggression, cannot respond effectively to restore stasis under severe threat. Where the aggressive drive would normally be able to 'fight back' to get back to a state of stasis, in these exceptional situations the aggressive response is either immobilised because of greater threat (you are outgunned) or ineffectual against it (the flood waters are too powerful).

The suspension of this aggressive response implies that the normal immune function of the psyche is now immobilised despite the severity of threat. Under threat, particularly existential threat, an extreme 'defensive' reaction should be mobilised. But if a defensive-aggressive response would prove even more dangerous, a greater existential threat, then this response cannot be mobilised effectively. If there is a gun at one's head the situation requires a quick evaluation of choice: compliance or suffer sudden entropy. But in a 'choice' of compliance, which may prove life-saving, psychic consequences are created in its wake. For example, symptoms of PTSD may develop over time which reflects this neuropsychological tension between a simultaneously mobilised response under threat that is also immediately immobilised under that same threat. If the playing field was level, faced with a real existential threat, one would ideally be able to respond effectively to neutralise the threat. However, when unable to respond effectively given the threat of violence, for example, this response if now rendered immobile and psychological sequelae often result. Whilst this example of PTSD is but one form of *psychical compromise*, it is the nature of all symptoms – the mind-body system 'negotiating' a compromise to optimise outcomes. Freud calls this concept a 'compromise formation', one of the manoeuvres of the mind-body system to find an optimised route through impossible internal conflicts.

The death drive concept has been controversial because as an initially metapsychological construct it proved elusive except where it combined with libidinal elements which were felt and conscious. By its nature, the death drive does not seek to be felt. It does not seek to be mobile unless under provocation. If this drive had cognition, it would say, "my job description is to stay out of sight and out of mind unless necessity draws me from my latent state into a felt presence". Necessity is defined, accordingly, as any impingement which threatens my state of quiescence or equilibrium. Leave me alone, I will leave you alone. Disturb this organism, and I will mobilise against you with all the force at my disposal *proportionate to the level* of disequilibrium. This drive registers a challenge to stasis and mobilises in proportion to the threat. We could say that small changes in homeostasis meet with small and incremental aggressive responses to restore stasis. Big threats to stasis will be met with big aggressive responses to restore stasis. It would make no sense from an energetic or economic point of view to expend enormous amounts of energy and effort to resolve a minor disturbance.

Memory has to work rapidly, efficiently, and be able to predict forward in order to be useful. Based on what has been encoded from past experiences, new experiences can be referenced against them to make forward predictions about what the likely outcome of something would or should be. But as Solms points out, the 'predictive brain' is revealed neuroscientifically to be 'lazy', at least over the long term, "vigilant for every opportunity to achieve more by doing less".[16] This makes intuitive sense, of course. Why would any intelligent biological system spend more energy to achieve less if it can achieve more by doing less? Darwin's insights into his notion of natural selection do not violate this code, since only under the *requirement* to evolve, the pressurisations of change or die, does adaptation get triggered beyond attempts to restore stasis. First, try get back (to the familiar) and preserve, then try move forward (and change) if that fails.

However, the extrapolation by implication that evolution suggests a multiplicity of organisms emerging from a single cell under the pressure of variation does not always fit itself neatly into the evolutionary evidence, according to some scientists such as the MIT-trained physicist Gerald Schroeder. Inter-species evolution is not the same as intra-species evolution. Nonetheless, Darwin had concluded his historical opus by suggesting that these laws of evolutionary pressures were identifiable.

They included reproduction and variability as a response to environmental challenge and change, the "indirect and direct action of the conditions of life", as he called it, the proliferation of life forms as the biological adaptation to fill any ecological niche that it can through its ability to keep adapting, "a ratio of increase so high as to lead to a struggle for life".[17] These notions describe organic life's capacity to evolve through 'variation' – suggesting that under conditions of environmental change and challenge, only those that can adapt will ultimately survive – with genes holding the identity of any living organism first, encoded through its genetic signature. One could suggest that this genetic template is a *conservative* template in that it determines a creature's objective identity and would prefer to resist change. An earthworm will look different from an eagle and will not become one. However, as science has in more recent decades demonstrated through epigenetics that genes can also be modified through life experience and that, as Kandel demonstrated, genetic memory can to some extent also be altered to accommodate environmental impingement.

Variation and Subjectivity

Darwin notes through his observations that species appear to evolve to enable adaptation to the impingements of reality, but implicit in these observations is that such evolution occurs, so to speak, from the *subjective* viewpoint of any organism in question. This is not to suggest, of course that lower organisms have sentience – but they do have a perspective on the world through their biological experience of it. And such a subjectivity is perhaps the precursor to more advanced forms of sentient subjectivity, with feelings as their main conduit and informant. Rather, under the pressure to survive, species of all sorts can make adaptation through epigenetic changes. Schroeder argues that inter-species evolution has no incontestable evidence to support it, "that evolution is channeled along these paths, working new variations into old original themes".[18] Evolution, argues Schroeder, "is not a free agent". The laws of biology, chemistry, and physics, the laws of nature, determine which structures can evolve. Schroeder makes the point that different phyla, genetically separate from the beginning of multicellular life, developed similar solutions to the challenges of environmental adaptation independently of each other, citing various developments in evolution, such as the complex acquisition of sight across species in a similar time frame. Evidence also suggests that there was a "burst of multicellular life at the start of the Cambrian, 530 million years ago" noted Schroeder, indicating that across a complex spread of capacity and forms, life emerged in a "single burst in the fossil record".[19] These and other indicators make a case that species did not necessarily evolve according to a linear timeline from simpler to more complex species, but that evolution *within* species is consistent with the actual data rather than a quantum jump from one to another through evolution. Nonetheless, whether within species, the evidence does appear to support the concept of variation, which remains as a key driver in evolution, suggesting that adaptation is built in from the ground up and had embedded what Freud would later term the libidinal drive or Eros, the life drive.

The idea of variation, or survival of the fittest, representing a gradual evolution from the simplest life form to who we are today, a bursting forth in all its grandeur, as Darwin put it, or whether evolution begins with an intra-species genetic template and proceeds from simple to complex within species as Schroeder would argue, is beyond the scope of this book. Also, interesting to note that Schroeder argues with theoretical and empirical conviction that the popular tendency to treat the scientific and the theological account of creation and evolution as inherently adversarial, and to dichotomise these positions is a false split; both the theological and scientific accounts, he demonstrates with flair and scientific validation, actually describe the same processes and in essentially consistent ways.

Either way, as far as our core concepts are concerned there is no contradiction between the two positions of intra- or inter-species variation, since we observe a drive to variation through epigenetic adaptation and its relation to memory in either case and within all species. Interestingly, biochemists such as Nick Lane, who has done extensive writing on the subject of the origins of life, also indicate that the notions of a linear trajectory of life from a single simple organism to complex multicellular life in all its varietal forms are not unequivocal in the evidence. Suffice to note that whatever the origin of organic life, and whether life formed itself or life was formed "having been originally breathed by the Creator into a few forms or into one",[20] as Darwin wrote in his conclusion, in observing how species could adapt to environmental impingements concords with the observation that all organisms, including human ones with a psyche, are governed by a drive that enables adaptation and one that strives to maintain its given form, if at all possible. Species evolve in the Darwinian sense within species, adapting to impingements as required through time. Adaptation versus conservation appears as a primal tension within all living systems. Freud's identification of a life drive and a death drive concords with these findings from biology and neuroscience and takes us forward in making sense of why aggression in humans can trend in perverse directions, developing a life of its own quality separated from its original purpose.

As we have discussed, species appear to have a capacity to evolve and modify themselves through changing parameters to meet the requirements of the external environment. Thus, Darwin writes in his concluding remarks:

> Thus from the war of nature, from famine and death, the most exalted object which we are capable of conceiving, namely, the production of higher animals, directly follows. There is grandeur in this view of life, with its several powers, having been originally breathed by the Creator into a few forms or into one; and that, whilst this planet has gone cycling on according to the fixed laws of gravity, from so simple a beginning endless forms most beautiful and most wonderful have been, and are being evolved.[21]

This magnificent statement suggests that evolution and adaptation could have emerged *within* any number of species and of course, there is no way for Darwin to know for certain what began the process, especially since as we now know, primitive cellular life did not evolve for two billion years. The distinction between intra- and inter-species evolution is not central to our discussion here – save to note that Darwin's notions of evolution through variation represent an adaptive mechanism for ensuring survival, a quality emerging through higher organisms and their functions, including psychic ones. Freud's insight into the life drive emerging after states of quiescence and the aggressive drive, in response to disturbances of quiescence, carries these biological trends into complex psychic function. They represent the juxtaposition of energy being spent in the service of homeostasis versus the energy required to adapt and grow, taking into account the 'economics' of life – achieve less with more if biologically viable. Regarding these primal tensions, Freud notes that there is invariably a circuitous path to death, "faithfully kept to by the conservative instincts",[22] these conservative instincts being represented by aggression and present always in these phenomena of life. He adds, "If we firmly maintain the exclusivity of the conservative nature of instincts, we cannot arrive at any other notions as to the origin and aim of life".[23]

The Great Advantage of Sex

The two conflicting trends of all life, between conservation and adaptation, present a paradox to life, and one inescapable given the currents that govern it. "Thus", says Freud,

> these guardians of life, too, were originally the myrmidons of death. Hence arises the paradoxical situation that the living organism struggles most energetically against events (dangers, in fact) which might help it to attain its life's aim rapidly – by a kind of short circuit.[24]

In other words, an organism wishes to die only in its own internal fashion and strives forcefully for the achievement of this aim. Every living thing wishes to exit life according to its internal developmental steps, and along its own internally-set time frame. So as we have seen, two kinds of instincts or drives emerge in life, the one that seeks to conserve and preserve in order to reach death by an internally dictated route and those, the sexual instincts, which are perpetually attempting to achieve a renewal of life.

One key mechanism to achieve the renewal of life is facilitated by the life drive's striving for coalescing into greater unities. Since we are told by the biochemists that genetic variation facilitates adaptation to complex and changing demands in the environment, it makes sense that the ability to combine genetic material with other cellular systems, from the outset of life, enables an advantage over life forms that do not have the ability to genetically combine and mutate. Genetic variation, and epigenetic capacity to switch genes off and on, enables 'natural selection' to facilitate survival. Natural selection is not about brawn or brute power, since a virus can better mutate and survive than a gorilla, and a virus can kill a gorilla more effectively than a gorilla can kill a virus. Sexuality is a most powerful drive because this (libidinal) energy drives the combining of genetic material through procreation, essentially the combining of genetic material that then promotes adaptation to changing demands of the environment. In fact, biochemists suggest that asexual organisms become vulnerable to extinction and according to the evidence do become extinct eventually (albeit over a few million years). Without generating chromosomes with different combinations – enabling adaptation to changing environments and conditions (including infection from parasites, for example) – adaptation becomes limited. Sex allows selection to act on all genes individually, says Lane, and hence selection, "like God, can now see all our vices and virtues, gene by gene. That's the great advantage of sex".[25] Lane explains that "Sex is needed, to maintain the function of individual genes in large genomes, whereas two sexes help maintain the quality of mitochondria",[26] mitochondria being the energetic source that powers biological cells and life itself.

Of course, there may be disadvantages to sex too – not only because it invites life-threatening and relationship-threatening consequences (children and conflict) – but because 'junk' genes can also get transmitted and create genetic problems down the line. But on the balance of things, nature benefits overall from genetic variation being a powerful mechanism for adaptation and selection that enables survival and development. Not surprising that this libidinal drive presses forward with such incalculable pressure and will stop at nothing to give expression to its fulfilment. But equally so, what benefits the species might be a significant mischief-creator for the individual. Libido unsettles equilibrium, creates pressure which requires release, and when fulfilled and discharged, the unpleasure created by the rising tension of the drive, fulfilled into pleasure of orgastic release, only settles for brief periods before recharging again to demand fulfilment all over again! In contrast to this pressure which unsettles individual equilibrium, lies the drive that strives to resist disruptions to homeostasis and in the most energetically *economic* manner either maintain or return to stasis via the shortest possible route.

Threatened with Extinction!

It was suggested earlier that according to the economics of organic life, any organism strives to achieve much with little resource expenditure. Reaction to an impingement, by this definition, should be proportionate to the demand of the impingement. But as we explored earlier, this is often not so in either personal or historical terms. The reader will quickly notice a problem and rightly object to this notion of economic conservativeness. Since how would this account for the many examples we witness of an aggressive-defensive reaction that is disproportionate to the trigger? How would this explain the Nazis using their resources to murder harmless civilians through a resource hungry system when their war effort and survival required every possible resource going into fighting enemies that had real power to destroy them?

We also notice such aberrations in our individual selves in any domestic dispute in which feelings are hurt. Who has not had the experience of 'over-reacting' to some provocation or perceived injury by those we love the most? Or couples in

divorce throwing half their estates away on needless legal disputes and fees mo-
tivated by anger and a desire to punish the other party? But we also read about
these excessive reactions in the news. Some years ago, following a fairly minor
road transgression, one driver was so enraged that he stopped his car, retrieved a
baseball bat from his boot, and proceeded to club to death the other driver. How
by any stretch of the 'aggression-as-conservation' theory could this make sense?
Obviously, such an event, taking place in a public and busy place, in view of many
people, identifiable clearly by his car, number plate, and person, would lead to
severe consequences for his life and future. How is this preservative? On a much
grander scale, how is it that the aggressor so often claims to be the victim?

On Thursday 24 February 2022 the unthinkable occurred. For the first time since
1945 and the end of the tragic war that cost 50 million human lives, a superpower
that had been the tragic victim of invasion and had lost 20 million of its people in
that war, used its military muscle to invade a sovereign country. Russia, the numerical and military Goliath invades Ukraine, the demographically and militarily
weaker David. Not only is Europe threatened with war once again, but the president of the invading country, perceived by most as the aggressor, Russian Vladimir
Putin escalates his invasion by threatening the use of nuclear weapons if the West
intervenes in the conflict. This presents an unthinkable scenario to the world and an
unimaginable escalation from an apparently rational superpower.

But Putin claims he is again the victim, that Russia is the one being bullied on
the world stage. This is not some arm-chair interpretation. Here is Putin's televised
speech to his people. In it, you will notice his conviction that Russia has been subject to the bullying and strong-arm tactics of the West, and in particular the United
States. As we navigate this address, the difficulty establishing who the perpetrator
is and who the victim is becomes apparent. Subjectivity appears to be everything.
Perspective is the defining factor here – aggression in the service of what is required to sustain and preserve. From an economics of energy point of view, the human and financial costs make little sense, and yet in this contemporary case study,
it provides a useful insight into the thinking and perceptions of the themes we are
exploring and represents a wider theoretical issue. Speeches such as this give us
useful data for our theoretical observations.

In Putin's speech to the Russian people, he speaks of the anxieties, worries, concerns, and "fundamental threats" to the security *and dignity* of Russia. I encourage
the reader to read the entire speech in Appendix B (I include further commentary),
as it is a useful and intimate rendering of perception, fusing cultural, political, and
personal narratives. The perception that NATO and the West are expanding their
military infrastructure closer to their border, extrapolating a view of an expansionist agenda putting Russia's territorial and cultural integrity at risk. Facing "cynical
deception and lies or attempts at pressure and blackmail", Russia is now facing a
perilous threat from NATO. This encroachment through neighbouring Ukraine is
perceived to be grave, its "military machine is moving and, as I said, is approaching
our very border".

From Putin's perspective, Ukraine is not under threat from Russia – Russia is under threat from Ukraine. Russia has 146 million citizens and a massive military capacity, including a wide arsenal of nuclear weapons that it is now threatening to use. Ukraine has 41 million citizens, no nuclear weapons or any military even remotely close to that of Russia.

Why is this happening? Referring to the collapse of the Soviet Empire, Putin reflects on the painful losses of that "weakness", showing him and Russia "that the paralysis of power and will is the first step towards complete degradation and oblivion". Interestingly – the Soviet Union became "weak" and in its degradation of power, says Putin, the former glorious strength and dignity of this superpower has become lost and it is a country and a proud people *threatened with extinction!* At best, subjugation by the strong awaits their fate, for those who refuse to comply, to subject themselves to a submissive place in the world order, "are subjected to strong-arm tactics". Russia is being bullied geopolitically. Is being subjugated. Forced increasingly into a state of vulnerability. The weak victim has to fight back to restore its geopolitical pride of place or it will perish. Putin goes on to substantiate his existential apprehension with the 'evidence' at hand, demonstrating what he calls a haughty arrogance of the West seeking to create nation-state servility, of "absolute superiority, a kind of modern absolutism, coupled with the low cultural standards and arrogance of those who formulated and pushed through decisions that suited only themselves".

Perception of a conspiracy of hegemonic imperialism, unrestrained by international norms and laws, indicates for Putin that this trend is imperilling the Motherland too. Many different examples of apparently imperialist war, each one with their own complexity and reasons, are lumped together in a shopping list of one single concept – there is a Them and there is an Us. This binary polarisation is present in many examples of individual and geopolitical aggression, and enables the aggressor to position themselves as warding off a threat to its existence. The Goliath is now the David, surrounded by enemies bent on existential challenge to the threatened entity. Note that like when the ancient Cain killed Abel because of his *feelings*, Putin refers repeatedly to pride, dignity, and feelings of humiliation. *Feelings!* Feelings justifying the escalation of a world war. Lumping many diverse and distinct historical events and conflicts, Putin goes on, citing numerous travesties of the West's use of brute power, from Belgrade to Syria to Libya to Iraq. Some would argue that Putin gives no context to these conflicts, no deconstructing of the unique elements in the buildup to these conflicts, no references to who the aggressors were in these conflicts, as for example, when Iraq under a reportedly ruthless dictator invaded a sovereign neighbouring country. The 'vulnerable under threat' narrative develops the polarisation of us and them, in psychological terms self and other. This differentiation, an ideological Markov blanket, if you will, creates the imperative, a no-choice reaction, to this perceived threat. From Putin's point of view, the external world threatens to breach the skin, and hence an immune reaction is warranted – mobilising the system uniquely enabled to defend against threat. Physical, mental, cultural, and geopolitical. The emergent qualities give rise to systems that require defence – aggression in the service of defence, even if nuclear war is the outcome. Sometimes this immune' response will activate even if it leads to a form of suicide, or in the Cold War lingo, Mutually Assured Destruction (MAD). But in a context in which "they have deceived us, or, to put it simply, they have played us…just lies and hypocrisy all around", such a response becomes justifiable.

Inch by inch, all over the world, Putin tells his people, forces are arraigned against the Russians. *They have played us.* Note the humiliation embedded in the narrative. We have been humiliated by the West, in their expansionist designs to annihilate the Russian entity and reduce it to a subservient and humiliated pawn of the West, spearheaded by what Iranian leaders often refer to as 'the Great Satan', the USA. "Therefore, one can say with good reason and confidence that the whole so-called Western bloc formed by the United States in its own image and likeness is, in its entirety, the very same 'empire of lies'". The Empire of some Great Conspiracy, one might frame it.

Whatever merit there is, the cherry picking of detail to support a preconceived narrative of subjective perception and positioning those details into a clustering of themes provides the authentic foundation from the vantage of the perceived victim, to respond and protect itself. To conserve what it can in the face of grave danger, as the West "immediately tried to put the final squeeze on us, finish us off, and utterly destroy us". Immediately tried to utterly destroy us. Fascinating inversion of the vast majority of countries around the world seeing Russia as the aggressor, the perpetrator in the Ukrainian invasion. Not so for Putin. He speaks of an impending doom, the attempts to *destroy our traditional values and force on us their false values that would erode us, our people from within…Nor will they succeed now!* Putin declares the importance of indelible memory, of threats from the West and invasions from history, when unprepared, and too late, the Nazis invaded the Motherland. The time now for being deceived in the face of such history is over and would not be repeated. Russia has *memory* and must go on the offensive to prevent a defensive risk of annihilation based on that memory. Encroachments from NATO that like the Nazis, would invade "without declaring war" can never be tolerated.

Memory Goes Nucleus

We see here an interesting rendering of memory, a fusing of geopolitical and personal memory. As we have discussed, memory has a critical function related to preservation. When memory fails, so too does survival. In the human psyche, it can be said: *Memory is the unconscious store of subjective perception.* Such memory is related to inherited experience (cultural, geopolitical, or personal) that creates the store against which reality can be checked and navigated forward. Last time I ate this poison berry, I became sick. Better not do that again, I am avoiding that bush. In order to accomplish this task, the mind has to 'go back', that is, to place itself in an old scenario in which ideational stores, ideas are accessed, which can be used to configure current experience and future action. Such future action is aimed at preventing threats to stasis and the risk of entropy.

As such, regression in the service of the ego, as Freud put it, becomes the normal and efficient method of psychic maintenance. Regression to the old, a revisiting the 'what-was', is facilitative because in accessing old ideational stores in this timeless mechanism, old affects are also triggered, as if they were in the present. Regression is therefore a revisiting of stored memory, in order to feedforward to manage impingement and threats and serve the interests of the subjective nucleus. This nucleus is both individual-specific, interest group-specific, and phyla-specific, serving the identity of any level under threat. Since memories are through the lens of any of these layers, they are subjective and individual reactivity to those memories, forged through the subjectivity that is embedded in all living matter, can never be accessed in any objective sense. We can never peer into your 'mind's eye' no matter the technology we may develop in any futuristic scenario.

The mind hides her secrets behind a veil inaccessible to any outside observation, except through inference. As the biochemist Nick Lane writes,

> Our life experience is written into synaptic networks, each neurone forming as many as 10,000 different synapses. If the neurone dies by apoptosis. those synaptic connections are lost forever, along with all the experience and personality that might have been written into them. That neurone is irreplaceable.[27]

This tragic effect for the individual suffering any form of brain insult or degeneration is also the determining factor for the exquisite beauty of subjective experience and its infinite variability that makes people so infinitely interesting, novel, and, in an analytic sense, object-seeking. Humans love attachments, especially those that are relatively novel, because subjectivity enhances experience through the mosaic of difference, or as the French might suggest, 'Viva la difference!' But, and it is a significant reservation, difference also promotes threat in the competition for resources and survival and the drive for preservation can counter this libidinal drive for attachment and the striving for gene-combining, often with violent effect.

As Putin reminded his country, memory was in play in his current decision-making. Referring to the Great Patriotic War against the Nazis, he remembers how in the first months of hostilities "we lost vast territories of strategic importance, as well as millions of lives. We will not make this mistake the second time. We have no right to do so". He remembers, and as we shall see below, some of these memories are personal. Referring to the nuclear option, he opined that "there should be no doubt for anyone that any potential aggressor will face defeat and ominous consequences should it directly attack our country". Ominous consequences – an implied threat of nuclear retaliation. If we are going to die at the hand of your sword, we will take you down with us.

> For the United States and its allies, it is a policy of containing Russia, with obvious geopolitical dividends. For our country, it is a matter of life and death, a matter of our historical future as a nation. This is not an exaggeration; this is a fact. It is not only a very real threat to our interests but to the very existence of our state and to its sovereignty.

We face a mortal threat says Putin. A matter of life or death. Not only for Russia but for Ukraine. "We had to stop that atrocity, that genocide of the millions of people who live there and who pinned their hopes on Russia, on all of us". Referencing memory again, Putin links current affairs to the association to the Nazi atrocities, "…to kill innocent people just as members of the punitive units of Ukrainian nationalists and Hitler's accomplices did during the Great Patriotic War". Interesting that the President of Ukraine in this invasion is himself Jewish – but for Putin the head of "neo-Nazi thuggery" is openly imperialistic in his designs and ambitions, just like Hitler. The struggling for survival is one between good and evil, "the showdown between Russia and these forces cannot be avoided. It is only a matter of time". Russia is not attacking anyone – Russia is defending itself from forces arraigned against it, orchestrated by the dominant United States and its proxies through NATO. It is a matter of defence, "a matter of defending ourselves. We had no other choice". It is forced upon him and his leadership to take action in defence. Its purpose is noble. "The purpose of this operation is to protect people who, for eight years now, have been facing humiliation and genocide perpetrated by the Kiev regime. To this end, we will seek to demilitarise and denazify Ukraine…" Note again the reference to *feelings*, humiliation, as part of the justification to invade, and even go nuclear if need be. "The outcomes of World War II and the sacrifices our people had to make to defeat Nazism are sacred". Memory holds sway in current reaction.

> The current events have nothing to do with a desire to infringe on the interests of Ukraine and the Ukrainian people. They are connected with the defending Russia from those who have taken Ukraine hostage and are trying to use it against our country and our people.

Memory compels him to aggress in the service of defence. Putin says, "I reiterate: we are acting to defend ourselves from the threats created for us and from a worse peril than what is happening now".

Putin asks his people to understand and work with him to prevent anyone interfering with their affairs and appeals to his soldiers to remember again their parents and grandparents sacrifices against the Nazis and to ally with him in 'defending' the Motherland against the neo-Nazis that have seized power in Ukraine and are busy "plundering" and "humiliating" its people. This is a war, essentially, of defence, to protect the Motherland from expansionistic designs by the Ukrainian "neo-Nazis" and the West through NATO.

Any interference will be met with a severe response: "Russia will respond immediately, and the consequences will be such as you have never seen in your entire history". Russian has truth and justice on its side, not the lies and brawn of the West, "when our saying on being 'all brawn and no brains' applies". In the end, through strength and courage the Russians will prevail "and reliably guarantee the security of our Motherland… and the invincible force rooted in the love for our Fatherland". The essence of Putin's speech and call to arms is that "Russia cannot feel safe, develop, and exist while facing a permanent threat from the territory of today's Ukraine". It is interesting to note the regressive elements in the speech too, of references to the Mother and the Father, and one wonders how the political and personal begin to intertwine in Putin's mind, perhaps sincerely believing the perils he faces and the requirement to defend himself and his country against the threats of annihilation and subjugation, humiliation, and defeat.

The Real Nazis and Perceptions of Victimhood

This narrative in world events carries noticeably similar themes and mechanisms when we analyse individual perpetrators of aggression too. Invariably, the most heinous of criminal acts of violence will be justified psychologically on the basis of victimhood, the perceived threat to integrity – and more often than not, such a perception is based on an old reality. The person was, in some subjective fashion, a victim.

Hitler's speeches in the 1930s and 1940s reflect this same narrative. Victimhood in the face of existential threat of annihilation justifying an aggressive 'defence'. Rationalised, the human mind has the capacity to turn rage into sublimated and rationalised narratives. As Panksepp notes, although RAGE itself is not cognitive (i.e., it is not a mental state that is created by information processing), "it is destined to become intertwined with cognitive influences through learning" and can hence suffer the mutilations of the rational in its service.

Back in the 20th century Hitler, in his (similar) narrative, opined:

> Only in those cases where the murderous lust of the Bolsheviks, even after the 30th of January 1933, led them to think that by the use of brute force they could prevent the success and realisation of the National Socialist ideal – only then did we answer violence with violence, and naturally we did it promptly.

Hitler rails against lies and deceptions, and "the failure to recognise the importance of conserving the blood and the race free from intermixture", to prevent the loss of the German people.

> "Unspeakable suffering and misery have come upon mankind because they lost this instinct which was grounded in a profound intuition; and this loss was caused by a wrong and lopsided education of the intellect. Among our people there are millions and millions of persons living today for whom this law has become clear and intelligible. What individual seers and the still unspoiled natures of our forefathers saw by direct perception has now become a subject of scientific research in Germany. And I can prophesy here that, just as the knowledge that the earth moves around the sun led to a revolutionary alternation in the general world-picture, so the blood-and-race doctrine of the National Socialist Movement will bring about a revolutionary change in our knowledge and therewith a radical reconstruction of the picture which human history gives us of the past and will also change the course of that history in the future" to bring about "the will to national self-preservation".

For, he remembers,

> How much blood flowed around this destination in vain! How many millions of German men, consciously or unconsciously in the service of this purpose, have gone the bitter road of rapid or painful death for more than a thousand years!

Hitler's narrative continues, reverting to cultural memory, how

> when the rest of the world took away the foreign capital of the German people, when they took all the colonial possessions, the philanthropic considerations of the democratic statesmen apparently had no decisive influence. "We have seen that, after more than 800,000 children died of hunger and food shortages at the end of the war, almost a million pieces of dairy cows were driven away after the cruel paragraphs of a dictate imposed by the democratic, humane world apostles impose us as a peace treaty. We have seen that one year after the end of the war, more than one million German prisoners of war were detained without any reason in captivity. We had to endure that far more than one and a half million Germans from their frontier areas were being wrenched from their belongings and whipped almost exclusively with what they carried on their bodies. We have endured the loss of millions of our fellow citizens without hearing them, or giving them even the slightest chance of further preserving their lives. I could add dozens of the most gruesome examples to those examples. So stay tuned with humanity. The German people do not want their interests to be determined and governed by a foreign people."

He reminds his people of the threat of

> international financial Jewry in and outside Europe should succeed in plunging the peoples once again into a world war, then the result will not be the Bolshevisation of the earth and thus the victory of Judaism, but annihilation of the Jewish race in Europe. For the time of the propagandistic defencelessness of non-Jewish peoples is over.

Referring to the humiliations of the Jews laughing at his prophesies, he expressed the feelings driving a need for domination. "I've been a prophet in my life very often and was mostly laughed at. At the time of my struggle for power, it was primarily the Jewish people who only accepted my prophecies with laughter".

Hitler goes on to identify not only the Jews as oppressors threatening his people but England.

> At that time England was the principal initiator of this struggle, England, which over a period of 300 years, through a continuous succession of bloody wars, subjugated roughly a quarter of the globe. ... Through the use of force they subjugated this continent of over 380 million people, and kept them subjugated. Only through force did they make one state after another pay them tribute and

taxes. Behind this force, of course, stood the other one, which scents business everywhere where a state of disturbance exists: our international Jewish acquaintances. In this manner England, over a period of a few hundred years, has subjugated the world; and, to make secure this conquest of the world, this subjugation of the people, England endeavours to maintain the so-called balance of power in Europe.

Once again we see the narrative of victimhood, England dominating global affairs, using brute force to subjugate the peoples of the world and of Germany. Death, humiliation, and annihilation threatened the integrity of the good people of Germany and their cultural superiority.

"To reach this goal, England conducted one war after another in Europe". After crushing the countries of France and Spain, they turned their power against Germany, he argues, "they then imagined that Germany must be, of necessity, the one factor which might possibly be able to unify Europe. Then it was that the struggle against Germany began, not out of love for the nations or their people, but only in their own most selfish, rational interests, behind which, as previously said, stands the eternal Jewry, which, in every struggle between nations, is capable of making profits and winning wherever there is confusion and wrangling. It is well-known that they have always been the instigators of unrest among the nations…"

It may be tough on the palate to read these sentiments but these sorts of geopolitical speeches give us important and useful data that narrows the gap between the personal and the geopolitical and I do not give them airtime except for the wish to understand scientifically what drives these types of perceptions, projections, and rationalisations. Is this data helpful, with a view to remedying the dizzying deluge of wanton violence and destructiveness we witness daily and have throughout human history? These speech extracts are a mosaic of some ideas that reflect a perception, and as difficult as it is to digest, a possibly genuine *perception*, that both Hitler himself and the German people have been victims of various conspiracies through history, leading to a diminishing, impoverishment, and humiliation of the German people. Like with Putin, the concept of reparation for perceived threat and sleight, for the Goliath experiencing himself to be the David, the heroic victim of a bullying conspiracy by the democracies, the West, the United States, the Jews, Ukrainian neo-Nazis, whoever can fit the descriptor of the Other as opposed to the Self, the Markov blanket separating self from external. What is often interesting is how often the reversion to *feelings* as reasons for waging war emerges – perceptions of humiliation, being laughed at, denigrated, driven by distress and anxiety. Feelings justify homicide, just like when the biblical Caine killed Abel because he *felt* humiliated and unfavoured.

In cultural terms, the grandeur of the mission and struggle for cultural survival in the face of annihilatory threats becomes the *casus belli* for waging war, not a war of aggression (if this oxymoron can be tolerated) but a *war of preservation*.

of aggression on both the individual the geopolitical stage are driven
ion of victimhood and rationalised as such with the historical and
ιt hand. The problem is that it often appears that the perception is
t. The problem also is that the motivation for aggression is often
.. υy factors unconscious, by motives that lurk in the shadows of individual
minds, coalescing into groups, coalescing into geopolitical alliances waging war.
Historians will justifiably scoff at these naive assertions – the complexity of geopolitical tensions and *realpolitik* being infinitely more complex than the simple
unconscious assertions of individuals in positions of power. And of course, there
is merit in this critique. But then again, geopolitical trends and *realpolitik* in group
psychology are also driven by individuals finding themselves in positions of power
and often striving for it over years, able to create on broader canvasses the mosaic
of projections that mortals can.

Freud recognised these links between the fundamentals of individual psychic nature and the emergence into greater unities of groups and societies, these emergent
systems never being free of instinctual roots. In fact, we should also note that there
is no such thing as an individual mind separate from other minds, from the outset
of life, both for the individual and the species. The systems and characteristics of
the individual mental apparatus is never therefore very far away from the mental
apparatus of bigger systems, from dyads to groups, and hence these carry more
primitive elements into these greater unities. During the First World War over 100
years ago, Freud wrote how groups carry the more primitive innate characteristics
of individual psychology in inescapable ways.[28] Notwithstanding that in contemporary neuroscience we are cautioned about simplistic correlations and extrapolations, with Panksepp suggesting that "RAGE, just like every basic emotion, is
regulated by many psychological processes and many brain regions", so drawing
simple conclusions about rage as a driver of war is unwise.

> It is tempting to believe that human anger contributes to the motivation to wage
> war, but that would be a gross overgeneralisation. Even in the heat of battle,
> tactically effective soldiers are not usually enraged, even though such passions
> surely emerge in the midst of hand-to-hand combat. Obviously, a great number
> of sociological, political, and historical considerations play a great part in wag-
> ing war.[29]

We are all likely to agree with this caution. On the other hand, conflict is not always
about hot anger, as the cold documents of the Nazis illustrate, and real-world politics
and its dynamics are also driven by humans with individual minds and motivations.
And in the individual and the emergent systems that arise from it, the laws of nature
govern this complexity. From simpler systems can emerge complex systems carrying the essential energies of the simpler systems, and these trends are noted in
both evolutionary theory and the modern sciences. This is everywhere in nature – as
in the drives that govern complex organisms carry essential qualities from simpler
life forms through evolution, as will be discussed further later. So, the matter of

complexity emerging from simpler layers, in this case not the complex organisms carrying essential elements from more primitive organisms but the emergence of multiplicity of minds in cultures, societies, and geopolitical realties is not so far-fetched. Indeed, the confluence of many variables might enable war, but at the end of the day, people and individuals in power carry the influences for these trends. Emergence as a property of social, group, and geopolitical systems reflects the trend of more primitive instinctual properties to find their way into more complex systems, much like we cannot reduce a liver or even a liver cell into an eight-cell embryo, but complex biological system do, of course, emerge from simpler ones and carry their energetic properties, as Freud discussed in his works on war and group psychology.

A biological living cell is more than the sum of its chemical ingredients, so too is being a group, couple, or family more than the simple sum of its parts, but these emergent systems are never free of their more primitive origins. As Freud wrote about the disillusionment and mortification in the First World War, "In reality our fellow-citizens have not sunk so low as we feared, because they had never risen so high as we believed".[30] The primitive mind is, in the fullest meaning of the world, says Freud, "imperishable"[31] and invariably finds its way into the mental life of both individual and greater unities – that is to say, attachments and groups of any kind, even civilised and sophisticated ones. Freud emphasised that the "essence of a group lies in the libidinal ties existing in it…",[32] the primacy of libidinal drivers underlying group psychology.

But Freud may have missed the developmental implications of his own later dual-drive theory that this is only true to the point a system coalesces. Once coalesced into a greater unity, be it a couple, a family, a group, or a nation, such a system, carrying its primitive drives, will seek to preserve itself, with the conservative drive taking centre stage away from the initial libidinal primacy. In marital breakdown, for example, we can note the paradoxical tensions between maintaining and preserving the system in the outer world whilst internal conflicts rage within as the individual preservation moves to centre stage. The initial ascendance of the life drive and libidinal elements give way to conservation and homeostatic demands. In fact, we could confidentially suggest that to one degree or another, in-group cohesion and survival invariably benefits from channelling hostilities and aggressions into out-groups, whether these derive from competition or rivalries to personal discontents and hurts. What we refer to as scapegoating is a preservatory mechanism to keep threats of aggressive elements within an in-group out, conferring a preservatory advantage. Although an in-group is initially forged from the pressures of the life drive, ambivalences invariably emerge – hostilities, rivalries, hurts, or envy – and the group benefits from these internal threats to cohesion being directed elsewhere. We can observe how the tension of the more primitive life and death drive pressures within the individual remains present in higher order systems.

Projection as Defence

As with individuals, groups can project outwardly. The matter of projection as a psychic mechanism has survival value. The ability of the psyche to preserve itself, to separate that which brings pleasure from that which brings pain, which it seeks to externalise. Freud made the point that in the process of projecting inner conflicts outwards, the psyche

> has separated off parts of its own self, which it projects into the external world and feels as hostile. After this new arrangement, the two polarities coincide once more; the ego-subject coincides with pleasure, and the external world with unpleasure...[33]

He adds that,

> We feel the 'repulsion' of the object, and hate it; this hate can afterwards be intensified to the point of an aggressive inclination against the object – an intention to destroy it... Indeed, it may be asserted that the true prototypes of the relation of hate are derived not from sexual life, but from the ego's struggle to preserve and maintain itself.[34]

Projection manifests so often in out-group prejudice and hatred, invariably directed at some 'other' perceived out-group. Hate is a derivative of the aggressive drive, a *subjective* manifestation of a feeling that reflects anger turned cold. Hate does not necessarily turn into manifest aggression but seethes quietly in the background, often unseen and unfelt to the outside world, until its shield is cracked by impingements that trigger it and turn it into a hot version of manifest anger or rage. Whilst Panksepp laments about issues of war that the causes remain complex and elusive, he notes:

> Of course, warlike tendencies in humans are ultimately accompanied by many hateful emotions, including avarice, spite, and triumph, not to mention behaviours such as raping and pillaging, but to the best of our meagre knowledge, most of these complex feelings, just like our jealousies, resentments, and hatreds, are not instinctual primary-process potentials of the ancient emotional part of the mammalian brain. They probably arise from higher brain areas through developmental and social learning. Other animals are not capable of the neocortical sophistication that we possess. As a result, most other animals are simply not able to have complex thoughts and feelings about such matters in the way that we do. But this is not to say that they are incapable of more simple-minded proto-resentments, proto-jealousies, and proto-hatreds. Still, elemental emotions like FEAR and RAGE surely flare on every battlefield, and these affects stem from the emotional systems that we share with all other mammals.[35]

Panksepp struggles to link the higher-order faculties of human with the 'mindlessness' of human violence through instinct. The higher order faculties that humans have, including thinking and feeling, which as Solms makes clear are also mechanisms of homeostatic efficiency and preservation, enable the links between innate drives of preservation to recruit ideation, memory, and thinking in its service. If I feel something, I need to explain it, and if there is no objective explanation, I can find data to fit my internal narrative that does explain it. Thinking, in other words, enables the linking and meaning to *become* represented.

It is evident in the data that at root *something* perceived by the human mind serves as the motivator for war and violent aggression that when able to recruit group or geopolitical trends can erupt into war. Without Vladimir Putin driving events in Ukraine because of his personal perceptions of victimhood and threat, would an invasion have been inevitable? Whilst the historians amongst us would baulk at the apparent naïveté of this question, at core we cannot deny all evidence that suggests human motivations drive conflict, even on the broader world stage and that personalities in positions of power have an undue influence on historical trends. As mentioned, primitive drives in the psyche do constantly have an effect on emergent systems and groups, since "the man of prehistoric times survives unchanged in our unconscious" and given neuroplasticity, the mind is susceptible to what Freud calls "involution",[36] that is regression to more primitive states, even in stages of higher development and civilisation.[37] The role of memory in mental life and psychobiological survival would also speak to this central concept, as does the advantage its relationship to consciousness bestows on navigating novel environments and stimuli.[38] Put together, non-reductionistic *emergence* of primitive human trends into more complex developed systems remains conceptually important and viable.

Whilst RAGE, to use Panksepp's neuroscientific nomenclature, is multifaceted and includes what we might term hot anger, cold predatory aggression, and aggression in the service of social dominance and hierarchy, we can also note that some aggressive-like behaviour, such as predatory aggression, is driven by a mix of the SEEKING system. That is, in Freudian terms, it has libidinal elements mixed or fused with aggressive drives. Neurobiologically, in other words, love and hate are never too far apart and can easily fuse together (think sado-masochism) or flip from one to the other (think when love is unrequited or a loving heart is broken through infidelity or breakup). The love can quickly turn to deep hate.

Hate is a strange emotion, since we might contend that the opposite of love is not hate – it is *indifference*. Love and hate occupy two sides of the same coin. Freud noted that,

> Hate, as a relation to objects, is older than love. It derives from the narcissistic ego's primordial repudiation of the external world with its outpouring of stimuli. As an expression of the reaction of unpleasure evoked by objects, it always remains in an intimate relation with the self-preservative instincts…[39]

The self-preservatory drive, the 'Death Instinct', leads the charge for preservation. This 'guardian of the peace' can be ruthless in its defence of the peace. Like the immune system of the body, it stores memory of pathogenic stimuli and aims to *anticipate* and annihilate their presence. The greater the threat, the greater the response to this threat, but as mentioned before, *from the vantage of the organism under this threat*. The immediacy of the response will be *triaged* against long-term costs – making the self-destructive aspects potentially secondary.

Since, as Panksepp reminds us "RAGE, just like every basic emotion, is regulated by many psychological processes and many brain regions",[40] we cannot define single motivators for an aggressive response, nor find any objective measure for it. It is subjective, albeit, often not consciously so. I italicised the notion of anticipation, since this links to memory and the mind's ability to store aversive *experiences* and recall them in the face of similar triggers. Since the unconscious is a reservoir of memory traces, and as Freud said, "consciousness emerges instead of a memory trace",[41] as the interface of the psychic skin between the inner and outer world, the Markov blanket of the mind, so to speak, the unconscious will hold memory of aversive triggers that can activate in the face of similar threats. The timeless quality of the unconscious means that current triggers that activate old memory traces will require a response as if it were in the present. Again, note the parallel to the immune system of the body, which retains memory (obviously through entirely different mechanisms to the psyche), so that it can efficiently attack and destroy invading pathogens more efficiently.

From the vantage point of an organism's subjectivity, there is an implication we have not yet identified and which requires elaboration. If an organism sees and experiences the world through its own lens, and then reacts accordingly, it is being as we might say in colloquial terms, "self-centred".

Notes

1 Solms, M. (2022). *The Hidden Spring*, p. 177.
2 Solms, M. (2022). *The Hidden Spring*, p. 253.
3 Freud, S. (1920). *Beyond the Pleasure Principle*, p. 338.
4 Freud, S. (1920). *Beyond the Pleasure Principle,* pp. 337–338.
5 Mills (p. 1), in Mills, J. (2006). *Reflections on the Death Drive*, pp. 373–382.
6 Solan (p. 197), in Solan, R. (1999). The Interaction between Self and Others: A Different Perspective on Narcissism, pp. 193–215.
7 Freud (1933a, p. 374).
8 Mills, J. (2006). *Reflections on the Death Drive*, pp. 373–382 (p. 374).
9 Darwin C. (2003). *The Origin of Species*, p. 87.
10 Darwin, C. (2003). *The Origin of Species*, p. 129.
11 Darwin's point captures this principle thus: "If under changing condition of life organic beings present individual differences in almost every part of their structure, and this cannot be disputed; if there be, owing to their geometric rate of increase, a severe struggle for life at some age, season, or year, and this certainly cannot be disputed; then considering the infinite complexity of the relations of all organic beings to each other and to their conditions of life, causing an infinite diversity in structure, constitution, and habits, to be advantageous to them…" (p. 129). "This principle of preservation, or the survival of the fittest", Darwin writes, "I have called Natural Selection. It leads to the improvement of each creature in relation to its organic and inorganic conditions of life; and consequently, in most cases, to what must be regarded as an advance in organisation."
12 Darwin, C. (2003). *The Origin of Species*, p. 129.
13 Nurse, P. (2020). *What Is Life? David Fickling Books*, p. 19.
14 Nurse, P. (2020). *What Is Life? David Fickling Books*, p. 20.

15 Freud, S. (1920). *Beyond the Pleasure Principle*, p. 303.

16 Solms, M. (2022). *The Hidden Spring*, p. 176.

17 Darwin concluded his historical opus by suggesting: "These laws, taken in the largest sense, being Growth with Reproduction; Inheritance which is almost implied with Reproduction; Variability from the indirect and direct action of the conditions of life, and from use and disuse: a Ratio of Increase so high as to lead to a Struggle for Life, and as a consequence to Natural Selection, entailing Divergence of Character and the Extinction of less-improved forms" (p. 459).

18 "We can conclude", says Schroeder, "that evolution is channeled along these paths, working new variations into old original themes" (p. 92). Evolution, says Schroeder, "is not a free agent".

19 Schroeder, G. (1997). *The Science of God*, p. 89.

20 Darwin, C. (2003). *The Origin of Species*, p. 459.

21 Darwin, C. (2003). *The Origin of Species*, p. 459.

22 Freud notes that there is invariably a circuitous path to death, "faithfully kept to by the conservative instincts, thus present us today with the picture of the phenomena of life. If we firmly maintain the exclusivity of the conservative nature of instincts, we cannot arrive at any other notions as to the origin and aim of life" (p. 311).

23 Freud, S. (1920). *Beyond the Pleasure Principle*, p. 311.

24 Freud, S. (1920). *Beyond the Pleasure Principle*, p. 312.

25 Lane, N. (2016). *The Vital Question: Why Is Life the Way It Is?*, p. 214.

26 Lane, N. (2016). *The Vital Question: Why Is Life the Way It Is?*, p. 241.

27 Lane, N. (2016). *The Vital Question: Why Is Life the Way It Is?*, p. 256.

28 See Freud's two papers (1915d). *Thoughts for the Times on War and Death; and also* (1921). *Group Psychology and the Analysis of the Ego.*

29 Panksepp, J. & Biven, L. (2012). *The Archaeology of Mind: Neuroevolutionary Origins of Human Emotions*, p. 161.

30 Freud, S. (1915). *Thoughts for the Times on War and Death*, p. 72.

31 Freud, S. (1915). *Thoughts for the Times on War and Death*, p. 73.

32 Freud (1921, p. 125).

33 Freud, S. (1915b). *Instincts & Their Vicissitudes*, p. 134.

34 Freud, S. (1915b). *Instincts & Their Vicissitudes*, p. 134.

35 Panksepp, J. & Biven, L. (2012). *The Archaeology of Mind: Neuroevolutionary Origins of Human Emotions*.

36 Freud (1915d, p. 73).

37 Freud (1915d, p. 85).

38 See Solms (2019).

39 Freud, S. (1915b). *Instincts & Their Vicissitudes*.

40 Panksepp, J. & Biven, L. (2012). *The Archaeology of Mind: Neuroevolutionary Origins of Human Emotions*, p. 156.

41 Freud (1920).

Chapter 5

Perversion of the Inner Guardian

On Narcissistic Injuries and Attacks

We are here stumbling into an area of psychology that is often associated with psychopathology, and colloquially with many things negative. Derived from the residual hangover and repetition of normal childhood centrality and self-centredness, "His Majesty the Baby",[1] some adults exhibit the self-centrality of childhood into their adult lives. Normal adults have their infantile narcissism "effaced", as Freud put it but some do not. Instead, as we shall discuss later, new forms of these infantile trends resurface in the adult in whom narcissistic injury plays a disproportionate role. Compensation through various psychological manoeuvres presents in the form of emotional reactivity as well as the grandiosity of the self.

The term narcissism was derived from a clinical description and chosen by Paul Näcke in 1899 to denote a *perverse* form of self-involvement. However, the term had in fact already been used by Havelock Ellis who first used the term in 1898 to denote a description of a "psychological attitude".[2] Whilst narcissism is often associated with either perversion or unsavoury characters or personality type, in its fundamental sense narcissism is not a swear word or even disparaging. It is a complement of mental energy that is required to preserve the self and give it identity and cohesion, in moderate quanta. Let us not forget that all life on earth is driven by energy, technically 'chemiosmotic', as the biochemists tell us, depending on proton gradients across membranes to drive carbon and energy metabolism.[3] But obviously, this energetic imperative is in the service of organismic preservation, or put differently, is a requirement for any self-organising system to keep itself in a self-organised state and resistant to entropy. This makes all living organisms narcissistic. The world *has* to be experienced, interpreted, and acted upon from the vantage of the organism doing the surviving. Solms puts this in different terms, noting that subjectivity underlies consciousness because without it, there is no self-organising entity able to differentiate itself from the external 'other'.[4] He writes

> consciousness registers the state of the subject, not of the object world. The sentient subject is first and foremost an affective subject. Only then can it experience perceptual and cognitive representations. That is why—to state the obvious—there

DOI: 10.4324/9781003452522-6

can be no objects of consciousness without a subject of consciousness to experience them. The subject of consciousness is primary. The secondary (perceptual
and cognitive) form of consciousness is achieved only when the subject of consciousness feels its way into its perceptions and cognitions, which are unconscious
in themselves. The pseudopodia of an amoeba, palpating the world, come to mind.

Narcissism in this fundamental sense, says Freud, "would not be a perversion,
but the libidinal complement to the egoism of the instinct of self-preservation, a
measure of which can be attributed to every living creature".[5] In this regard, psychoanalysis and biochemistry concur with evolution and Darwin's notion of natural
selection, that the energetics of all life permeated throughout the genealogical tree
into higher and more complex organisms. The essentials are not lost, including
the idea that all living entities, even microbial ones, are narcissistic, experiencing
the world through their own lens and determining adaptive strategies to survive it.
Along with other authors such as Solan, I propose to consider narcissism (and its
preservation through aggression) "as one of the psychic envelopes that function as
the 'immune system' of our familiar sense of self while being permeable to excitations with the nonfamiliar other".[6] 'Death-work for Freud was ultimately in the service of restoring or reinstating a previous state of undifferentiated internal being',[7]
that being a state in which tension is reduced or eliminated. The death drive, in
this reading, is not merely a force acting against arousal or pleasure but one which
aims to restore quiescence when internal equilibrium is disturbed. As authors such
as Mills write, 'Freud did not argue that death was the only aim of life, only that it
maintained a dialectical tension in juxtaposition to a life principle under the ancient
command of Eros, yet the two forces of mind remained ontologically inseparable'.[8]
Solan's point is that within the normal sphere of mental functioning, narcissism
functions to maintain integrity of the core self in response to impingements that
upset this equilibrium. Put in the terms of physics, narcissism represents the ego's
Markov blanket that enables cohesion of the self to form, to represent the self to the
self and to the external world, and to fly the flag of self-identity. This differentiation of self and other is essential to any living organism knowing what is 'me' from
what is 'not me', a psychic skin essential to survival. "I am this! This is who I am
and what I am! I am different from you, from anything Other. I am a subject in the
world who perceives, experiences, remembers! From that memory, I can construct
the world!" Narcissism is the envelope of selfhood, the 'I' of the ego. Libido is directed in two directions from the outset of life: to the self as an object and to objects
in the external world. Object-libido and ego-libido represent two dimensions of the
flow of mental energy. "We have recognised our mental apparatus as being first and
foremost a device designed for mastering excitations which would otherwise be
felt as distressing or would have pathogenic effects", Freud wrote.[9]

Infancy and Oceanic Bliss

In human terms, the ego or "I", signifies a representation of this Self both *to*
the self and to others in the external world. It should be remembered that the

character of this "I" forms over time, but in the early years of infancy it is governed by a powerful precedence over all. In the mind of the infant, it holds a grand and special place in the universe, demanding total attunement (from the mother), placing itself at the centre of her focus and attentions and demanding nothing less than her perfect and devoted responsiveness to it. In this regard, an ego-ideal, as Freud put it, forms for the perfectly attuned mother meeting the demands and needs of the infant – and she is perfection idealised. When this goes well, the infant finds themselves at the centre of what Margaret Mahler thought of as a state of bliss: "We might visualise that these scattered foci of memory deposits form little islands within the hitherto *oceanic* feeling of complete fusion and oneness with the mother, in the infant's semi-conscious state".[10] A state of reverie and contentment, this peace being broken by impingements on occasion, but soothed quickly by the mother to restore stasis. When this goes well, the idealised mother absorbs a great deal of object-libido, and in turn, the infant introjects this idealisation into ego-libido, since, from the infant's perspective, the mother is an extension of self and psychically indistinguishable from self. But as Winnicott also noted, the baby can be ruthless, treating the mother "as scum, an unpaid servant, a slave; she has to love him, excretions and all... so having got what he wants he throws her away like orange peel..."[11] leading to states of disequilibrium in the mind of the mother.

The merging of the mother's and the infant's minds is a necessary part of attunement and responsiveness in the early part of life, even though this can create secondary problems for the mother into whom a freely flowing barrage of mental contents and projections from her infant leave her in a state of constant psychic disequilibrium. This is a unique situation in life in which the mind of one human and the mind of another is merged in a necessary and healthy sense, but this leaves little defence for the mother against constant challenges to her mental stasis. Such a state will by its nature tend to activate a response in the mother to restore equilibrium – aggression as we know being this mechanism. This can channel in three ways: the mother can direct her hostility at the infant and impact the infant through maternal acting out, a rare scenario since nature protects the infant above all else (think shaken-baby syndrome, for example). The hostility can be turned inwards, which leads to post-partum depression in the mother and is fairly common. Or a displacement of her activated hostility can and usually is at least partly directed into the father, the least damaging option to mother and baby but often devastating to the couple relationship over time (more detail of these mechanisms can be found in my paper on the Phallic Container in the Post-partum Couple[12]). In this merged state, the object-ideal and all the libidinal energy cathected onto it (her) also creates a great quantum of ego-ideal and libidinal energy cathected to the infant's own ego. The infant lives with primary narcissism in which it occupies pride of place in the universe, a state of feeling highly valued and finds itself "possessed of every perfection that is of value".[13] This normal state of self-idealisation is of course unconscious and primitive but fuels the centrality of the infant's own ego as one idealised in its gratifications.

It would be a delightful outcome for the infant if such a state could remain intact in perpetuity. However, the frustrations of reality quickly begin to impose themselves and intercede between the idealised state and the discomfort of the real world. Whether due to a frustrating mother, or of course, the infant's own bodily persecutions and inevitable aches, pains, and internal discomforts due to somatic demands, the state of peace and idealisation is constantly challenged and periodically shattered. Sometimes, for internal or external reasons, the infant's mental capacity to metabolise and sustain beyond its threshold for such impingements is challenged and instead, the mental skin is breached. This experience is injurious to the idealised perception and forms collective assaults on the primitive narcissism of the infant. Neither the mother nor hence the self is so perfect. But alas, it is as if the infant might fantasise that if not for this imperfection, everything would still be ideal! The infant's idealised ego is being assaulted and challenged, leading to perceptions of injury, sometimes even mortal and irrecoverable injury, that the perfect state of object-libido is being frustrated and hence momentarily withdrawn from the maternal object. But also then ego-libido is withdrawn from the infant's own ego, merged as it is with the maternal object in the early months. Narcissistic injury in this sense leaves traces via memory impressions that if only the frustrations of life that disturbed the oceanic bliss would cease in their threats and attacks, the 'I' would get back to an idealised and perfect state, possessed of every perfection that is of value.

It is interesting to note how common this sentiment appears to be in the justifications and motives of aggressors in both the personal and geopolitical space. Hitler and Putin in their own speeches make these points powerfully, that the attacks and encroachments of some other reality require a response to restore the values, way of life, and the very existence of their states. If only these challenges did not exist, their own self-valued and idealised positions would be *restored*. Like the infant's mechanism for such restoration, crying and screaming and flailing induce response from the environment, driven as we have discussed by an aggressive drive, which aims to return to an idealised and perfectly narcissistic state, without the dysregulation of reality taking this away. Aggression as an inner state *drives* the mechanism of restoration, from the subjective perspective of the infant. The exact pathway this aggressive pressure will forge will depend on a number of factors available to the infant or child at the time it is required, both developmentally (an infant cannot decide to run away but it can decide to close its mouth or scream) and in terms of resource options available to it in the external environment (is mother available and responsive for example). Regarding the former point, Freud's connecting of the psychosexual focus given a child's age and stage creates somatic foci for libidinal energy to cathect, or attach itself in a manner that becomes relatively fixed. These 'fixations' are returned to repeatedly via memory imprints to enable forward predictions about the likely outcomes of the subjective interface with the environment. In the terms of neuroscience, "the fundamental task of the ego is to make predictions—to make predictions as to how it can meet its multiple needs in the world" and to periodically update these predictions when old patterning fails in a new world context. What might have worked screaming for the mother in infancy when kept waiting for a feed might not work as well when repeated compulsively in the restaurant thirty years later when kept waiting by the waiter, even when the same *feelings* are triggered and the memory returns to this fixation point.

The Ego and Memory

I mentioned that memory traces carry the impressions of early injury, and of course, the many variables that influence how experience is perceived and navigated give rise to unique subjectivity in the infant. "The ego", writes Solms, "therefore, is fundamentally bound up with memory".[14] The importance of the memory system to how these impressions are retained for later use cannot be overestimated. A system without memory carries no sustained narcissistic injury nor will rely on aggression at any future point to manage old injuries and threats. A system without memory carries no repetition of affective reactivity to early experience, since from the subjective point of view of that organism, there is no history at all. Experience is fleeting, momentary, and disappears from the organism's playbook. There is no unconscious, no regression, and no return to the past to motivate any reaction. In both personal and geopolitical life, memory is always in the mix of current reaction and is often brought up in both conscious and unconscious ways to justify an aggressive position. Hitler remembered the humiliations and betrayals of the Versailles Treaty that ended WW1, and Putin remembered the humiliations of the West post the cold war, and the injuries this brought to the proud Russian nation-state. The ego-ideal relates also to group psychology, Freud notes, in that in addition to the individual side, this ideal has a social side, and also the common ideal of the family, a class, or a nation.[15]

Often, injuries that affect the ego-ideal are unconscious and remain accessible only through psychological intervention or if encoded early enough in life, part of a non-declarative store of memory trace that can never be made fully conscious but which still occupies a place in triggering emotional reactivity. Memory is critical in its role in forming the unconscious, and since as Freud noted, "conscious emerges instead of a memory trace", the vast reservoir of memory traces are contained in the system unconscious, held in check by defensive systems, and especially repression. I will return to the nature of repression shortly, since without it the integrity of the mind would be compromised. But for now we can note the observation of how history tends to repeat itself through repetition, revisiting old injuries, often relentlessly, in the avowed service of survival. The need to efficiently recognise pathogenic threats to both body and mind, and by extension groups or cultures, becomes baked in through memory and the emotional response to memory. In its pure form, we could say that without this immune system in both body and mind, that is the mechanism of aggression driven by memory, life would be short and brutish.

Repetition Compulsion and Memory

Such is its nature, that the repetition compulsion presents enigmatic challenges: why would such a function be at all adaptive? It is well understood by now that under its influence all manner of psychopathology is manifest and that if we were to distil the purpose of psychotherapy, it is to undo the compulsive nature of repetitive patterns from historical antecedents that continue to exert undue and often negative influence. In often destructive ways, these repetitions exert their influence relentlessly, a puzzling phenomenon that on the face of it had no adaptive value for the individual. What possible benefit could accrue to a person repeating patterns in their life that bring loss, pain, or damage. Is nature this disingenuous? If some adaptive value is to be found, it must be for the benefit of evolution or the species would be seriously compromised if the mind was programmed by mindless repetition of no inherent value. Natural economics suggests that there is no function in body or mind that is entirely superfluous to adaptive function. Repetition, in the mental sphere, is no exception to this rule – but why would it return to the very impingements that evoked disequilibrium to begin, and revisit them again and again, violating inherent logic of any organism that will avoid impingements that threaten equilibrium? Part of the answer to this paradox lies in the theoretical and empirical assistance we get from Kandel and his work on memory, which function is to encode neuroanatomically circuits that act to remind the organism of experiences *beyond a critical valence* that were aversive and threatening. Minor aversive stimuli will trigger a response that is temporary. Prolonged exposure, beyond a critical threshold, appears to create circuits of encoded ideation, which being able to recruit emotional centres of the brain can serve as immune identifiers in the mental realm.

Memory provides to the mind a foundation for psychic immunity and gives to the mind what the memory of the somatic immune system gives to the body. Both mental and physical systems use aggression to respond to potential threats, employing memory to identity the signature of these threats. The immune system of the body is aggressive but uses biological processes for conservation. The mind utilises aggression as its chief mechanism to neutralise sources of disequilibrium, or what it perceives to be the signature of a pathogenic trigger. In the somatic realm, "immunological memory" is the ability of the immune system to respond more rapidly and effectively to pathogens that have been encountered previously, and reflects the preexistence of a population of antigen-specific lymphocytes. This ability to identify potential pathogens in the somatic realm is mirrored in the mental one but in what could be seen as an apparently self-defeating way.

Memory lies at the heart of the repetition compulsion, a pattern to which the mind can return again and again as a mechanism aimed at encoding past 'pathogenic triggers', and alerting the individual to their risks at recreating disequilibrium. A symbolic activator of the past injury/aversive event is likely to then trigger the internal aggressive drive because the aggressive drive is the mind's mechanism whose aim is restoration. Memory is the mental representative of the body's immunological memory, and aggression its means of defence. Nonetheless, its aim remains benign, merely the restoration of stasis. However far the reality of the destructive effects of such a response might be, proportional to the internal identification of the degree of threat it poses to the self, its aim may be regarded as intrinsically and ultimately benign. Memory, containing the building blocks of the Unconscious, serves the function of recognition; ideation whose purpose is to identify pathogens that have previously incurred injury to that individual. Aggression is the response to such unconscious identification, aimed at eliminating the threat and returning to stasis. The peculiar characteristic of repetition, and the repetition compulsion identified by Freud, appears to be bound up with this function, of returning repeatedly to the memory of what is pathogenic, identifying signatures that trigger this memory, and then seeking to neutralise the threat. In this fashion, the unconscious silently gears itself towards scanning for and identifying threats and, when necessary, acting against them. In the somatic realm, this response had no effect on another person, but is murderous to pathogens venturing against it. But in the mental realm, the pathogenic trigger is invariably attachment-based, another person representing a pathogenic trigger, against which a response must be mounted. Early object representations suffer projection, attributing to even neutral objects some of the experiences of early imagos, particularly parental ones.

But it is also clinically obvious that not all objects are tarred with the same brush. Some associative elements carry much greater emotional value and must exist to remind the person of a familiar pathogen; and by such association external objects, pathogenically neutral to the outside observer, become tainted with such internal representations. The age, gender, build, and mannerisms of an external object can trigger by association a memory trace, such ideation recruiting affect to give expression to previous early experience. At times, a sensory stimulus, such as a smell or sound, appears to have the power to trigger a memory trace to life, even when such sensory memory is rooted in ancient personal history, long 'forgotten' to consciousness. At other times, such as in extreme trauma (violence, car accident) the density of experience in the process of the trauma leads to memory trying to encode the events, but in a situation of helplessness to effect outcomes. Accordingly, the recruitment of all the senses into the inputting of memory facilitates unconscious identifiers being established for an 'immune' response which is immobilised – the aggressive response remaining ineffective at re-establishing equilibrium because it cannot be enacted. This may be either because one is helpless to affect outcomes or the threat of violence prevents any normal retaliatory response. This freezing of the immune response to an acute and annihilatory threat may prove so overwhelming that a pathological post-traumatic response is affected, with all the symptom profile that is so familiar to clinicians working with post-traumatic effects. The link between somatic and mental responses should not, it is increasingly recognised, be separated, since the mind utilises neurochemistry to register its discontents and impingements, from which the encoding becomes unconscious memory, the reservoir of ideation that forms the foundation of mental immunity. Whereas trauma originates externally, drives originate from within the mind and are constant, and impinge not from without but from within, and as such, as Freud noted, "no flight can avail against it".[16]

We are developing links between experience, subjectivity, and memory, to which the human mind can return repeatedly when under threat of disequilibrium. Narcissism reflects idealised subjectivity. In the normal course of development, the experience of injury beyond the infant's temperamental threshold will imprint as permanent memory traces, as aversive enough to require adaptive return to it. Testing new experience against old references serves an adaptive purpose. Solms, points out, that

> ... long-term memories serve the future. Once the midbrain decisions triangle has evaluated the compressed feedback flowing in from previous action, what it activates is an expanded *feedforward* process which unfolds in reverse direction, through the forebrain's memory systems, generating an *expected context* for the selected motor sequence. This is the product of all our learning. In other words, when a need propels us into the world, *we do not discover the world afresh with each new cycle*. It activates a set of predictions about the likely sensory consequences of our actions, based upon past experience of how to meet the selected need in the prevailing circumstances.[17]

Solms elaborates, drawing on Panksepp's neuroscientific modelling, that there is an evolutionary bridge between these two aspects of experience which are "inherently valenced perceptions qualified by specific feelings". Over this evolutionary bridge, in Panksepp's view, consciousness becomes extended into perception in general, "since it contextualises affect".[18] We are seeing here a dovetailing of contemporary neuroscience and Freud's observations of how valenced perception, influenced by memory of the system Unconscious, stored particularly in response to aversive experience as Kandel discovered, and amplified through the perception of subjectivity, leads to injury or threat to the integrity of the self, an ego-threat to narcissistic integrity. Injury of this sort will demand by all the laws of physics and evolution, a response to either restore or adapt to restore.

The failure of love, that is object-love, upon which the integrity of the ego depends, even in, and perhaps especially in early primitive states of infancy, threatens also then ego-libido, since these two remain intertwined from the outset of life. To love is to be humbled. "A person who loves has, so to speak, forfeited a part of his narcissism, and it can only be replaced by his being loved".[19] Since loving unrequited leads to impoverishing of the ego and loving returned restores narcissistic supplies to a happy state, we can see the role narcissism and narcissistic injury can play through the *perceived* failures of maternal attunement in infancy (or through the failure of love in later life), or through persecutions of the infant's own body, but which the mother is unable to remedy quickly enough. This leads to the product of all our learning – as Solms explains,

> ...when a need propels us into the world, *we do not discover the world afresh with each new cycle*. It activates a set of predictions about the likely sensory consequences of our actions, based upon our past experience of how to meet the selected need in the prevailing circumstances.[20]

What needs to be added here is that emotion in memory is not held like a can of pressurised deodorant waiting to be pressed into release. Rather, memory traces are stored in a neurological reservoir as ideation, idea traces or memory traces as it were, that trigger emotional responses or affects emerging finally as feelings,[21] according to what those traces represent *to the individual*, not in any objective sense or through the lens of anyone else who may have shared the experience, including the mother of the infant. If experience is by definition subjective, as we have suggested above, then the emotional valence attached to ideational stores or memory traces will be affected by this personal lens of what those experiences *meant* for the individual. Hate, in this sense, derives not only because of love's frustration but as Freud noted, "from the ego's struggle to preserve and maintain itself".[22] Hate is older than love, preceding attachment in theory as stasis precedes the challenge of stimuli that impacts the organisms from outside itself, but also from the constant stream of instinctual energies impinging from within and against which there is no barrier.

Love and Hate

Hate is a subjective derivative of the aggressive drive and linked to ambivalence, the flip side of love. Faced with the frustrations of imperfection of the idealised object, and hence discovering these in the idealised self too, creates *feelings*. It may seem trite to suggest that humans suffer from feelings, since to many this is as self-evident as is breathing. But psychology and neuroscience over the decades has not always found comfortable agreement that this rather intangible variable can be considered in any scientific sense, since by definition feelings are subjective and objectively unmeasurable. Behaviour therapy and its refinements over the years have eschewed the role of feelings in psychopathology or its treatment since the inner world cannot be reliably or objectively measured. Psychoanalysis has taken a different course, recognising the centrality of feelings and the role they play in the mental life of humans. Affects can be unconscious as can drives and instincts. But feelings become registered and felt, since it is in the nature of feelings that they must be felt. And someone has to be doing that feeling, or at least, having those feelings. An aggressive response can occur in the absence of feelings or any sentient consciousness – such as when a shark attacks a surfer or a dog bites a rival. But anger is different – for there has to be someone, an ego, registering that feeling of anger as it surfaces from the unconscious activation *and its associations* into the conscious awareness.

The juncture at which affects or unconscious associations become felt as feelings is unmeasurable in any objective sense, though debate as to the neurology behind this bridge abounds in the neuropsychoanalytic literature. The fly in the ointment is, so to speak, subjectivity and its cascade effects through association. If it were possible to suspend subjectivity for a moment, we might note that ego-libido represents a quantum of mental energy that promotes the self. Like libido attaches to the external object, or strives to, so libidinal energy attached to the self-acts to create a vested interest in the self, its promotion in a world competing for all manner of resource. This drive in its normal course could be regarded as benign, narcissism that serves the interest of the individual by enabling a coherent sense of self to emerge and with it a specific set of self-references in relation to the world. I am this type of person. I vest character and personality and values in being this type of person. This *I-am-ness* becomes a reflection of core sense of who and what it is to be you in the world, and in relationship to others. Identity is of course an evolving phenomenon, but also, core elements within the identity of an individual persist through the life cycle.

If narcissism forms the fuel for the 'envelope' of selfhood and self-identity, then injury or threat to this envelope is likely to trigger a response in *its* defence. The primitive and developing ego requires a portion of libido to cathect inwards, to be directed at itself for a survival imperative to be created, to drive a prioritising that there is an I. Object-libido, the love and attachment needs for the mother, are partially inflected thereby also to the infant's own ego in the form of ego-libido. This is enabled since the mother and infant remain inseparable, a dyad of psychic merger in which mental contents can move freely between the mother and the infant. Winnicott opined that there was "no such thing as a baby", a phrase that carried considerable initial surprise but later clout paradigmatically in psychoanalysis. "There is no such thing as an infant, meaning, of course, that whenever one finds an infant one finds maternal care, and without maternal care there would be no infant".[23] Kahn in his preface to Winnicott's book, noted that:

> For Winnicott the paradox of infant-mother relationship lay in that the *environment* (mother) makes the becoming self of the infant feasible. Winnicott was the first among analysts to point out the obvious fact that a mother cherishes, enjoys and *creates* her baby: not only in the somatic inside of her womb, but also in the early stages of the infant's finding and realising of its innate *givens* of endowment and the person it will differentiate and actualise into in *time*.[24]

Winnicott himself mused later that more generally we could say that in life the "centre of gravity of the being does not start off in the individual. It is in the total set-up".

Just like in-utero, where physical merger is in place, so in the post-partum period the mind of the baby and the mind of the mother are inseparable, a merger without a psychic barrier. At least, this would be true in an ideal state – since sometimes the frustrations of the infant in mis-attuned relationship with its mother can lead to defensive separation from her and attempts to find alternative minds through which it can find attunement. Only with the passage of time, and the 'hatching' (to use Mahler's phrase) of the infant into the world, does it begin to develop a mind separated from the mother. Mahler noted, that this "separation-individuation phase is a kind of second birth experience ... a hatching from the symbiotic mother-child common membrane. This hatching is just as inevitable as is biological birth".[25] But the question Winnicott asked is important too:

> What precedes this? We sometimes loosely assume that before the two-body object relationship there is a one-body relationship, but this is wrong, and

obviously wrong if we look closely. The capacity for a one-body relationship follows that of a two-body relationship, through the *introjection* of the object.[26]

The essential notion that two minds find each other, so to speak, and *create* merger through common purpose, suggests that this is a normative but essentially psychotic state. Two minds coming to merge without mental barriers, even if temporarily through the first months of development, is an unusual state, except in psychosis where mental boundaries between the internal and external worlds break down. But in the post-partum period, it is normative and necessary, but with costs for the mother whose mind is, effectively, activated or induced to metabolise and respond, to make links by the baby when in states of disequilibrium. It means that the baby's instinctive love and drive to attachment with the mother will also enable some libidinal attachment to the self. The infant's own ego benefits from 'self-love' as it were, in which ego-libido is directed to the baby's own narcissism, or at least forms the foundation of narcissistic self-love.

That is, even in the primitive stages of psychic development, the idea that the infant is an 'I' having 'me' experiences creates the foundation for subjectivity in a more complex sense than that of simpler organisms whose subjectivity is without sentience. Through the experience of the infant, impingements that disrupt this state of love and 'oceanic bliss' carry a disproportionate valence relative to an older child or adult. For the infant, a pin prick, for example, represents in the moment its whole world, and this prick is a threat to its whole world. For an adult, a pin prick represents partial experience, a fragment of a much larger whole. But an infant does not benefit from perspective yet, and frustrations are amplified through helplessness and as yet unformed meaning, or more aptly, *meaninglessness*.

Meaninglessness in this context signifies that an infant cannot yet make meaning out of novel experience, particularly aversive novelty. *Meaning* has to be created out of nothing. Without reference to experience in memory, what something represents, the infant creates its own inferences through its primitive lens. The division of experience between pleasure and unpleasure creates for the infant the sense that unpleasure is bad and threatens the cohesion and integrity of the primitive self. There are few defences yet in place to hide behind, except primitive defences of denial and repression, an attempt to form a mental shield against stimuli that are too negatively powerful. Fundamentally, the threat to the narcissistic envelope is initially binary – it is pleasure-good or unpleasure-bad. Pleasure-good is associated with sustenance and nourishment for aliveness, and unpleasure-bad is a signal of the need to activate a restorative response to prevent threat and annihilation. "Indeed", said Freud, "it may be asserted that the true prototypes of the relation of hate are derived not from sexual life, but from the ego's struggle to preserve and maintain itself".[27]

Psychic Meaninglessness and the Primordial Soup

From the perspective of adults, and especially parents, the most meaningful moment in life must surely be the birth of a child. There is not much in life that can top the significance of making life, of partnering with nature or God to create a living being, especially in one's likeness. The miracle of life is seldom lost on new parents, witnessing something so deeply meaningful as to be beyond the purview of words. It is profoundly *meaningful*.

Unfortunately, this is not true from the perspective of the infant being born. Quite the contrary, *meaninglessness* appears to be the first and primary mental state of the infant entering the world. I am reminded of one of the oldest descriptions on record of cosmic evolution that portends the laws of nature and the inexorably forward flow of time from a state of formlessness to form. Through the flow of time disorder is propelled into self-organising systems. *Creatio ex nihilo* (creation of something out of nothing) begins with the notion that the cosmos itself and all within it are governed by the laws of nature, and that these laws that are seen to apply at the broadest macro-processes of cosmic life are also present in the tiniest of micro-processes within the tiny planet called earth.

Genesis 1:2 presents an initial condition of creation – namely, that it is *toyhu va voyhu*, formless and void: "Now the earth was unformed and void, and darkness was upon the face of the deep". This coincides, as we now know, with the scientific view of cosmic evolution too, a recent discovery that until Einstein's groundbreaking insights saw the cosmic order as a constant and eternal. Now, we discover in science that the cosmos and all within it had a start point, a beginning. With the advent of expansion after the Big Bang (a one time and inexplicable cosmic event), we uncover the flow of time driving chaos into order and ultimately into self-organising systems, aptly described more recently in science in Friston's Free Energy Theory and self-organising systems. The free-energy principle in physics suggests that energy will strive to become self-organised, as will all systems in nature. Once organised into a self-system, it will seek to maintain and preserve itself.

This character of cosmic life, and ultimately of organic life too, also provides insight into the trajectory of mental life and serves to introduce the rest of the section, which describes a process of forming and filling, turning the formless and void into mental structures and forms able to make psychological meaning of the world and to navigate it. The first task of the infant is to begin a process of making meaning out of this state of *meaninglessness*, in order to navigate and survive it. The life drive, or libidinal drive, seems to prompt this teleological thrust from a chaotic mental state in which there is no meaning into a more organised mental state in which systems of 'knowledge' about the world begin to coalesce into fragments of coherence. The moment some interpretation of this meaningless state is made, the infant faces two competing tensions of energy – adapt to this new meaning and then try preserve the new normal or keep on modifying the meaning made to enable further adaptation.

This tension between adaptation and acquisition (of new meaning and knowledge) and the striving to either restore or maintain homeostasis is at the core of the human psyche. This polarity that Freud described, is not static – but a constant tension around laying down foundational blueprints for how the world works and how to navigate it to survive. The subjectivity of how these traces form is driven and influenced by the uniqueness of each infant and their somatic realty, psychosocial milieu, temperament, and so on – influencing how memory is laid for future reference. Given the emotional amplitude of early infancy and the greatness of chaos (an individual 'primordial soup', as it were) compared to order that comes later, gives us the clues as to why in states of regression the emotional amplitude of the adult personality will appear so disproportionate to current observable reality. I use this notion of the 'primordial soup' both tongue in cheek as a metaphor for the process of the infant's mind but also because the tendency in the cosmos and in all cosmic laws indicate a trend from absolute chaos into order, with order becoming a feature of all cosmic systems. Once ordered, they strive to preserve themselves as self-organising systems, holding then the familiar polarity of homeostasis versus entropy that governs all systems in nature, including biological and mental ones. The tendency in nature to strive for order out of chaos leads to self-governing systems that are able to initially differentiate self from other and then *strive* to maintain self from other. Striving to maintain the self as a self-organising system means that self-identity will require preservation from the vantage and perspective of the system once formed. The mystery of the universe is that the universe itself, and all its contents are governed by the same principles and laws. Chaos converts over time into order. Once established, that order seeks to preserve itself from entropy using energy. Homeostasis requires energy, or work. Adaptation driving evolution also requires work. In the human psyche, libidinal drivers push the organism into a constant state of tension and work as a by-product of making sense out of the chaos, interpreting it, and adapting to it to ensure its survival. Making meaning out of *meaninglessness* implies the acquisition of knowledge, or at least a form of knowledge that enables any organism to subjectively have an experience that it can evaluate and respond to in the pursuit of survival. This gives the impression of cognitive function that supposes rationality. However, even a basic organism has to use some form of 'knowledge' to navigate its environment, even if by knowledge that is instinctive or reflexive. The brain of that organism still has to learn, encode, store, and retrieve to navigate.

Enter the Aplysia

It is 1939 and the young nine-year-old Eric Kandel whom we have discussed above is forcibly expelled from his family home in Vienna as the Nazis take control of the city.[28] His family targeted for being Jewish left an indelible impression on the young Kandel's mind. Intuitively, we would all regard it as obvious that such an event as soldiers throwing a family out of their home would make an impression on a young nine-year-old. But as many great thinkers, from Freud to Einstein, notice very simple things and reflect upon them, the young Eric wondered why and how this memory entrenched itself, as if seared into his neuronal structure for permanent retrieval and access. Kandel considered this apparently simple process more deeply and this seemingly 'minor' question ended up having deep significance. Kandel set out in his early career to locate Freudian psychoanalysis in the brain and became a leading psychiatrist and neuroscientific researcher, eventually winning

the Nobel Prize in medicine for his decades of research. Kandel's Nobel Prize winning research delved into memory, using the *Aplysia* sea slug to study the effects
of environmental impingements on learning, noting this creature's large neuronal
structure to observe changes.

What he found was interesting. Aversive stimuli, such as an electrical shock, engage neuronal and neurochemical changes that are temporary if the aversive event
is short. But if the aversive stimuli are prolonged, new neuronal circuits emerge
to permanently record and store as memory the stimuli that requires avoiding if
pain is to be circumnavigated in the interests of efficient future survival. In other
words, even primitive organisms with basic neuronal structures have to acquire
'knowledge' to navigate complexity in their environment. This does not suggest
consciousness or sentience in a conventional sense, or the stuff we read about in
encyclopaedias, but rather the capacity to acquire and store information that can
be referenced as a forward-thinking guide to future encounters. Those organisms
able to achieve this in a relatively competitive space of time have fulfilled the
requirement of adaptation through evolution where the conservative first response
to maintain homeostasis is breached. One could assume that if homeostasis is not
breached, and the organism is able to maintain stasis using its current mechanisms,
then adaptation via change, in this case neurological change, would not be required
since the work required to adapt is greater than the work required to maintain.
Converting a meaningless state into a meaningful one requires the acquisition of
knowledge about the internal and external environment and perhaps challenging it,
not unlike the cosmos itself moves from chaos into order.

Of course, a young infant has none of these functions available to it, yet some
form of knowledge has to be acquired if it is to make meaning and navigate the
challenges of the external world and its own internal world. At this young age,
knowledge is acquired and driven by feeling states, changes to homeostasis that
require remedy. *Feelings* are central to linking internal states and external impingements to the mind so that work can be performed. Let us remember Freud's
significant point that, and concurring with Solms' modern neuroscientific views,[29]
"the psychical representative of the stimuli originating from within the organism
and reaching the mind, as a measure of the demand made upon the mind for work
in consequence of its connection with the body".[30] Crying induces a response in
the mother and the infant quickly discovers that feelings are improved from bad
to good (or sometimes not) when an adequate response is achieved. Feelings, as
Solms has argued, lie at the core of the available psychic mechanisms in the advanced mental systems of the human mind and derive from *Id* sources that enable
the most effective feedback loop for the organism.

The Id, as Freud termed it (the "It" translated from the original German), suggests
that the wellspring of affects and feelings derive from primitive and unconscious
mechanisms of the mind designed ultimately to facilitate the two primary evolutionary mechanisms available for survival – conservation of homeostasis or adaptation for a new normal. Keep in mind that from a biological point of view, the most
successful species are those that maintain the right balance between constancy and

change, according to Paul Nurse, a Nobel Prize winning geneticist and cell biologist. Notwithstanding that Solms notes a distinction between homeostatic, emotional, and sensory affects,[31] I put these together because they each still serve their main function of either maintaining states of 'what is' or adapting to generate new states via adaptation or what Darwin calls 'variation'. Some evolutionists argue that variation begins randomly, that random genetic variations survive because they work better in changing environments. One could put this the other way around, suggesting that without a *drive* towards variation, adaptation to changing environments would be impossible. Certainly, as mentioned earlier, biochemists such as Lane examining the origins of life suggest this, that the best way of describing evolution is the idea of it pushing, driving, forced, and needing to happen. Variation is not always passive.

Self-organising Systems

Survival within the challenges of the real world requires work for any self-organising system, including that of the mind and body to maintain itself. The individual self-organising system, in other words, must maintain as best homeostasis as it can within a given set of parameters to survive but must also be able to adapt to pressures and impingements that exceed the threshold for homeostasis in order to better survive. If cold, we shiver to warm up. But if we cannot warm up simply by shivering, we have to figure out a way to generate warmth, either by creating it externally, moving to a warmer environment, or simply putting on a jersey. If a jersey is not immediately available, planning to acquire one becomes a mental step of thinking. If there are no shops at hand, a substitute will be required, perhaps say an animal skin or creating a woollen covering out of sheep wool. But this form of survival applies to the individual self-organising system within its habitat. At a broader level, survival of the individual benefits enormously from being able to replicate itself and create other self-organising systems that represent the same identity coalescing against anything differentiated as Other. Darwin's observation of the power of reproduction as a driver of species suggests that preservation of the self is enhanced through reproduction of the self-species and in this manner, preservation of the self-organising system (in this case the human one) is improved. Hence, what Freud understood as the libidinal drive, that internal pressure of the sexual instincts seeking to replicate and reproduce explains why built in to the organism is a state of constant (sexual) tension which can only be discharged temporarily before this powerful driver and motivator will recharge again. This creates cycles of inner sources of tensions which seek further discharge.

It is an endless cycle of the libidinal drive in ascendance, a residue of the evolutionary imperative to preserve the Self through adaptation, creating and procreating as a mechanism to ensure both individual and species survival. "Natural selection acts", says Darwin,

> by the preservation and accumulation of variations, which are beneficial under the organic and inorganic conditions to which each creature is exposed at all periods of life. The ultimate result is that each creature tends to become more and

more improved in relation to its conditions. This improvement inevitably leads to the gradual advancement of the organisation of the greater number of living beings throughout the world.[32]

Darwin also acknowledges that some organisms have retained their homeostatic blueprint for eons of time without ever heeding the requirement for adaptation and evolution, presumably because homeostasis as a choice remained possible under the pressures of the environment, without compromising survival. In fact, more recently Lane observes that for some two and a half *billion* years simple cellular life did not evolve at all! Nonetheless, this thrust of Eros is perhaps the residue of adaptation or die that occurs when the threshold for homeostasis is breached. However, left unchecked, a rampant drive to adaptation would render the organism vulnerable to losing its own core identity and ultimately contribute to its own demise. Homeostasis provides the tension to maintain some balance, to preserve the organisms first and foremost against demise and yields only in the face of the species-requirement to adapt.

This tension between the life and death drives is never lost, a constant internal struggle felt within the individual psyche, in which the struggle for creativity and procreativity tensions against homeostasis and quiescence. Survival of the self depends upon survival of the species which represents the self, and which differentiates itself from the not-self. In the competition for resources, which are naturally limited in space, time, and substance, differentiating Self from Other provides the impetus for better survival, not only in the individual but also in the species. Groups provide safety, nation-states provide safety, and identity within group provides safety through identity and adherence to the group by common cause. 'Othering' becomes a natural mechanism to identify self as differentiated from other, an impetus for better longevity in the natural battle for resources. As we also know, Othering can also become destructive.

Energy, Life, and the Singularity

What gave the impetus for a speck of infinite density, known as the Initial Singularity, to start expanding into the Big Bang and the universe as we know it is unclear and perhaps unknowable as Nature seems adept at hiding many of her secrets. Nor is the transition from the inanimate to the animate, "originally breathed by the Creator into a few forms or into one" (as Darwin put it), "and breathed into his nostrils the breath of life, and the man became a living being", as Genesis puts it, easy to discern, those quantum leaps from a state of ultimate homeostasis to organic life. Nonetheless, in all these emergent states we note the evolution of tensions between a drive to maintain a given state and a drive to adapt to a new state under the pressures of reality. Freud initially thought of these tensions as related to the reality principle versus the pleasure principle of mental drives, the

general tendency of our mental apparatus, which can be traced back to the economic principle of saving expenditure of energy, seems to find expression in the tenacity with which we hold onto sources of pleasure at our disposal, and in the difficulty with which we renounce them.[33]

Forces appear to inhabit the organism, now organic and animate, which are capable of adaptation, a creative energy that enables both psychic and biological adaptation to reality via epigenetic modifications and psychic manoeuvres. Could this quantum energy that emerged ex-nihilo that emerges to promote adaptability, including through a reproductive process which serves both individual needs to survival through familial and group adhesion and also serves the species survival be linked to Freud's observation of the libidinal drive? Whatever the deep origin of this drive, we note its power to enable creative and procreative impetus originating in a force capable of adaptation for survival.

In contrast, we are assisted by Friston's Free Energy Principle that all systems are scaled-up versions of a basic self-preservatory mechanism and will invariably strive to minimise free energy if it can. This suggests that self-organising systems are conservative literally by nature, and once forming into self-cohesion with imbedded subjectivity, will strive to minimise free energy and will change to achieve this, *if it can*, as Solms notes: "All the quantities in a self-organising system that can change will change to minimise free energy".[34] And therein we seem to encounter an apparent paradox: Friston's Law states that systems will change, *in other words expend energy*, in order to conserve energy. Systems will adapt (change) in order to remain the same (to conserve and maintain). This paradox lies at the core of the psychic apparatus too and Freud's grappling with its paradoxical drives – one that can make change in the service of not making change. Perhaps more accurately, a drive capable of adaptation and change only when conditions for stasis are challenged by the reality principle and its impingements and demands.

Once the drive to adaptation has achieved its goals, activated when the conservative drive cannot maintain stasis in the face of impingements, which is to restore a (new) steady state and its job momentarily complete, the organism can return to maintaining itself. The conservative drive whose raison d'être is strive for homeostasis without adaptation, that is to maintain a steady state, returns to exert its influence over the organism. The study of the origin of life through biochemistry seems to agree with this point. From the outset, says Nick Lane, primitive organic organisms favoured stasis for billions of years and only made change for adaptation when forced to through environmental changes and the challenges these presented. Stasis first, adaptation after, new stasis. Two fundamental tensions that drive all living matter: a drive to maintain stasis and a drive for adaptation. Lane makes the point that:

Only rarely is natural selection a force for change. Most commonly, it opposes change, purging variations from the peaks of an adaptive landscape. Only when the landscape undergoes some kind of seismic shift does selection promote change rather than stasis.[35]

In the complexity of the psyche, we note therefore Freud's observations about two principle drives in constant tension and conflict from the advent of the animate, in both organic and cosmic terms, between what Freud termed the life drive and the death drive, originating in the most basic of life forms. When this tension loses sustainability, through age or the organisms ability to either conserve or adapt, then entropy follows and the system trends towards demise. In fact, as Nurse makes the point, without being responsive to inner and outer change, through what Solms' accents as *feelings* in order to be able to detect changes and respond, the future for us "might turn out to be rather brief".[36]

Bion and the Alpha Elements

So we have noticed two fundamental forces at play in nature – one adaptive and one conservative – in the human psyche these appear represented by the life drive and the death drive. The life drive is adaptive, creative, and procreative and the death drive, as Freud termed it, conservative and maintaining of mental stasis. An infant born into mental chaos, order-as-yet-unformed, carries the same tension of opposite energies – striving to maintain stasis whilst adapting as best it can when this fails. Making meaning out of the primal state of *meaninglessness* is the first step in a developing subjectivity. Other theorists have described this process of making order from chaos in the life of the infant. Wilfred Bion, an influential English medical doctor turned psychoanalyst who was involved in the world-renowned Tavistock Clinic in the UK, recognised this conversion process of the 'undigested' into the 'digested', and wrote of conversion of beta into alpha elements, using the mind of the mother as a container for converting the undifferentiated psychotic-like state of mental chaos into more processed and metabolised beta elements that form the foundation of thinking and mental order. He wrote:

> Beta-elements are stored but differ from alpha-elements in that they are not so much memories as undigested facts, whereas the alpha-elements have been digested by alpha-function and thus made available for thought. It is important to distinguish between memories and undigested facts—beta-elements.[37]

What Bion is identifying is the forward-driven conversion process of the raw sensory experience of an organism, in this case the infant, who is compelled to make some (rudimentary) meaning out of experience and the constant flow of sensory impressions bearing upon it. The Alpha-function operates to convert sensory impressions and emotions in their various manifestations from raw and essentially meaningless into those more manageable, meaningful, and sensible to thought. That is, they get digested and therefore made useful for mental thinking,[38] or what is more currently described as 'mentalising' by recent theorists such as Peter Fonagy.[39]

The puzzling question of how the sensory impressions flowing into the sensory apparatus are converted to meaning is one that Bion grappled with. Which is another way of thinking about how mental order emerges from the chaos of primitive bodily and sensory experience for a human infant, or how order emerges from more primitive states of chaos in general. In humans, referencing emotional experience or feeling states is critical but only in so far as these elements can be filtered and assisted through a containing parental mind, usually in the form of the mother. This ties in to the thankfully normal 'psychotic' state of mental merger that exists in the dyadic relationship of the mother and her infant.[40] We might also be reminded here of Winnicott's point that there is no such thing as a baby, at least not in the abstract, away from the mind of its mother. One could suggest that there is no such thing as a baby's *mind*, at least not in the abstract without a maternal mind to enable a metabolic function and the making of meaning.

Despots and Dictators

The conversion of the undifferentiated experience into differentiated experience and knowledge that is stored as memory to be accessed to negotiate life forward lies at the heart of development. Information is key to these processes, since genes code information and signalling pathways transmit information, as the biochemist Nick Lane puts it, "within cells, between cells, between organs, between whole organisms, between populations of organisms and even between different species across whole ecosystems".[41] However, such information development and transfer does not *begin* as learning through any cognitive or intellectual function, since these are as yet undeveloped, but through *feelings*. Albeit primitive, feelings, nonetheless, lie at the heart of learning from the outset of life. The infant feeling cold, or hungry, or lonely knows of this experience because it *feels* these impingements and sensory stirrings. If agency is possible, feelings prompt action for remedy, but the infant in its helpless and undifferentiated state can only remedy through the promptings of feeling states that register disequilibrium. In the early months of life, *feelings become knowledge*. In adulthood, it often seems as if cerebral knowledge drives feeling states, through the interpretation of events. But the developmental reality is that the cherry picking of the data in adulthood to create templates of rationalised knowledge often suits underlying emotional drivers, which come first. This becomes important in deconstructing why ideological posturing is so convincing for all sides of an argument and people cling tenaciously to one or other side of a vexing issue. However, ideology can be a fickle master, often changing according to or following emotional experience. It also may provide some insight into how the Hitlers and the Putins of the world can use every conceivable scientific and ideological justification for pursuing an essentially emotional agenda. This tendency is not unique to despots and dictators. It is a paradox of human pride in rationality taking precedent over emotion and being its tamer; yet at core the human mind is primary a feeling-driven organ and the higher cortical functions emerge from that powerful internal driver that Solms poetically describes as the 'hidden spring' at the source of consciousness. Feelings guide the push to psychic order and somatic equilibrium. Feelings drive the push from the undifferentiated state of *meaninglessness* to an ordered state of meaning. In Bion's terms, the path to this knowledge is in the conversion of beta-elements into alpha-elements, the unmetabolised into the metabolised. Such a process raises the question of why humans have developed thinking at all. Why think?

Thinking and Perversity

Freud posited that a process of "thinking"[42] developed as a form of ideational representation which made it possible to tolerate an increased tension of stimulus "while the process of discharge was postponed". Thinking, or more accurately ideational representations (sensory imprints in primitive organisms), enables a small amount of cathexis to accompany less (actual) expenditure of energy. Thinking, in this sense, was an unconscious mechanism that interfaced between "impressions of objects" and the organisms need to adapt to them. Thinking can therefore be thought of as the mediator between the internal and external worlds. We can then formulate 'thinking' as representing ideational impressions for even primitive organisms that can in some form represent their environment and its demands without constantly expending energy to fight them off or evolve to adapt better to them. The infant, even in its early primitive post-partum state, can form ideas about its world and in some form of thinking *represent* these ideas internally. Thinking derives in this sense from sensory impressions and the tension from the outset between the two competing drives. Between the environment and its demands and the forming mental apparatus with its capacity for consciousness and memory, lies the body – the conduit for all impressions of life. The mind presents itself as the formidably efficient system for serving its needs and triaging bodily survival above all else. However, as we shall explore later, once formed the mind has the ability to develop a 'life of its own' quality, representing the world *as-if* it can independently represent the world without having to reference it. That suggests that the mind can invent the world through psychotic phantasy or represent it ideationally in ways that are not bound by the reality principle. Emotional valence triggered by such associative capacity can be disproportionate.

This notion suggests that either of the primary drives we have been discussing can become *perversified*, not in the narrow sexual sense of perversion but in the broader sense that a drive that becomes separated from its original purpose may trend to become perverse. No longer is the mind serving the demands of the body in order to ensure survival, but rather *creating* the world through old representations with an emotional valence that is governed by internal processes rather than external reality. The tension between stasis and adaptation, imbedded in all living matter from the outset, governed by the free-energy principle and the requirement to minimise the expenditure of free energy, becomes exceeded in the mental sphere. In this sense, it has become perverse, separated from the quantity of demands for stasis or adaptation. The immune system in the somatic realm has evolved to protect the body from pathogens that seek to colonise it and in so doing damage it. The conservative drive in the psyche serve this same purpose, to detect, recognise, codify, and react to impingements or mental pathogens that seek to unsettle it. The distinction between the immune system of the soma being in many senses 'objective' and even measurable versus the immune system of the mind being entirely subjective and not measurable, is not to imply a separation of the two. Since, in some respects the emergence of subjectivity is also an 'objective' process in more primitive organisms. The perspective of the 'I' doing the experiencing, no matter how primitive the organism, can be observed in how an organism 'perceives' and responds to threats or changes in its state. In humans, we run into the problem of subjectivity being infinitely more complex and hence apparently not observable, but subjectivity is in any event an 'objective' mechanism driven by the principle of self-organising systems to develop efficient mechanisms to manage survival.

In the complex systems of humans, the mind performs its work by virtue of its relation to the body and when perception dominates over reality, this principle is not negated. Rather, perversion of a sort has formed, the splitting of the internal world from its proportional relation to reality. In this sense, perception can *become* reality, not in the sense of denial of reality (as in psychotic states) but in the ideational representation that triggers an emotional response. It is worth remembering, that Freud did not view the need by an organism to reduce to nothing or at least keep the sum of excitations that flow upon it as low as possible in a purely *quantitative* sense. "It appears", he suggests, "that they depend, not on this quantitative factor, but on some characteristic of it which we can only describe as a qualitative one".[43] This *qualitative* element implies that from the perspective of the organism, an interpretation gets made about a stimulus or impingement that requires some form of evaluation in order to determine a course of action. This subjectivity permeates all living organisms in simpler or more complex ways, suggesting that once the quantum leap is made from the inanimate to the animate, an element of subjectivity must emerge, from which a system in becoming self-organised must have a view point of its relation to the world, *viewed through the lens of available means*. Any organism's available tools will determine how the environment is perceived and managed, depending on what faculty it has for doing so. An infant has senses and a sensory apparatus but is born in an undifferentiated mental state and relies on primitive mechanisms to evaluate and respond to the world. Whilst physically the self-organising system of the body is in full swing, the mental apparatus is emergent, taking shape through the sensory systems of the body, a fluid and evolving system in-making. That is the nature of the neural system and its mental emergence. Neuroplasticity, the ability of the brain to form new connections (and prune old ones) enables memory traces to form according to individualised circumstance and subjective experience of it. Cells themselves carry chemical memory traces, chemical imprints of their past experiences, according to Nurse, but in the exponential complexity of their combining, subjective memory traces form too at higher levels of neurological and psychological complexity.

The movement from psychic disorder and undifferentiated experience into order and meaning is not automatic, even if the libidinal drive exerts a pressure along this path – it requires both internal processing and a context of the mother-infant dyad. Winnicott's notion that there is 'no such thing as a baby' speaks to this concept of the essential requirement that every living infant has to make meaning out of primary meaningless mental states but can only achieve this by using the mind of the (m)other to assist in this metabolic function. In Bion's terms, this turning beta into alpha elements is not automatic from a content point of view – it is only automatic in that the natural propensity of the mind is to make form out of formlessness, to mentally organise the chaos in order to survive it. The exact mechanisms of this need not concern us here but important to note that the drive to make meaning out of meaninglessness, to convert chaos into order follows the energetic trend in nature to both maintain a self-organising system and to be able to adapt when this cannot be sustained. A baby crying induces a response from the environment, catalysing adult action to address sources of disequilibrium that the infant themselves cannot action. In doing so, subjectivity is forming, a perspective of feeling states that are most effective in both maintaining stasis and driving creative adaptation for change when these are not satisfied. Development versus stasis – or progression versus regression becomes written into the future of all humans.

Regression in Psychoanalysis

Why *regression*? In dynamic terms, regression is a revisiting of old reference points contained in memory, the building blocks of the unconscious, and old experience is referenced to make responses to current impingements or challenges, to *feedforward* as Solms puts it. Regression to old familiar states activates what Freud termed the repetition compulsion; we are obliged under the pressure of environmental challenge to revisit old reference points to efficiently respond forward. Feelings become the guide, affects stirred by ideational representations formed during the early stages of mental development, the making of meaning from the primal meaningless state. In this sense, primary narcissism dominates – that is, *everything* must be understood and experienced solely through the lens of the infant's own 'I', or 'ego', as primitive as this might still be in the early stages of life. Perspective that differentiates self from others and other's experience from one's own is a developmental achievement that only emerges with time, in the human psyche even over years, and some would argue over a lifetime. Of course, primary narcissism is benign and does not seek to create conflict with anyone beyond inducing a response to restore equilibrium where the helpless infant cannot for its own account.

If benign, as opposed to malignant forms of narcissism dominate the early stages of life, and the evolving forms of identity that the narcissistic thrust demands, we are left to puzzle how benign and healthy forms of narcissism morph into malignant forms later in life? How does a weedy, oversensitive would-be artist turn into a tyrannical dictator of epic merciless proportions in the form of Hitler the Nazi? The notion that for an infant the emotional magnitude of an unpleasure experience is not nuanced and tends to be ungraded, since without perspective a threat is a threat, unfiltered through the mitigating effects of life experience and cognitive capacity. Is hunger, cramp, or loneliness any different a threat to strangulation or apnoea? In venturing to suggest that from a young infant's point of view there is little to differentiate the one from the other, I risk reaching conclusions through the unobservable. However, we can recognise in clinical work that the more developmentally primitive the origin of an emotional response, the greater the likelihood of increased intensity. The 'as-if' quality of adult regression into the earlier templates of memory and the emotional triggers attached to that memory indicate to us how significant the perception (ideation) is and how intense the emotional triggers activated by them from early primitive experience. Memory in the unconscious is never 'in the past'. It remains in the present, 'as-if' it were now, no matter the passage of time. This Freud recognised in his discovery of the Unconscious and its quality of being timeless. Memory only has an adaptive function if it can operate in the present 'as-if' it *was* the present, rather than a Kodak moment referencing the past. What purpose would that serve? A memory bank of pleasant life experiences? A catalogue of reminisces? Nature giving the mechanism of memory a pride of place in the mental apparatus is for good developmental reason. Without it we could not survive. And the added function it serves is not merely that we remember how to navigate to a familiar toilet in time of need, but that any stimulus that represents a threat to survival and integrity of the psychic Markov blanket requires a mechanism to both identify it and respond to it.

Trauma, Regression, and 'Linking'

A man diving under the table in response to a car backfiring outside makes no sense to an objective observer. It is a disproportionate response. However, if one knows that this man is a veteran of war, we gather that he is suffering Post Traumatic Stress Disorder in psychiatric terms and is diving under the table as a reaction in the present to something traumatic from the past. It is as if this past has no reference to time passing. For an infant, it is perhaps not surprising that the amplitude of experience coming from every sensation and impingement is novel and hence also much greater, requiring linking and containment to enable the effects to be mitigated. Positive experience and the libidinal cathexis for the love object is likely intense, but so too the impact of anything injurious. As we have discussed, meaning has to be forged and achieved – it is not automatic for the primitive mind of the infant. The encoding of experience into memory will carry the residues how this meaning is made and forged. Nonetheless, how do we square a hyper-reaction to an apparently benign stimulus? One of the links in this chain of events is in fact what has been termed 'linking'. Between raw sensory experience and reaction are a few steps mediated internally through memory and the affect that is associated with such memory.

'Linking' is a technical term that Wilfred Bion[44] used to refer to the child and the mother enabling the child to make links between emotional experience and events and how they are mentally processed. This is not automatic. They require the mediation and processing of the mother's mind for the infant to be able to make meaning of experience, particularly aversive experience. And links that the mother attempts to make for the infant can be 'attacked' in the mind of the infant if meaning is failed.[45] If the baby does not find soothing from the maternal intervention, frustration and disequilibrium may prevail and hence trigger an immune response. When this happens, the aggressive function is activated in attempts to restore states of disequilibrium. Says Bion,

> These attacks on the linking function of emotion lead to an over-prominence in the psychotic part of the personality of links which appear to be logical, almost mathematical, but never emotionally reasonable. Consequently, the links surviving are perverse, cruel, and sterile.[46]

In reality, if the infant has experiences of any sort, meaning is made of that experience through the mediation of the mother's mind. The baby can form primitive connections that assist it to make emotional meaning. Without this mediation, *meaninglessness* will tend to predominate – and the threshold may be breached for the infant's capacity to tolerate or metabolise this experience. The infants has two choices – make meaning out of the meaningless through the assistance of the mother and her mind and turn inwards to try make meaning out of the *meaningless* state of dysregulation.

We should not be surprised that even a partial resort to making meaning from a primitive mind will create distortions that might persist in memory, a future-forward lens through which later experience becomes interpreted. If the infant, for example, is experiencing frustrations because of gastric impingement that causes discomfort and pain, and meaning cannot be made of this through remedy and the soothing through the mother, these sensations of discomfort leave the infant feeling as if they are being persecuted from within, or simply persecuted when the inner and outer worlds are still diffuse and undifferentiated. This *meaning* to the infant is that the world in which it is now a habitant is a persecutory place, a bad place, a place which cannot be trusted. If this experience is not remedied and meaning is not made, the young mind will encode this experience as memory, to be referenced in the future. Life is a poison berry that should not be eaten twice! However, it is not necessarily *that* specific poison berry that is encoded as a poison berry that should not be eaten twice. This differentiation involves the mental capacity for encoding we would expect from an older child or adult. Rather since for the young infant, this is the totality of their experience in the moment rather than being only partial, the threat to psychic integrity and survival may be experienced as much greater. It therefore depends on developing the *feedforward* process that we mentioned earlier that Solms identifies, which unfolds in reverse direction, through the forebrain's memory systems, generating an *expected context* for future reactions.

The lessons for the mental apparatus to navigate future survival depends on being able to lay down such memory traces of the sources of aversive impingement but more so, to make *meaning* out of them in order to better navigate these in the future, and, moreover, to future-proof *efficiently.* It bears repeating, that this encoding and memory as reference has no objective signature. The meaning being made by the infant is from their own subjective experience of the experience of whatever aversive ails them. The complexity of this subjectivity is as nuanced as each person's different face. Universal attributes reflect similarity and commonality (we all have ears, mouth, noses, and eyes in roughly the same arrangement) but each human face is distinct and unique. Perhaps some temperaments, the subtleties of the infant's own body and sensitivities positioned in a context of the maternal dyad and her mind and its projections, make for a distinct and endlessly divergent individual subjectivity, within the parameters of normative developmental capabilities and function. This adaptive mechanism of the human psyche is efficient and for the most part highly adaptive to navigating mentally a complex world. But to Darwin's point, the organism must either resist impingement to maintain homeostasis or adapt to it in order to enable survival. In this sense, 'survival of the fittest' is not necessarily about who can run faster from the proverbial sabre-toothed tiger, but how any organism can adapt to new challenges and become 'compliant' to these demands in order to master the stimuli and develop a new accommodation, a new normal, which in turn will require preservation. Sometimes, as Freud noted in a letter to Einstein in 1933 addressing the question Einstein put to him about war,[47] that the "organism preserves its own life, so to say, by destroying an extraneous one". The drive of preservation turns to destructiveness but only, theoretically, *in an effort to better preserve itself.* "The death instinct becomes an impulse to destruction when, with the aid of certain organs, it directs its action outwards, against external objects. The living being, that is to say, defends its own existence by destroying foreign bodies". Like the body, the mind requires a mechanism to defend itself from perceptions of injury and threat, albeit from the subjectivity of the individual mind.

The disproportionate intensity that an infant experiences, driven by the complete nature of the experience, as opposed to something aversive being partial in experience, gives it a disproportionate valence in the *feedforward* process. Compound this quantitative element with the requirement of subjectivity to make meaning out of the *meaningless,* leaves early templates of experience not filtered through that infant's meaning and memory, constantly being referenced in new experiences through the life cycle. If an infant who suffered terrible colic carries memory of the world being a persecutory place, then when older and learning to use the potty may struggle with anxiety that the defecation that makes the internal become external carries threatening elements that are dangerous. Encopresis, keeping the faecal matter internal, or expelling it but demonstrating anxiety about the potty or its contents may flow from this early template.

The reader will no doubt be critical of the simplicity of these examples, and rightly so, because falling foul of my earlier point that individual subjectivity is complex and uniquely individual, such global interpretations are thin. But I include it here merely to demonstrate the layers of psychic development that become influenced by early experiences and which manifest traits, behaviours, symptoms, and characteristics that appear to the adult world mysterious and often out of keeping with other members of the family.

Perversion

Earlier I mentioned the link between ideas that evolve in the infant to form representations of the world and the influence of subjectivity in how these ideas form and are filtered, together with their emotional valence. I suggested that in this 'life-of-its own' quality that enable perversion of both principle drives to emerge. A perversion may be defined as "a distortion or corruption of the original course, meaning, or state of something", as in "the thing which most disturbed him was the perversion of language and truth". The implication of this definition, which we can consider acceptable theoretically, suggests that an impulse or flow of impulses is diverted from an original aim into or onto some other object or part object. Freud wrote extensively of this process in sexuality and how an impulse on track for an object meeting with an internal resistance due to anxiety will divert its aims onto a part object, obscuring the original impulse and instead finding safer cathexis in a more harmless object or part object.

Desire is a powerful driver in the human psyche, and its origins in childhood development introduces complicated developmental challenges in the navigation of these trends. The *psycho-sexual* aim of early childhood is forced to traverse some rocky terrain in its aim of cathexis with the loved object. Desire for the love object and the wish to possess it, the parents usually, is met with various powerful instinctual and environmental taboos. Incest being a primary internal taboo long embedded through generations over millennia remains the single most powerful prohibition in the human psyche. Two powerful but contradictory pressures then drive the child's development – and these contradictory pressures strive for both libidinal cathexis with and possession of the object whilst such an achievement would simultaneously violate the prohibition of incest.

External pressures also make their appearance in the form of rivalries, or at least perceived or imagined ones, from the opposite sex parent and other rivals in the child's environment. These threats have strong impacts on generating anxieties and ambivalences that are resolved through partial or total repression of the aim of the impulse. Sometimes, however, repression arrives too late and the child is forced to rely on finding another route for the aim that renders the impulse harmless. It is worth repeating that in the nature of energetic conservation, in which energy cannot be lost or destroyed but only transformed, in the psychic realm too an impulse cannot be simply switched off or stopped in its tracks – defensive manoeuvres are required, and at times these divert the impulse way from the original object towards a more harmless object or part object. This can be a part of the desired object, or a representation of them through an item of clothing, or a part of their body such as their foot, rather than their genitalia or body as whole. Such psychic manoeuvres enable the impulse to find some form of expression without violating either an internal taboo or an external threat. A foot or shoe fetish, for example, represents a safer attachment of an impulse to a part object that no longer invokes threat. If this tendency is powerful enough and embeds itself, this fetish becomes entrenched in the adult sexual life too. The fetish becomes a requirement for arousal or completion of the sexual act. This *disavowal* of the original aim of the impulse enables psychic functions with reduced anxiety against potential threats. Disavowal suggests to the conscious mind that there is no impulse towards the object and that if there was one it is safely and innocently discharged. However, as this dynamic entrenches itself, we are left with a psychic loop in which libidinal drives are contained in a circuit that forms part of a cluster we term the perversions. Technically, a perversion is really the separation of an impulse or drive from its original aim and its deviation from its original course through a *repetitive* tendency even in the face of discomfort or regret. Disavowal drives perversion away from its original course and renders it, consciously at least, relatively harmless.

Sex and Its Combinations

Much of the discussion around perversion centres on the sexual drive and its deviations from its aim. Commonly, we associated perversion with sexual deviance, or at least deviations from heteronormativity and the ultimate evolutionary aim of copulative reproduction. This is not an ideological statement – rather, reproduction depends on heteronormativity to ensure the best possible reproductive outcomes for life. At a species level, Lane points out that sex, that is the ability of complex organisms to combine their DNA, enables deviant cells to be sidelined in the course of evolution, a mechanism to ensure viability. Cellular and DNA cloning seems like an easier option for reproduction but according to the biochemists would lead to extinction as genetic flaws reproduce.

Albeit over millions of years, the strategy of self-reproduction is apparently not the best for ensuring reproductive survivability over time. In this sense, sex and a sexual drive is embedded in an evolutionary advantage from the outset of even the most primitive organisms and underlies Freud's emphasis on the sexual drive as one of the key drivers of human development. Through sex, that is essentially the biological strategy of combining DNA to ensure better advantage in survival, we see the strategy of adaptability emergent from life's primitive outset. In other words, in the face of environmental changes, primitive life faced the simple choice of adapt or die. Over many eons of time, adaptability embraced the strategy of combining DNA to better push survivability – and sex was born, so to speak. This created the one of two key mechanisms of all living matter, including the human psyche in all its complexity. First conserve and maintain homeostasis – and if that fails seek mechanisms to adapt and create new normals for conservation. Without this normative pressure, life would die out fairly quickly. The nearly eight billion people on earth suggest that this evolutionary strategy has worked well.

But of course, human sexuality is not bound by these species-level aims, nor is the individual sexual drive geared solely in the direction of reproduction. All manner of pleasurable benefit accrues to sexual expression outside of these aims and for the most part sexuality is engaged not in some preparatory process but because the pleasure of tension release is in itself highly rewarding. The intensity and power of the sexual drive perhaps derives from the role it may have played in ensuring organismic adaptation and the impetus for survival in an intensely dangerous environment but this has not remained its sole purpose. Separated from reproduction, the sensual nature of the entire body from infancy accrues all manner of both physical and mental pleasurable experience, the bonding derived from it sustaining adaptation and survival. Like a thirsty plant, human beings require touch to sustain them mentally. This same power and intensity of this drive that sustains is also met with powerful resistances that can cause the aim of the drive to deviate from the object of desire to a more benign part of the object or other item that unconsciously represents the object. Cathexis of this energy onto that part object can become fixed and persistent. This disavowal of the original path enables a compromise to be reached that does not (and cannot) inhibit the sexual drive but at the same time finds a path and aim for it that is more benign and perceived as safe. Safe in this context means it avoids violating the incest taboo or other internal prohibition. Such is the nature of a perversion, the essential separation of the sexual drive from its original (more threatening) object to a compromised benign one. Separated from its original path enables psychic balance to be restored at the time the fixation was set up. However, its persistence through the adult cycle of life can create distortions that no longer serve psychological balance.

Perversion of Aggression

As the sexual drive can become perverse, so too can the aggressive drive suffer perversion. This can occur when there is a separation of its original aim of restoring stasis, as the guardian of the mind, to a fixated response under pressure and provocation. It emerges in current conditions from the perspective of its original fixation. The original fixation is governed by the conditions of the age and time and available defences and resources for managing it. As mentioned, the valence of emotional experience for a helpless infant is disproportionately intense because from its subjective point of view, its entire world is contained in that experience, and the limitations on remedial action require a mental response that registers the existential threat that the infant might *feel* in response to states of disequilibrium. The aggressive response aims to divest from a threatening attachment or attack it (think of Bion's point about the infant's attacks on *linking*) to restore equilibrium and comply with the dictates of the conservatism mechanism – one that maintains a window of mental comfort in the similar way that temperature regulation maintains a zone of somatic comfort.

As mentioned before, psychic comfort has no objective parameters by which to measure it, with self-report itself being the only way to know for certain what someone feels and the intensity with which they feel it. However, even this has limitation since we know from depth psychology that the subjectivity of experienced mind is not invariably *of* one mind. Unconscious determinants and conscious ones can surprisingly *not* coincide – two parts of the mental apparatus pursuing different and sometimes opposite agendas. The conflicts of mind are well known, with instinctual promptings and feelings meeting with internal resistances and prohibitions, and these mental conflicts are the source of neurotic symptoms and difficulties in life. The mind is never, we have come to understand, free of internal conflicts, not only between those that are conscious and those that are unconscious but also between different parts of the unconscious itself. Love and hate can meet with powerful tensions from the outset of life when unconscious systems are entirely dominant in the young infant and consciousness can barely be thought to exist yet. Even under such conditions, the infant emerges with conflicts and tensions between satiation and frustration.

Freud grappled with the question of aggression, or the 'destructive' impulses as he often referred to them, and at times it appears in his writing that he never quite recognised the implications of his deep insights regarding this drive that he captured in his significant book Beyond the Pleasure Principle. Writing in 1915 and again to Einstein in 1933, Freud wrote in his papers Thoughts for the Times on War and Death and in his letter to Einstein on War (1933), how civilisation was no obstacle to barbaric cruelty and in fact may lend itself to a capacity to scale destruction through culture and intellect.[48] Interestingly, Putin's speech I quoted earlier and subsequent actions in the invasion of Ukraine reflect the universal tendency of peoples under the leadership of those in power. Groups can also become governed by their own perverse projections of victimhood, standing up to a perceived perpetrator and the threats they appear to perpetrate. Freud, back then, elaborated that we should not be surprised at the fluid exchange between individuals in leadership and the collective, for when

> the community no longer raises objections, there is an end, too, to the suppression of evil passions, and men perpetrate deeds of cruelty, fraud, treachery and barbarity so incompatible with their level of civilisation that one would have thought them impossible.[49]

It is worth noting that although Freud himself escaped the Nazi holocaust by leaving Vienna for England just before the war broke out, four of his sisters who remained behind were murdered by the Nazis.[50]

This contradiction of the most highly developed of peoples and nations becoming capable of the most heinous of barbaric cruelty must originate like everything in the laws of nature and its dictates. Freud expressed this aspect of nature in his writing to Einstein[51]: "In reality, there is no such thing as 'eradicating' evil", he wrote. The deepest essence of human nature consists of instinctual impulses and drives which are of an elementary nature, similar in all people and which aim at the satisfaction of certain primal needs. "These impulses in themselves are neither good nor bad", Freud said. "We classify them and their expressions in that way, according to their relation to the needs and demands of the human community". Geopolitical perspective becomes everything. As Bob Dylan wrote, "Steal a little and they throw you in jail. Steal a lot and they make you king". It is often context that judges the expression of these primitive impulses, but nonetheless these basic impulses underpin much of what we see on the bigger stages of life.

It is true that these impulses undergo a lengthy process of development through childhood[52] and are inhibited, directed towards other aims and fields, become commingled, alter their objects, and so on. These instincts are subject to reaction-formations, the turning into the opposite as a disguising of their true origin and aim. War and its violence have a way of laying bare these instinctual impulses, splitting the world into not only the good and the bad, but the Self and the Other, those who identify and hence support versus those who are in opposition and hence are a threat to be turned enemy. Freud asks rhetorically,

> Should we not confess that in our civilised attitude towards death we are once again living psychologically beyond our means, and should we not rather turn back and recognise the truth? Would it not be better to give death the place in reality and in our thoughts which is its due, and to give a little more prominence to the unconscious attitude towards death which we have hitherto so carefully suppressed?[53]

The essential point here, Freud reminds us, is that when groups coalesce around, particularly identities and agendas, no matter how civilised and ideologically justified, they never escape the essential roots of their nature. Individual's drives and instincts find their way into greater complexities and group dynamics. The geopolitical is never free of nature. This reality is difficult to acknowledge, admits Freud, but consoles Einstein with the notion that, "To tolerate life remains, after all, the first duty of all living beings. Illusion becomes valueless if it makes this harder for us".[54] We are instinctual creatures never far from our true natures, and driven by these energies and forces despite our capacity to think. Thinking and all its manifestations remain under the guidance of innate and primitive drives but often form themselves through reaction-formations into their opposites. Violence in the service or peace in the geopolitical realm is often rooted in the notion of 'killing with kindness' in the personal realm.

Such reaction-formations abound in the psychic realm, originating in the individual psyche but ironically under the pressure of the life drive to create identities through group adhesion; a powerful antidote to the alpha-male dominance in nature is the collectivisation of the weaker into groups. Such group identity carries the emergent properties of the individual psyche, subject also to the reaction-formations and projective capabilities of the individual. In this human capacity, we begin to see the origins of scaling aggression through numbers and later in history through technology. Weapons enable scalability of the destructive impulse which originating as a conservative instinct to protect the individual finds itself *no longer the master of preservation but the slave of collective projection.* Such becomes the driver towards war when historical circumstances accumulate and converge that enable personal projections to cross the group divide and its tendency to 'other'. The projective mechanism of the personal wends its way through the collective and in turn group cohesion, the propensity to self-organising as a system, facilitates adaptation and survival. But invariably, if behind every perpetrator is the perception of being a victim, so too in group aggression perceptions of victimhood invariably appear to underlie the perpetration of scalable destructiveness. Hitler's speeches, or more recently in history that of Putin, demonstrate the often probably genuine perception of this victimhood behind the often touted *necessity* to aggress against the perceived source of threat – Jews, Ukrainians, blacks, gays, women, and the other sports team, the target is removed from the original and usually unconscious source of the injury – it is now subject to perversion.

Group Identity and War

Some may object to this characterisation that a psychic mechanism internal to the individual by its very nature can somehow mutate into the group narrative. How can a group use a collective defence mechanism originating intra-psychically? Such an apparently tenuous leap is made possible by the general driver of the life drive and its tendency to coagulate in broader and broader collectives (in the interests of sustaining strength against threat) that enables individual mechanisms to penetrate the collective psyche and through emergent layers operate as if it were the same. In-group and out-group dynamics are as an extension of the self-organising systems that Friston's Law addresses, in the interests of sustainable survival. If systems remain disorganised at any concrete, physical or psychic level, entropy becomes more likely. The group character becomes governed by the same tendencies of the leadership in the group and imbibes its issues. Said Freud of the First World War,

> Two things in this war have aroused our sense of disillusionment: the low morality shown externally by states which in their internal relations pose as the guardians of moral standards, and the brutality shown by individuals whom, as participants in the highest human civilisation, one would not have thought capable of such behaviour.[55]

Obviously, collectives gather because of a resonance of similarity of issue, and if 'pinning ones colours to the mast' facilitates group identity and an in-group adhesion, so too is sustaining of that individual within the collective improved. *Unitas veritas*, the motto of many military and sports teams – 'In unity there is strength' – remains the motto of almost every group defining itself against threat, the collective of the vulnerable against the existential threat of a perceived sinister external. Under such threat, even the most advanced and culturally developed of groups and nations, often highly refined, will regress to the utmost barbarity in the pursuit of survival not of the fittest, to paraphrase Darwin, but of the most threatened. The strongest who knows he is strong does not need to aggress unless there is a threat to that dominance, and hierarchical aggression is activated. And often the strongest, the most endowed with resources, perceive themselves to be increasingly under threat. Dictatorship invariably brings vulnerability and history demonstrates that invariably those dictators that yield the greatest power find themselves increasingly isolated and resorting to greater use of control, restriction, and violence to keep such threats at bay. Julius Caesar's famous line in the Shakespearian play, "*Et tu*, Brute?" represents the great vulnerability that accrues to those who wield power and the realistic threat that tyrants face in their attempts to retain their grip on power and resource. From the outside, the tyranny of the aggressor is felt and obvious to all who fall prey to it. But from the inside, tyrants feel vulnerable for both individual psychic reasons and because the pressures of reality impose themselves in the human state. People will invariably resent the power of the few, unless justice and equity are perceived to be present. This paradox of dominance and tyranny represent for us how so often in human history the greater the use of power to sustain the powerful, the greater develops their vulnerability over time. Throughout history, the tyrants become the victims, once time has run its course. Equally, tyrants resort to greater use of aggression and violence as their perceptions of vulnerability increases.

I had another personal experience of these contradictions of making sense of who perceives themselves to be the perpetrator and who the victim. Even under the height of Apartheid in South Africa, President PW Botha, known as 'Die Groot Krokodil' (the Great Crocodile), lamented over his fear of becoming the victim of forces arraigned against his country and its people. In his infamous Rubicon Speech of 1985, he declared

"But let me point out at once that since South Africa freed itself from colonialism, democracy has already been broadened and millions of people who never had a say in Governmental affairs under the British Colonial system, have it today… I am not prepared to lead White South Africans and other minority groups on a road to abdication and suicide. Destroy White South Africa and our influence, and this country will drift into faction strife, chaos and poverty", he stated.

Note the narrative drifting from Botha and Apartheid as perpetrator to the threat of being and becoming the victim.

Since then we have had to contend with escalating violence within South Africa, and pressure from abroad in the form of measures designed to coerce the Government into giving in to various demands. Our enemies-both within and without-seek to divide our peoples. They seek to create unbridgeable differences between us to prevent us from negotiating peaceful solutions to our problems. Peaceful negotiation is their enemy. Peaceful negotiation is their enemy, because it will lead to joint responsibility for the progress and prosperity of South Africa. Those whose methods are violent, do not want to participate. They wish to seize and monopolise all power. Let there be no doubt about what they would do with such power. One has only to look at their methods and means. Violent and brutal means can only lead to totalitarian and tyrannical ends.

The inversion of perpetrator and victim is apparent in this data, and of course the subjectivity intrinsic to which pole one inhabits.

Notes

1 Freud, S. (1914). *On Narcissism,* p. 85.
2 Freud, S. (1914). *On Narcissism,* p. 65.
3 Lane, N. (2016). *The Vital Question: Why Is Life the Way It Is?,* p. 286.
4 Solms, M. (2017). What Is "The Unconscious", and Where Is It Located in the Brain? A Neuropsychoanalytic Perspective, pp. 90–97 (p. 92).
5 Freud, S. (1914). *On Narcissism,* p. 66.
6 Solan, R. (1999). The Interaction between Self and Others: A Different Perspective on Narcissism, pp. 193–215 (p. 197).
7 Freud (1933, p. 374).
8 Mills, J. (2006). Reflections on the Death Drive, pp. 373–382 (p. 374).
9 Freud, S. (1914). *On Narcissism,* p. 79.
10 Margaret, M.S. & Gosliner, B.J. (1955). On Symbiotic Child Psychosis: Genetic, Dynamic, and Restitutive Aspects, pp. 195–212 (p. 197).
11 Winnicott, D.W. (1949). Hate in the Counter-Transference, pp. 69–74.
12 Perkel, A. (2006). The Phallic Container in the Couple: Splitting and Diversion of Maternal Hate as Protection of the Infant, pp. 13–38; Perkel, A. (2008). The Phallic Container in the Post-partum Couple: Splitting and Diversion of Maternal Hate as Protection of the Infant.
13 Freud, S. (1914). *On Narcissism,* p. 88.
14 Solms, M. (2017). What Is "The Unconscious", and Where Is It Located in the Brain? A Neuropsychoanalytic Perspective, pp. 90–97 (p. 93).
15 Freud, S. (1914). *On Narcissism,* p. 96.
16 Freud, S. (1915). Instincts & Their Vicissitudes, p. 115.
17 Solms, M. (2022). *The Hidden Spring: A Journey to the Source of Consciousness,* p. 141.
18 Solms, M. (2022). *The Hidden Spring: A Journey to the Source of Consciousness,* p. 143.
19 Freud, S. (1914). *On Narcissism,* p. 93.
20 Solms, M. (2022). *The Hidden Spring: A Journey to the Source of Consciousness,* p. 141.
21 Solms, M. (2022). *The Hidden Spring: A Journey to the Source of Consciousness,* p. 181.
22 Freud, S. (1915). Instincts & Their Vicissitudes, p. 136.
23 Winnicott, D.W. (1975). *Through Paediatrics to Psychoanalysis, Collected Papers.*
24 In Winnicott's own reflections he thought through the implications of his utterance: "What then precedes the first *object* relationship? For my own part I have had a long struggle with this problem. It started when I found myself saying in this Society (about ten years ago) and I said it rather excitedly and with heat: 'There is no such thing as a baby'. I was alarmed to hear myself utter these words and tried to justify myself by pointing out that if you show me a baby you certainly show me also someone caring for the baby, or at least a pram with someone's eyes and ears glued to it. One sees a 'nursing couple'…" Considering this he reflected later, "In a quieter way today I would say that before object relationships the state of affairs is this: that the unit is not the individual, the unit is an environment-individual set-up. The centre of gravity of the being does not start off in the individual. It is in the total set-up" (p. 99).
25 Margaret, M.S. & Gosliner, B.J. (1955). On Symbiotic Child Psychosis: Genetic, Dynamic, and Restitutive Aspects, pp. 195–212 (p. 196).

26 Winnicott, D.W. (1975). *Through Paediatrics to Psychoanalysis, Collected Papers*, p. 99.
27 Freud, S. (1915). Instincts & Their Vicissitudes, p. 136.
28 Kandel, E. (2006). *In Search of Memory: The Emergence of a New Science of Mind*.
29 See Solms, M. (2017). What Is "The Unconscious", and Where Is It Located in the Brain? A Neuropsychoanalytic Perspective, pp. 90–97.
30 Freud, S. (1915). Instincts & Their Vicissitudes, p. 122.
31 Solms (2017, p. 92).
32 Darwin (p. 124).
33 Freud, S. (1911). Formulations on the Two Principles of Mental Functioning, p. 39.
34 Solms, M. (2022). *The Hidden Spring: A Journey to the Source of Consciousness*, p. 177.
35 Lane, N. (2016). *The Vital Question: Why Is Life the Way It Is?*, p. 196.
36 Nurse, P. (2020). *What Is Life? David Fickling Books*, p. 119.
37 Bion, W.R. (1962). *Learning from Experience*, p. 9.
38 "Alpha-function operates on the sense impressions, whatever they are, and the emotions, whatever they are, of which the patient is aware. In so far as alpha-function is successful *alpha elements* are produced and these elements are suited to storage and the requirements of dream thoughts. If alpha-function is disturbed, and therefore inoperative, the sense impressions of which the patient is aware and the emotions which he is experiencing remain unchanged. I shall call them beta-elements. In contrast with the alpha-elements the beta-elements are not felt to be phenomena, but things in themselves" (p. 6).
39 Fonagy, P., Gergely, G., Jurist, E. & Target, M. (2002). *Affect Regulation, Metallisation, and the Development of the Self*.
40 Bion noted, "To learn from experience alpha-function must operate on the awareness of the *emotional experience*; alpha-elements are produced from the impressions of the experience; these are thus made storable and available for dream thoughts and for unconscious waking thinking. A child having the *emotional experience* called learning to walk is able by virtue of alpha-function to store this experience. Thoughts that had originally to be conscious become unconscious and so the child can do all the thinking needed for walking without any longer being conscious of any of it. Alpha-function is needed for conscious thinking and reasoning and for the relegation of thinking to the unconscious when it is necessary to disencumber consciousness of the burden of thought by learning a skill. If there are only beta-elements, which cannot be made unconscious, there can be no repression, suppression, or learning. This creates the impression that the patient is incapable of discrimination. He cannot be unaware of any single sensory stimulus: yet such hypersensitivity is not contact with reality" (p. 8).
41 Lane, N. (2016). *The Vital Question: Why Is Life the Way It Is?*, p. 141.
42 Freud, S. (1911). Formulations on the Two Principles of Mental Functioning, p. 38.
43 Freud, S. (1924). The Economic Problem of Masochism, p. 414.
44 Bion, W. (1963). *Elements of Psychoanalysis*, pp. 1–4.
45 Bion, W.R. (1959). Attacks on Linking, pp. 308–315.
46 Bion, W.R. (1959). Attacks on Linking, pp. 308–315 (p. 315).
47 Freud, S. (1933). Why War?, p. 211.
48 Moreover, it has brought to light an almost incredible phenomenon: the civilised nations know and understand one another so little that one can turn against the other with hate and loathing. Indeed, one of the great civilised nations is so universally unpopular that the attempt can actually be made to exclude it from the civilised community as 'barbaric', although it has long proved its fitness by the magnificent contributions to that community which it has made. Writing in 1915 and again to Einstein in 1933, Freud wrote in his papers Thoughts for the Times on War and Death (1915) and in his letter to Einstein Why War? (1933).

49 "Nor should it be a matter for surprise that this relaxation of all the moral ties between the collective individuals of mankind should have had repercussions on the morality of individuals; for our conscience is not the inflexible judge that ethical teachers declare it, but in its origin is 'social anxiety' and nothing else. When the community no longer raises objections, there is an end, too, to the suppression of evil passions, and men perpetrate deeds of cruelty, fraud, treachery and barbarity so incompatible with their level of civilisation that one would have thought them impossible" (Freud, S. (1933). Why War?, p. 280).

50 Cohen, D. (2009). *The Escape of Sigmund Freud.*

51 Freud wrote to Einstein: "In reality, there is no such thing as 'eradicating' evil. Psychological—or, more strictly speaking, psycho-analytic—investigation shows instead that the deepest essence of human nature consists of instinctual impulses which are of an elementary nature, which are similar in all men and which aim at the satisfaction of certain primal needs. These impulses in themselves are neither good nor bad. We classify them and their expressions in that way, according to their relation to the needs and demands of the human community. It must be granted that all the impulses which society condemns as evil—let us take as representative the selfish and the cruel ones— are of this primitive kind" (p. 330).

52 Freud adds: "These primitive impulses undergo a lengthy process of development before they are allowed to become active in the adult. They are inhibited, directed towards other aims and fields, become commingled, alter their objects, and are to some extent turned back upon their possessor. Reaction-formations against certain instincts take the deceptive form of a change in their content, as though egoism had changed into altruism, or cruelty into pity. These reaction-formations are facilitated by the circumstance that some instinctual impulses make their appearance almost from the first in pairs of opposites—a very remarkable phenomenon, and one strange to the lay public, which is termed 'ambivalence of feeling'. The most easily observed and comprehensible instance of this is the fact that intense love and intense hatred are so often to be found together in the same person. Psycho-analysis adds that the two opposed feelings not infrequently have the same person for their object". "It strips us of the later accretions of civilisation, and lays bare the primal man in each of us. It compels us once more to be heroes who cannot believe in their own death; it stamps strangers as enemies, whose death is to be brought about or desired; it tells us to disregard the death of those we love. But war cannot be abolished; so long as the conditions of existence among nations are so different and their mutual repulsion so violent, there are bound to be wars. The question then arises: Is it not we who should give in, who should adapt ourselves to war? Should we not confess that in our civilised attitude towards death we are once again living psychologically beyond our means, and should we not rather turn back and recognise the truth? Would it not be better to give death the place in reality and in our thoughts which is its due, and to give a little more prominence to the unconscious attitude towards death which we have hitherto so carefully suppressed? This hardly seems an advance to higher achievement, but rather in some respects a backward step—a regression; but it has the advantage of taking the truth more into account, and of making life more tolerable for us once again. To tolerate life remains, after all, the first duty of all living beings. Illusion becomes valueless if it makes this harder for us" (p. 299).

53 Freud, S. (1933). Why War?, p. 299.

54 Freud, S. (1933). Why War?, p. 299.

55 Freud, S. (1915). Thoughts for the Times on War and Death, pp. 61–89.

Chapter 6

Geopolitics Meets Freud

The Personal and the Political

I listened to PW Botha's words from the discomfort of a cold prison cell in the biting winter of a Johannesburg Highveld Prison, a speaker on the wall broadcasting his speech to prisoners. It was a time of great civil unrest and equally great repression, the heightening of the standoff between the Apartheid State and the disenfranchised majority. The latter was being brought together under the leadership of the United Democratic Front (UDF), the internal and on the face of it legal front for the still banned African National Congress (ANC). Nelson Mandela was still in prison, indefinite detention, interrogation, and torture were widespread, and riots, teargas, and violence had become normative. In every corner of the land, there were protests, mass meetings, and violent confrontations between police, soldiers, and civilians. The ANC had organised every layer of society through civil groups, women's groups, student groups, unions, and anti-conscription groups, amongst many others. There was no corner of society left aside in the quest to take on the almighty rule of the National Party government.

It was 1985 and I was in solitary confinement and nursing some wounds from being thrashed with a riot policeman's quirt, flesh missing from my right arm where the end of the rubber gouged out a small piece of me. Without glass to cover the bars, the cold Johannesburg air sliced through and gripped me like a wild predator. Here I was sitting in that cold, hungry loneliness, feeling somewhat vulnerable in the hands of an all-powerful state security apparatus, being held for an indefinite period without recourse to lawyers, the courts, or any means to determine my own future. In the hands of this all-powerful State apparatus, many had died and I was struck by the strange irony and paradox of the situation.

Since only a few years previously, Dr. Neil Aggett (a medical doctor and activist who was white) had been tortured and murdered in detention, even as a young white student my skin colour was no longer a protection – it was now clear that anything could happen. I had also managed to have some fleeting and forbidden whispered conservations earlier with some of his colleagues now also in detention, who had themselves been brutally tortured. One of them said he had been mentally prepared for electric shocks *or* suffocation by a canvass bag. But he had not been

DOI: 10.4324/9781003452522-7

prepared for both techniques to be used simultaneously.[1] The ironic part of the scene that I was sitting in was that PW Botha, with his powerful army and state security apparatus, was essentially describing being threatened by a skinny student who was utterly powerless in their hands, yet in Botha's mind I was the one using violent and brutal means leading to tyrannical ends. I understood the bigger narrative, of course, that this was not about me versus the State – but nonetheless I was struck then how the question of perception of who is the perpetrator and who is the victim was apparent. In the circumstances I found myself I certainly *felt* the victim. But here was the President telling me, essentially, that he was. Taking pictures at a peaceful student protest had turned ugly as the riot police teargassed and charged the students, beating and arresting whoever they could. The violence and terror was felt by the unarmed students. And yet, the police and who they represented saw them as the existential threat.

We might be forgiven for wondering who are the victims and who are the perpetrators, a question that seems to emerge constantly in geopolitical narratives and inter-group conflicts, equally as it does in individual conflicts between strangers and between spouses bonded by love. Roughly a year after my first detention, I was again arrested in 1986 and held under the notorious detention without trial laws, in this case under the State of Emergency allowing for indefinite detentions without trial. This event was not because of any protest. The Security Police invaded my apartment at 3 am, and conducted a search. A few hours later, after working their way through every piece of paper, book, and crumpled tissue in the dustbin of the small flat, they took me into their custody. They suspected I was involved with the ANC, the underground organisation spearheading the anti-Apartheid struggle and who were still banned at that time. It was a serious offence to belong or 'further the aims'. A mine worker at the time had engraved the words "Viva Mandela" onto his tin mug at work and ended up with a four-year jail term for furthering the aims of the banned ANC. A friend of mine spent seven months in solitary confinement, eventually being charged and subsequently convicted for 'furthering the aims of a banned organisation'. She had been putting up posters.

A few days into my detention, I was fetched from my solitary confinement cell and driven by my two Security Police interrogators to their offices. I found myself sitting handcuffed against a wall of an unremarkable office being interrogated by two Security Policemen, threatening me with all manner of personal injury, periodically lunging and screaming at me when dissatisfied with an answer to their questions, as I braced against the wall, the handcuffs biting into my wrists. Once again, this time in a far more personal way, I was struck by the question of who felt themselves to be the perpetrator and who the victim. Of course, neither cop feared me personally. I was entirely powerless, isolated, cold, hungry, anxious, and utterly in their hands. They were legally protected, armed, and untouchable with every conceivable power in their hands to do whatever they wished, including torture if needed. And yet, as the interrogations unfolded, it became apparent that these two men, both I gathered being family men, married with children whom they loved, genuinely believed themselves and their families to be under threat – from the 'swart gevaar' (black danger) and their alliance with the 'rooi gevaar' (the 'red danger' of the communists and their Soviet Allies at the time). The forces arraigned against the South African State appeared to them to be formidable, and under every bush, as the joke went, some or other threat lay in wait to take over the country through violence and create the conditions for the pending bloodbath.

They could detain people for endless periods of solitary confinement, interrogate them (in some cases torture and murder), because they perceived themselves to be victims of an existential threat arraigned against them. I, of course, and many like me at the time, felt ourselves to be the victim, helpless, vulnerable, and utterly powerless. How could these two men, in the intimacy of an interrogation room (interrogation and torture can be very intimate and up close), perceive me to be the threat and them the victims? But so they did.

Back to PW Botha's speech of the year before, this inversion of the narrative, from my perspective sitting in a cold lonely cell, was intriguing, a narrative of victimhood and existential threat. Botha stated in his speech

> But let me remind the public of the reasons why Mr Mandela is in jail. I think it is absolutely necessary that we deal with that first of all. When he was brought before court in the sixties, the then Attorney-General, Dr Yutar, set out the State's case inter alia as follows: "As the indictment alleges, the accused deliberately and maliciously plotted and engineered the commission of acts of violence and destruction throughout the country ... The planned purpose thereof was to bring about in the Republic of South Africa chaos, disorder and turmoil ..." They (Mr Mandela and his friends) planned violent insurrection and rebellion... A document was produced during the Court case in Mandela's own handwriting in which he stated: "We Communist Party members are the most advanced revolutionaries in modern history ... The enemy must be completely crushed and wiped out from the face of the earth before a Communist world can be realised."

This extract at the height of the South African civil war in 1985 again finds itself in the good company of the speeches from other tyrannies of history – the perception of vulnerability in the face of increasing threats that seek to dysregulate the cohesion of the order and disrupt the system towards entropy. Such is the nature of revolution that the ability of the system to adapt in an evolutionary manner is overtaken by the pressures of disruption to the given order and represent to it an existential threat. First conservation, then adaptation. The destructive drive brought into service of the individual and its representation through the collective. This quantum jump in emergent properties from the somatic-biological to the psychological does not stop with the individual, since under the pressures of Eros, the aggregation of individuals into collectives, in-group, generates stretch, survivability against impingements from both the natural environment and other self-organising group or collectives. In the most primitive form, the unconscious narrative is often defined as "who is not with us is against us", and only under the pressures of civilised discourse and attempts by the collective to scale back the threat of annihilation in direct proportion to the modern scalability of aggression, may help us understand why human violence has decreased over time, if Stephen Pinker is to be believed.[2] Perhaps, a driver of a moral compass in modern societies is that the threat of annihilation is reduced by non-aggression as a modality rather than increased, whereas in earlier epochs of history a lack of aggression would render a group vulnerable and under a greater threat of annihilation as a group. Strength through aggression has been replaced to some extent by strength through non-aggression. But evidence also suggests to us that human instincts do not easily succumb to our attempts to subdue them. Threats to systems always remain and groups, like individuals, are subject to constant impingements that disrupt equilibrium and cohesion and threaten entropy of the self-organising system.

Victimhood and Its Narratives

The separation of a drive from its original source into a self-perpetuating repetition, like the perversion of sexuality, emerges in the perversion of the aggressive drive also – violence and destruction that is for its own sake, bearing little connection to the underlying logic or rationalisations that are used to justify it, and invariably presented to the self and the world as victimhood in defence. The striking finding on analysing so many of the sentiments of consensus-held tyrants, dictators, murderers, and bullies is that the narrative of victimhood permeates virtually without fail. Unlike the comic books where the villains take pride in being the villains, in real life the villains see themselves as the victims in their narratives, and ironically, they often appear quite so in their personal (his)stories. Equally interesting, is that so often in both personal and geopolitical narratives those who once were victim are often to be counted amongst those who perpetrate when the balance of power tilts in their favour.

We seem to note that the guardian of homeostasis and preserver of the self becomes torn from its original roots to develop a life of its own quality, in which the unconscious drivers are so deeply disavowed that there is scarcely any obvious link between them. The Hitler commanding supreme and absolute power in his pursuit of expansionist domination through all and any means is a far cry from the weedy inept emasculated artist wannabe of his early life, and even more so removed from the helpless ineffectual boy with his terrible beatings and weak mother unable to challenge the patriarchal authority of his father's violence, far from his expressed dictates to German youth rallies, how "In our eyes, the German boy of the future should be slim and slender, quick like a greyhound, tough like leather, and hard like Krupp steel". An image further from Hitler's own person and biography would be hard to create – but does capture his own emotional system of defences and how he sought internally to eradicate any vestige of vulnerability and fragility.

Victim to Perpetrator

I put Vladimir Putin into this narrative not because he parallels Hitler's extreme right wing ideologies but because whether on the politically left or right internal worlds find themselves projected onto and into ideological and political narratives. Where opportunity and history coincide, these projections take on real-world effects, and sometimes on a global scale. Putin's history is reportedly fraught with challenge and injury, and with speculative interpretation, it is possible that his short height created a vulnerability, leading to the oft-created cult of personality that men in power who carry internal vulnerability seem to do. This image of a tough, outdoorsy, and sporty alpha-male (like with the Italian dictator Mussolini during the Second World War) was accompanied at times with his demonstrating his physical prowess and taking part in unusual or dangerous acts, such as extreme sports and interaction with wild animals. Some speculate that this was part of a public relations approach that, according to Wired Magazine, "deliberately cultivates the macho, take-charge superhero image". In 2007, a Russian tabloid published a huge photograph of a shirtless Putin vacationing in the Siberian mountains under the headline "Be Like Putin". Is the cult of personality a simple political strategy or a more significant reflection of compensations for perceived inadequacies? Some commentators apparently have accused Putin of seeking to create a cult of personality around himself, an accusation that the Kremlin has denied, though it has been thought that some of Putin's activities have been staged, and he is reputed to be self-conscious about his height, which has been estimated at between five feet one inch and five feet five inches tall.[3]

Putin was born in 1952 in Leningrad, Soviet Union (now Saint Petersburg, Russia), the youngest of three children. Leningrad and the German siege of Leningrad during the Second World War carries, of course, great significance as a symbol of the genocidal intent of the Germans and in turn the Soviet experience in a war that cost over 20 million military and civilian Soviet lives. Putin's birth was apparently preceded by the deaths of two brothers, one of whom born in the 1930s, died in infancy, and a second, born in 1940, who died of diphtheria and starvation in 1942 during the Siege of Leningrad by Nazi forces. Putin's mother was a factory worker and his father was a Soviet Navy conscript, who was reportedly severely wounded in 1942 having transferred to the regular army. During the War, Putin's maternal grandmother was killed in 1941 and his maternal uncles also apparently disappeared on the Eastern Front.[4]

It is perhaps no surprise that given the personal and political history, this man should experience himself as a small David fighting the threat of annihilatory Goliaths, actual losses, and threatened losses. Nazism had created such vulnerability and trauma to his people both personally and nationally, symbolised in the trauma of Leningrad, yet how strange that once in power himself this man would recreate the traumas of his history by inflicting them on others. Inverting the victimhood of his history, he perpetuated or assisted in the sieges and scorched earth violence on the people of Aleppo in Syria, for example, and later on the cities of Ukraine, encircling and attempting to starve people into submission through bombardment from the air and through complete resource deprivation on the ground. We could suggest an interpretation of a Leningrad scenario in which the dominance is inverted, reversing his internal narrative of the threats Russia faces at the hands of an 'expansionist' NATO, and the privations of the West, threats of loss so familiar to his history. In February 2007, Putin criticised what he called the United States' monopolistic dominance in global relations, and "almost un-contained hyper use of force in international relations". He said the result of it is that "no one feels safe! Because no one can feel that international law is like a stone wall that will protect them. Of course such a policy stimulates an arms race". This came to be known as the Munich Speech, one that the NATO secretary called "disappointing and not helpful". We note the interesting intersection of the personal with the political, and what may be interpreted to be the real personal internal and national vulnerability and history of loss to persecutory Goliaths, that even in his prosecution of war with overwhelming strength against Ukraine, his internal 'little David' fighting against all odds appears to persist. The victim has once again morphed into the perpetrator, but as if there is little connection between the prosecution of violence and the internal state of victimhood. It is now on a world stage and clothed in the machinations of ideology, history, military, and geopolitical analyses and assessments. From the point of view of those prosecuting the war, it is rational.

Perversion of the aggressive drive can be observed to have taken place in both these biographical vignettes, with inversion of the unconscious vulnerability into a disavowal of the original impulses designed to protect the self from impingements and loss. Such can be said of the *aim* of the drive, but indeed, as we observe, not of its *effects*. The nature of perversion is that aims and effects become separated and the preservatory agenda gives way to one so destructive that the scalability of aggression becomes tragically violent, creating the intra-species annihilation so counter-intuitive to humanities ongoing survival.

In its purer manifestation, aim and effects of the drive converge. A libidinal or aggressive impulse is psychically generated to drive adaptation or stasis and it achieves its intra-psychic aim by effecting a response that is proportionate and meets the inner need. *Feelings* register the need and the changes brought about by meeting it. Remember, that Freud's comment, "Feelings represent a demand upon the mind to perform work…". We *feel* better once the need is met and equilibrium is reset. With perversion, the aim of the impulse and its effects become separated both in terms of what is achieved by its discharge but also quantifiably in its proportionality. Invariably, disavowal leads to the inner valence, or affective charge becoming greater and the destructive effects out of proportion to the internal need.

Scalability of Affect

An infant screaming to induce a response and bring about a restoration of a state of disequilibrium creates a converging aim and effect as contentment is restored. But if this restoration is incomplete, a regression in adult life might involve a terrible rage and vengeance on other people when feelings of abandonment and persecution are present. The problem that emerges as we observe the diverging of the aim of *affect* to restore stasis through meeting a need, from its effects when the threshold for managing its frustration is breached, leads to the disavowal and separation of aim and effect. No longer does the effects of a drive carry any direct proportionality to its origin. This perversion can be said to enable a circular internal narrative to spin on its own axis, and once separated from its source psychically-speaking, can be free to ramp up scalability. The inner feeling, trapped as it were in a circular orbit within the unconscious, reacting in the now *as if* it were a reaction to the original insult or injury, creates an internal scalability of the affect and in turn appears to enable a scalability of its external effects. Freud had argued that a *quota of affect*, corresponding to the notion of an instinct, can become detached from an internal idea, that of a memory trace of previous experience, and influence current emotional reactivity in ways that are disproportionate.[5]

Ideation, the memory trace of an experience, and the quantum of affect or instinctual energy associated with it, can become separated. The formation of the substitute for the ideational portion (of the instinctual representative) comes about through a displacement, this transformation not leading to a disappearance of the underlying affect or instinctual energy, but a channelling of it onto substitutive objects or symbols which can enable a safer discharge of this (unresolved) emotional energy. Other transforming mechanisms are possible, such as reaction-formation (intensifying of the opposite, like killing with kindness, to cause discomfort to someone to whom hostile feelings are present, for example, by treating him or her in a way that is extremely kind or helpful), or through recruiting of a somatic area for the emotional energy to be represented. Essentially, these mechanisms provide routes through which affects originating from one source become separated from the ideation or memory trace attached to it and instead are discharged onto alternative objects or through substitutive mechanisms. Hitler the boy being severely beaten faces (by technical definition) deep hatred for the (paternal) object abusing and humiliating him and for the (maternal) object in her 'feebleness' not stepping in to protect him. I suggest the term 'technical' because violent disruption of homeostasis through pain, fear, humiliation, loss of control, etc. *must* evoke an aggressive response to restore equilibrium, but under these extreme conditions of trauma, cannot be effectively mobilised. The aggressive redress is rendered helpless, creating the conditions for the intense mobilising of (aggressive) affects that cannot be usefully discharged. The rendering of conditions for the creation of the later perversion of the drive displaced onto some other enfeebled symbol that must be hated (the Jew, for example), who represents both the danger of the ineffectual self that must be destroyed, but also a less threatening object (than the violent castrating father) onto which the destructive impulse can be displaced.

The Guardian Becomes Perverse

Psychic manoeuvres are invariably *overdetermined*. Whereas perhaps primitive humans were better off in knowing no restrictions to instinct, Freud noted, "to counterbalance this, his prospects of enjoying this happiness for any length of time were very slender".[6] Group cohesion of any sort demands a psychic mechanism for the internal regulation of instinct or it soon leads to conflict and entropic failure. Civilisation as we know it benefits enormously from internal regulation and the sublimation of primal drives into what we might think of as higher order aspirations. But then again, we never entirely lose the primacy of the drives embedded in the mental apparatus by nature.

Managing internal psychic tensions is neither easy nor energy-efficient. The mind does not always find simple linear solutions to its challenges and conflicts but relies on various defences being brought into play simultaneously to manage psychic tension. The layers of infant and childhood development enable different 'solutions' to weld together into mental strategies that compound layer upon layer of manoeuvres to manage internal and external conflict. This is especially so when the quantum of affect associated with dysregulation is overwhelming to the defences. Auxiliary mechanisms appear to be brought into service to bolster the original and potentially failing mechanism. Fuelled by the emotional intensity of the infant or child, whose experience in the moment is much more total than the partial experience of an adult, these psychic manoeuvres 'swell' disproportionately, become scaled-up as the energy is discharged into substitutive objects. Armed with these psychic strategies of survival in the face of overwhelming affects, some unconscious and some experienced consciously as *feelings*, the mind strives first to preserve itself from disintegration and fragmentation. These self-protective manoeuvres are, under such conditions, adaptive *from the subjective vantage of the victim at the time, and in many senses proportional to the experienced threat*. But as time passes and the circumstances change, the tendency of the psyche to regress to old points where these memories are fixated leads to maladaptive effects despite the noble intent of the original aim. *The guardian has become perverse.*

As limiting as psycho-biographies can be, as opposed to detailed case studies of patients in analysis or depth psychotherapy, when used accumulatively their stories become suggestive of trends from which observations can be deduced and to which theoretical observations can be tested. The historical biographies of geopolitical tyrants can be put together with the stories of those perpetrating violence or destructiveness, such as prisoners on death row or serial killers. Over and over, the observation of the link between perceived or experienced injury and aggression is compelling. In many cases, the requirement of subjectivity as a point of valence for the injury is moot – since consensus in such cases would be present that this individual suffered enormous abuse and/or neglect in infancy and childhood and there is no requirement for subjective perception to see the victim in the perpetrator and as a driver behind later depravity or perversion. In other cases, the victim element requires more subjectivity and the individual experience more intra-psychic interpretation for sense to be made of the scaled aggression against others later in life. This association of injury and aggression seems so common and fits with what we might expect theoretically, that I now regard it as a universal principle of mental functioning. Where Freud, Darwin, and the biochemists seem to agree is that from the outset of living matter two primary energetic forces have been in play. These two primary drives have permeated their way through higher and more complex layers of multi-cellular organisms and ultimately into the psychic realm of the human mind. Applied clinically, we notice that there appears to be no perpetrator without injury, no unbridled destructive impulse without a history of the threshold for mental disequilibrium being breached. In such instances, defences are configured, and ideational circuits established which stored in memory are activated through associative processes. Triggers activate these fixations to emerge in the present as if through the lens of the *past-in-the-present*.

As mentioned, the System Unconscious has no reference to time. Memory behaves in the present as if the passage of time between original injury and the current state does not exist. Whilst all this appears to tie together some of the effects we observe in disproportionate destructiveness, we encounter an oft-repeated objection to such a link: why do two people raised in the same house by the same parents, sometimes even who are twins, emerge with such different personalities? The sibling of a serial killer may seem quite normal and certainly there is no apparent correlation between the aggressors of the world and their siblings being of such character.

Orchids and Dandelions

Two observations can be drawn on to address this issue: firstly, I have made the point that subjectivity lies at the core of experience and the interpretation of adversity, as it does for any organism, even the most simple and primitive, interpreting the world around it from its subjective point of view. This is no simple fob – since subjectivity is created through experience that is uniquely individual, and majorly nuanced, and as Solms noted, affects, although inherently subjective, are typically directed toward objects: "I feel like this *about that*".[7] The complexity of an infant's early *subjective* experiences cannot be generalised nor its nuances and complexities ever be grasped except through the lens of that infant.

However, even with this consideration, it is hard not to notice that some infants are temperamentally more sensitive than others and experience adversity though a lens that seems to amplify the experience. It is as if they experience life in a heightened way. Thomas Boyce, a developmental paediatrician, has made some interesting observations in his work with troubled children in child-development research.[8] His research into temperament has offered useful insights into how some babies experience life as if they *feel* the world at greater intensity, a divergence of temperament. This suggests that some infants are primed for greater sensitivity than others. The cause of this heightened sensitivity might be for neurobiological reasons, often influenced by early arousal and stress (of labour, birth, and immediate post-partum challenges). These children are referred to as 'orchid' children because they are more sensitive and experience the sensory world as if it were amplified. But if nurtured in warm and contained environments, they can thrive to become creative and unique adults. But if raised in an environment that is less warm and containing, they can struggle through life with heightened emotionality, stress, and problems. On the other side of the spectrum are the Dandelion children, hardy and resilient like weeds, can thrive in any environment and appear more impervious to disequilibrium or impingement that might unsettle an orchid child. It makes sense that such children might psychologically interpret hurt, trauma, neglect, and humiliation in a less sensitising manner than the orchids who might internally amplify these same insults. Teasing a Dandelion, for example, might elicit a throwback defence. The orchid, however, might feel deeply hurt and register this insult as an aversive event to be stored in memory.

By association, activating these old hurts become the triggers for aggressive outpourings, at times directly, or in extreme cases through perversion of the aggressive response using defensive strategies. These can include displacement, reaction-formation, sublimation, and projection – with often fatal effects. The aim of the defence at source was to protect the individual psyche from feeling or being damaged but can end up perverse and split off into often terrible displacements of in-group and out-group polarisation. In this mode, it is as if anyone not with the person is against them. Extending this dynamic into in-group identities at teenage gang level, ideologies, or religious or nation states, the extension of this mechanism can have destructive effects, scaling on the spectrum to genocide. The Markov blanket so endemic to systems in the universe creates psychological currents in higher order human beings that induce self-organisation. It also by extension creates a response to anything that threatens entropy to that system, such a threat being invariably interpreted *from the vantage point* of the self-organising system – that is, from its subjectivity.

The peculiar use of subjectivity from non-sentient systems nonetheless applies. Human subjectivity takes on a sentient consciousness and for those with sentient consciousness who are temperamentally more orchid-like and sensitive, reactivity in subjective experience is likely to be heightened. Accordingly, so too the aggressive response to re-regulate and protect the system from entropic demise will be greater. Heightened sensitivity drives a greater subjectivity and hence a greater restorative response. As Solms explains this dimension, the internal body also has to be represented to the self, and so "the objects and the subject of perception combine, and so objects are always perceived by an experiencing subject".[9] Put in different biological terms, Paul Nurse relates this capacity to what he calls our 'self-conscious mind',[10] that is our ability as humans to reflect and adjust our behaviour when our worlds change, and also makes sense for the evolutionary benefit that accrues to *feeling states* being registered and reflected on. In essence, then, heightened sensitivity in body and mind will combine to generate a subject with more intense feelings, tending to also then greater reactivity when homeostasis is experienced or perceived as unsettled.

The Conscious Id

We are pulling together various concepts here. These include the notion that *regression* to an earlier state of mental development is possible; going back to earlier stages of development is achieved through accessing memory, which is stored as a reservoir of ideation; these stores of ideas are particularly good at representing aversive experiences that will require avoidance (into the *feedforward* process of the future) to ensure survivability; these memories must be readily and efficiently accessible by the mind, even when such regression is not fully conscious.

In fact, the functioning of the human mind presupposes that greater efficiency is achieved by a short-circuiting of conscious evaluation. A reflex has greater efficiency to a stimulus than does its *cognitive* evaluation. The Id (the "It" in English) is the part of the psyche that Freud notated to represent this unconscious reservoir and which Solms argues through current neuroscience lies at the core of consciousness. The 'conscious Id', as Solms described it, suggests that better efficiency is gained through the registration of feelings in a direct route from the unconscious. When states change, feelings can register these changes and categorise them into feel "good" or feel "bad". This is evidently what conscious states are *for*, Solms argues, "Conscious feelings tell the subject how well it is doing. At this level of the brain, therefore, consciousness is closely tied to homeostasis".[11]

This suggests that deeper representations of the brain-mind originating in brainstem structures work as a conduit for sensory perception and evaluation. This neurological system will be driven by affective intensity, since these sources are primarily sensory-affective. Senses and feelings play a significant role in adaptation and help link the unconscious with the conscious parts of the psyche. Says Solms, consciousness ultimately can be understood to emerge from internal brain structures that generate experiences of sensory dysregulation and is inherently *affective*. That is, it is feeling-driven and more related to instinct than cognition.[12] These observations lend support to the notion that subjectivity drives perception, and in two ways: by definition that the self-organising system must view threats to entropy from its own perspective; but also because *affective* experience drives conscious evaluation which in turn can be directed at objects that are not necessarily responsible for the source of disequilibrium. The mind can, in other words, be triggered by affect and emotional experience derived from a deeper limbic system source and convert these feelings into mental and cognitive representations in the external world. The higher-level brain structure of the cortex therefore enables humans to *represent* feelings, and 'stabilise' the objects of perception that allows emotional memory to be *represented* in the form of ideas or what Solms call 'mental solids' and Freud called object-presentations.[13] But this also suggests that humans must make post-facto meaning out of what they feel, and so ideologies, rationalisations, and even theories will be subject, literally, to these emotional drivers. Feeling precedes thinking and appears to drive much of how thought gets constructed. It also suggests that as humans we suffer an internal pressure to make cognitive meaning out of underlying feelings and emotional experiences and attach superstructures of ideas to them. Words and language, we could add, emerge to represent internal states and give meaning to these cognitive superstructures.

The implication of this aspect of the science is that internal feeling states originating in efficient homeostatic regulation, drive higher-order perception and the ideational representations that yield to them. Higher levels of thinking, ideology, ideas, political causes, and so on are unfortunately never free from such drivers, and in fact these cognitive elements in which we place such enormous value and pride are in a sense the slaves to a deeper master. We are forced to make meaning of deeper feelings through representing them as mental or cognitive ideas, and often attaching them to external causes and ideological positions that assist in this process. But as much as displacements, reaction-formations, and sublimations abound in managing more primitive drivers, we are never free from what lies beneath. We might suggest that feelings are invariably the human master – ideology and ideas its slave. Civilisation is welded together by the need to master internal states as a promotor of evolution and to avoid premature entropy but this veneer, as we know from history, is a thin one and can too easily succumb to the dictates of its underlying and unconscious emotional master. It is like a gourmet meal, no matter how elegantly prepared, is still driven by the need to eat.

Attack to Conserve

As mentioned, internal feeling states must be turned into more conscious and cognitive meaning to be useful. But also, objects in the external world *can come to represent* feeling states or affects originating in the unconscious, and which are stored as representations of prior experience. Projection of inner states onto the external world makes sense since inner perceptions and the outer world of reality benefit from being aligned. It is conducive to survival that feeling too cold aligns with the outside environment being too cold. If these misalign, the mind must create conditions for alignment.

The implications of this for how the aggressive drive manifests in the external world is significant, since extreme emotional reactions can be activated due to internal feeling states, influencing perception of an object or event in the external world, and retaliating against it as a form of restoration. It is as if from the ego's internal representation, its modus operandi might be construed as 'attack to conserve'. This internal representation suffers feelings, as Freud would suggest, through narcissistic interpretation of impingements that have unsettled equilibrium. Narcissism suggests that the psyche has a representation of *itself* in the world, not only of a representation *of* the world in itself. If the external environment is perceived as humiliating or threatening due to frustrations or impingement from the environment, so too the ego can form an internal representation of itself in relation to these experiences. The world can be perceived as bad and threatening. But so too can the ego represent itself as weak and vulnerable. If feelings of hostility are activated in response to bad things happening, and these bad feelings cannot manifest, then by the law of conservation of energy these feelings can leave the infant or child feeling bad in themselves – it is not the world that is bad, I am bad! I am weak. I am pathetic! This internalisation of the bad engages introjection as a defence to manage the bad feelings, redirecting them away from the target object (usually the mother) and instead finding a safer path inward. A compromise is reached whereby the external object upon who the infant depends is preserved and the badness is turned inwards. Later, anxiety and depression may manifest, or aggressive enactments outwardly, but at the time preservation of the love object is achieved and the internal self becomes represented in ways that preserve the object. Later, associative triggers may catalyse these (unresolved) feelings and set in motion a process where the internal representation of the self, a form of narcissistic representation of the self in the world, is activated.

It is on the one hand so obvious and intuitive that humans represent themselves to themselves in relation to the external world, and that these internal representations (or maps of the self as a self-organising system and identity) carry significant psychological weight. It is also not surprising that unique amongst the species, humans have the capacity to form internal representations of their internal feelings states and transform these feelings states into words, images, and fantasies that represent these internal feelings states. Instinctual energies are filtered through higher cognitive facilities to enable civilised social cohesion and functioning to occur. Unique amongst the species, the human psyche can form representations of itself in relation to the world, and recruit these representations in the service of imaging both the (narcissistic) self and the external environment.

These representations or internal maps invariably suffer the distortions of subjectivity, recruiting ideas, ideologies, and data to suit the underlying *affective* driver. The 'conscious Id', as Solms constructs it, makes a neuroscientific case for the notion that affect *precedes* cognition, that feelings underscore the representation we have and then create of the world. 'We *feel* therefore we are', to parody the Cartesian position that thinking makes reality. Rather, neuroscience in convergence with Freudian psychoanalysis is suggesting that the human mind tends towards cherry-picking the (cognitive) data, based on unconscious emotional experience, to create cognitive representations of the world. The evidence for cognitive belief appears through this mechanism to be driven by emotional experience. The science would suggest that it is not 'cogito, ergo sum' ('I think therefore I am') as Cartesian philosophy might suggest, but 'I am, therefore I think'. Cognitive representations derive from experiences of the world that require internal representations to be formed, to enable efficient feedback systems to evolve that can represent complex events and stimuli in efficient ways. Often, these cognitive superstructures become represented through the use of language and the words of language – the value of words being, as Solms puts it, to represent the relation between things, to *re*-represent them abstractly.[14]

If you are exposed to an item that may or may not be threatening, for example a knife, the context will interface with your own experience and evaluation of the stimulus. Are your associations positive and non-threatening? The knife represents cuisine and cookery, an enabling item with creative potential. Or, the knife is in a stranger's hand walking toward you on a mountain path. In quick intuitive evaluation, instant flooding of associations will form 'in the mind's eye', enabling extremely rapid and efficient focus to form that can trigger a response to neutralise the potential threat – prepare to aggress (fight) or prepare to run (flight) or prepare to submit (comply). The neurobiological efficiency with which this cascade occurs begins with a feeling and proceeds to recruit cognition in its service. But of course, this model of flight-fight does not account for subjectivity in the mix, the mediation of the self-representation in between the stimulus and the response. If the self-representation is stronger and considers one's capacity to fight the (lone) potential aggressor (smaller than me) threat (*I* have a gun in my belt) fight in defence of homeostasis (to stay alive) might predominate. If the self-representation is weak (he is bigger than I), has co-conspirators with him (I am outgunned and unarmed), the evaluation might be to flee or freeze and comply with demands in an attempt to preserve the self.

But often, the middle ground is demanded – you cannot fight (outgunned) and you cannot run (they are right upon me, have the element of surprise, are over-whelmingly aggressive, have nothing to lose) then using internal representation of one's own personal strategies for survival will mediate (take my money and leave me alone!). This simplification does not do justice to the complexity of such a situation of the neuropsychological processes that are activated. But it does at least represent the concepts. It represents subjectivity in consciousness, how we feel and represent ourselves, even if originating from an unconscious source driven by feeling states that are triggered by old memories and associations. Through this cascade, cognition is recruited to form images, ideologies, *theories* that validate and make sense of felt experience. If all men are *felt* to be bad to a woman who has experienced sexual abuse, this deeply triggering memory of helpless rage will find theoretical constructs and data to verify the internal representation. Felt experience that has been embedded psychically to represent the threats of the external world.

Ideological Surrogates

Hitler being thrashed by his hard father whilst his mother sat 'helplessly' outside the door unable to intervene (or from the vantage of the little boy perhaps choosing not to intervene) may have created representations of the world as a demeaning, humiliat-ing, unprotected place in which the self forms representations of being feeble, weak, and emasculated. Derived from this emotional source and its psychic representation of the self *in its relation to* the world, ideological surrogates in the external world for good and bad can become representatives of the internal world. Symbols of power, strength, and masculinity (and restoration of phallic) strength and prestige in the world built from the ashes of geopolitical and national humiliation and defeat, a concordant world of the internal and the external can be seen to emerge in this case.

Eric Kandel speaks indirectly to this point when noting that the conversion of short-term memory into long-term memory, the stuff of the unconscious, requires the activation of genes, particularly when encoding aversive stimuli. In each case "modulatory transmitters appear to carry an attentional signal *marking the impor-tance of a stimulus*".[15] In response to that signal "genes are turned on and proteins are produced and sent to all the synapses". This is interesting, since the neurosci-ence suggests that what the organism perceives or experiences as aversive will set in motion this neurological cascade aimed at encoding into memory the aversive association. Another way of thinking about this is that when faced with a threat or impingement perceived or experienced to be aversive from the *subjective perspec-tive* of an organism, it will recruit the attentional signal activating the neuronal cascade. In Kandel's work, the research involved physical shock as the trigger for 'unpleasure' (to use Freud's term).

But the recruiting of such a cascade in the human psyche need not necessarily involve physical unpleasure, although often does in infancy, given the embodied nature of human experience. In fact, we might argue that so much of human unpleasure and trauma originates in the mental realm as the organism grows. In infancy, of course, the chief origin of trauma starts somatically, but separation from the mother, an entirely mental process, creates significant distress and trauma also, even in the absence of immediate physical dysregulation. Psychical dysregulation to the human organism carries, over time, even greater valence in the ordinary course of living than does the somatic. A heart broken in love can have greater deleterious effects than one damaged through poor diet.

Needs are complex and often about satiation of our mental and energetic requirements – including for sex and intimacy. A striking quality about the unconscious is its ability to encode and retain memory of aversive *experiences* when they are subjectively perceived, and even single aversive experiences can become encoded into long-term memory. "Indeed", says Kandel, from a neuroscientific point of view, "after a single exposure to a threat, the amygdala can retain the memory of that threat throughout an organism's entire life".[16] This central role of the unconscious is supported by the finding that, as Solms argues, the "unconscious evaluation of a frightening stimulus precedes conscious, cortical evaluation of fear…"[17] and that this source of conscious experience is bridged through the (subjective) experience registered consciously as *feelings*.

The interesting question that the neuroscience opens up relates to the bridging between the objective and the subjective. The objective evidence is there for how aversive threats and experiences are encoded into memory but always from the vantage of the organism. In this sense, an objective cascade is subjectively triggered. This admittedly broad use of the concept of subjectivity seems nonetheless to carry through into the sentience of human subjectivity and the role that *perception* of a stimulus plays in evaluating a felt experience as benign or malignant. The conscious evaluation of whether the gun someone is pointing at you is real or plastic will have a determining role in how that threat is constructed and reacted to, and as Kandel noted, the striking feature about fear is that it can readily become associated with neutral stimuli through learning. Once this happens, the neutral stimuli itself can become a powerful trigger of long-term emotional reactions in people. As many neuroscientists would now agree, and as Freud's pioneering observation noted, most of our mental life is unconscious and becomes conscious only through words and images, or accessing ideation (the memory traces of the Unconscious). This accessing of old memory traces occurs through paying attention or usually only by introspecting via a reflective mirror, usually a psychotherapist that can notice links between the external and the internal. Interpreting these links enables the unconscious to become conscious and hence 'worked through'. But feelings can be triggered more directly when associations in the present that activates an unconscious association in the present, narrowing the gap between what has been encoded in the past with what is current in the present.

Earlier, I linked individual atrocity, geopolitical atrocity, and the self-preservatory drive. Some may object to this simplification of history, and rightly so, since alignment of many other variables is required for this to occur. But to those who say, yes, this is all very well, but not everyone subject to such childhood abuse becomes a Hitler in the world, even when geopolitical realities align, it may be retorted, precisely, because not everyone *is* Hitler! His subjectivity defines his experience in its unique psychic configuration and this is the jaw-dropping complexity and its elusive quality – but it is also *magnifique*! The 'hard problem' of science, how something objective (like neurones) becomes subjective is understandably still complex. Since the moment we engage with subjectivity, we run into the paradox of how by definition of its quality, we cannot know it. No-one can ever know how you feel or experience something, without your report of it.

Violent Crime

This element of subjectivity as an evolutionary imperative protected by the aggressive drive can appear inverted in many cases of violence – especially that typed as 'mindless violence' by any common-sense objective observation. David Michael Barnett was sentenced to death on 2 May 1977 in St. Louis County, Missouri, USA for the double murder of his adoptive grandparents, whom he stabbed to death as they returned home from church. He then proceeded to steal money and their car.[18]

He later confessed to these crimes and was sentenced to death for each of the two murder counts and consecutive life sentences for the robbery and armed criminal action counts. At the time of the murders, Barnett had been living with friends and had apparently spoken several times to them about his grandparent's car that they were going to rent to him. On the morning of the murder, he made his way to and broke in to his grandparents' house, who were away attending church services, apparently through a bedroom window. He then proceeded to sit down on the couch, watching television, and falling asleep. When Barnett's grandparents returned home, he was waiting for them. First, he confronted his grandmother and pushed her down in the hallway, then pushed his grandfather to the floor and grabbed a knife that was lying on the nearby kitchen table. First kicking him in the head and then stabbing him repeatedly in the neck area, Barnett reportedly inflicted ten stab wounds and numerous cuts to his grandfather's neck, face, and hands. Now satisfied that he had killed his grandfather, he returned to the kitchen to get another knife and then began stabbing his grandmother in her neck as well. Once again, Barnett returned to the kitchen to get more knives. This time he retrieved two knives with which he continued to stab his grandmother until she, too, was killed, reportedly suffering 12 stab wounds to her neck and numerous cuts to her face. After the attack, Barnett concealed one of the knives by placing it between two mattress pads in his grandparent's bedroom, went to the bathroom and washed the blood off his hands. He then took the car keys to their car and some cash from his grandmother's purse, made sure they were not breathing, and left the house. He proceeded to lower two of the shades in the house, locked up, and drove off in the victims' car. Early the next morning, police officers found the victims' car parked in a residential area of Glendale, and interestingly, Barnett reportedly walked up to the uniformed officers and confessed that he had committed the murders.

On the undisputed facts of the case the level of violent depravity is striking. The intensity of the violence, the 'overkill' elements, the apparently mindless blood-lust on the one hand coupled with a considered aspect makes attempts at meaning appear pointless. But a quick glance at the killer's childhood history creates a long list of meaningful elements. Amongst them, maternal abandonment, poverty and neglect, depravity in all areas of his life, glimmers of hope through early adoption coupled with subsequent abandonment here too. Later adoption was coupled with sexual abuse, disbelief by a police officer when Barnett and his adoptive brother tried to report the perpetrator for paedophilia (providing a photograph as evidence, which was returned without action), and physical violence and privations. Interestingly, both the adoptive father and grandfather (whom he later killed) wore similar signet rings and used to smack him on the head, inflicting pain and injury, creating an association in his mind of these perpetrators being in a similar conflated and overdetermined space in his mind. Whatever triggered the final violent enactment is unclear but it does seem from later reports that there were words and probable frustrations that unconsciously unleashed all the accumulated injuries this boy was victim to in his childhood. He did not seem to experience himself as perpetrator. Rather, he seemed to experience himself as a victim of intense and ongoing abuse and neglect creating ongoing psychic need to re-regulate. The aggressive drive would have likely been in constant overdrive but with no direct route for effective environmental induction for remedy or change fixated at disproportionate affect levels. Whilst all perpetrators claim victimhood as a motivator for their crimes, the unmistakable facts in so many of these cases are precisely that experiences of dysregulation abound in their histories, amplified through their subjective lens.

The link between feelings (of injury) and retaliatory aggression in defence of the 'subject' is not simply about modern-day serial killers or geopolitical tyrants. It appears embedded in the psychic DNA of humanity. In fact, so fundamental appears the juxtaposition of two competing and conflicting tendencies of life itself, of all organic matter, that as we shall see there is no escaping this psychic and social tension. By definition of life's energetic foundation, which we will explore further in a bit, embedded in mental process, is the tension between conservation (keeping things the same) and adaptation (change), which leads to inevitable in-group out-group tendencies of the self-organising system governed by the free-energy principle. Differentiation of the internal from the external, the 'us' from the 'them', enables humans to feel safer and more secure. Interesting to note with humans, however, unlike other species, is that psychic subjectivity and dominance of feelings as the central mechanisms for regulation of the mind-body system sensitises humans to taking concrete action in the service of intangible threats activated through feelings. It is fascinating to consider that the first recorded homicide in human history speaks volumes to the fundamental and primitive nature of this characteristic. The first recorded homicide in human history is not about physical threat, territorial integrity, protection of the clan or its resources, or defending the fatherland or motherland. It is about, strangely and simply, feelings!

The First Homicide – Biblical Murder and Feelings

The story of Cain's murder of Abel and its consequences is told in Genesis and perhaps represents a *leitmotif* of this primary human condition and its mental drivers for aggression. In the text, you can notice the buildup of the dynamics from which the aggression gets activated. The interesting reference to "his face fell" as a direct indicator of his emotional reaction, his feelings, signifies to the reader the central role that purely emotional reactivity can play in the genesis of the aggressive drive.

> And the human knew Eve his woman and she conceived and bore Cain, and she said, "I have got me a man with the Lord." And she bore as well his brother Abel, and Abel became a herder of sheep while Cain was a tiller of the soil. And it happened in the course of time that Cain brought from the fruit of the soil an offering to the Lord. And Abel too had brought from the choice firstlings of his flock, and the Lord regarded Abel and his offering but did not regard Cain and his offering. And Cain was very incensed, and his face fell. And the Lord said to Cain,

> Why are you incensed,
> and why is your face fallen?
> For whether you offer well,
> or whether you do not,
> at the tent flap sin crouches
> and for you is its longing,
> but you will rule over it.

> And Cain said to Abel his brother, "Let us go out to the field," and when they were in the field Cain rose against Abel his brother and killed him. And the Lord said to Cain, "Where is Abel your brother?" And he said, "I do not know: am I my brother's keeper?" And He said, "What have you done? Listen! Your brother's blood cries out to me from the soil. And so, cursed shall you be by the soil that gaped with its mouth to take your brother's blood from your hand. If you till the soil, it will no longer give you strength. A restless wanderer shall you be on the earth." And Cain said to the Lord, "My punishment is too great to bear. Now that You have driven me this day from the soil I must hide from Your presence, I shall be a restless wanderer on the earth and whoever finds me

will kill me." And the Lord said to him, "Therefore whoever kills Cain shall suffer sevenfold vengeance." And the Lord set a mark upon Cain so that whoever found him would not slay him.

Ronald Hendel, Professor of Hebrew Bible and Jewish Studies at the University of California, Berkeley, writes a compelling interpretive narrative about the theme of sibling rivalry as a motif in the theological narrative.[19] Hendel refers to this in two themes: sibling rivalry per se and also the upending of the hierarchy between siblings. In the biblical story, Cain has several motives for murdering his brother Abel, including feelings of jealousy that God accepted Abel's offering over Cain's, but for Cain and his offering there was no regard, with God defying expectations and accepting only the youngest son's offering. In addition, the normal hierarchy of the firstborn and younger child is turned upside down, a reversal of what would be expected. This inversion of roles adds depth to Cain's response when God asks, after the murder, "Where is your brother Abel?" Cain replies, "I do not know; am I my brother's keeper?"[20] Cain is rejecting the obligation to care for Abel; instead, he murders him. And it is Abel's blood, shed in violence, that calls out to God and implicates the murderer. Cain, who brought his sacrifice "from the fruit of the ground" and has shed his brother's blood on the soil, is now himself cursed "from the ground". No longer a farmer, he becomes a wanderer, exiled from the fruitful soil and dwelling in the Land of Nod (literally "wandering"). Having lost his family, his livelihood, and his home, he now dwells outside of civilisation, a rootless vagabond. The theme of feelings driving aggression, even where the result ends up being self-defeating is contained in this depiction of the first recorded homicide.

Once again, it bears repeating that this act of humanity's first recorded murder is one driven primarily by feelings and a perception of injury. The feelings of injury appear to be due to both the father (Adam) and the father's father (God) creating the conditions for feelings of humiliation, rejection, abandonment, and diminishment. All of these represent no significant threat of physical or territorial harm and all are feelings confined to the mental-emotional realm. This is an interesting choice of story to narrate an underlying lesson of human functioning and the foundation of the destructive effects of a primarily conservative and self-protective mechanism. The ego, or 'I' that suffers the narcissistic injury, represents the centre of the self-organising system that is the human mind-body system. This follows Freud, and Solms' modifications of the notion of consciousness deriving as the interface between the internal and external environments, like the mental projection of the surface of the skin, a separation barrier of sorts. The underlying drives that govern the psyche, the conservative aggressive drive and the adaptive mutating libidinal one, produce energy that ends up as (subjective) feelings for which there is not any objective measure. By their definition and nature, feelings have to represent the perspective of the system to which they apply themselves, and so are objectively unmeasurable, except through self-report, and the underlying principle of the pioneering 'talking cure' of psychoanalysis and most modern therapeutic systems. This also makes the energetic quality of both drives maddeningly elusive and intangible yet singularly powerful drivers of a 'felt-sense'. Sexuality and aggression dominate the psychic landscape with utmost intensity, these drives finding their way into consciousness and the experience of feeling something that requires work for the mind to re-regulate.

The Energy of Feelings

The question remains, however, as to how it is possible for something so intangible as an 'energy' to be simultaneously so strongly felt as if it were something concrete and tangible. The irony of these drives is that without subjective report, they do not appear to exist. There is no measure for someone feeling horny or hateful (even if there may be some objective signs of these states, such as arousal or tumescence or flushing, elevations in blood pressure, Galvanic Skin Response, and so on). How then can intangible, non-observable, non-objective energies translate into subjectively concrete felt feelings? Physics is not unfamiliar with such paradox – since energy and matter, as Einstein notated are interchangeable. The neurobiology of hormonal influences is well understood, but the quantum step from the objective to the subjective remains complex and elusive. Nonetheless, these primary drives present powerful in-built mechanisms for conservation and adaptation of the human self-organising system. Without the psychic inputs and its feeling states, the body could not survive, since there would be no *felt* measure of states of disequilibrium. This point that Solms makes about the 'conscious Id' based on contemporary neuroscience adds value to the link between the primitive elements of all organic life and their emergent qualities in highly complex somatic and psychic systems. In this context, it also makes little sense to speak of a separation of mind and body since the integration of these systems is what governs homeostasis and survival. The mind creates awareness of internal states in relation to external stimuli, both physiological and emotional. The mismatch between these elements creates disequilibrium that demands a response for work to re-regulate. However, the nature of memory and the system unconscious leaves particular excessive experiences stored for future quick reference.

The psychic system of energetics seems at once both as real as the day is long and entirely nonsensical from a scientific point of view. Feelings are as real to the subject as they are elusive to the observer. Energy has both an intangible quality and yet in some respects also a measurable one. Life itself, it would seem to the biochemists' eye, relies on the transformation of energy to enable the shift from the inorganic to the organic. This is not too different from many neuroscientists lament about the 'hard problem' in neuroscience, since according to Kandel, "What science lacks are rules for explaining how subjective properties (consciousness) arise from the properties of objects (inter-connected nerve cells)".[21] This is no small problem. It relates to the property of emergence, how complex system can emerge from simpler underlying structures and processes, and yet in this trajectory of growth from simple to complex, the reverse can never be achieved. The egg can never be unscrambled or put back into the shell. Life is asymmetrical in its propensity to drive forward with time. Whilst we grapple with this problem in the mental apparatus around consciousness and the experience of subjectivity, life itself struggles with this problem. The 'hard problem' of consciousness also connects to the transformation of the inanimate to the animate. How does life itself manage to emerge from organic molecules that are lifeless in any biological sense? The combining of all the raw ingredients for life does not in any way manage to achieve the creation of life. This transition from the inorganic to the organic, from the inanimate to the animate, shrouds life forces themselves in the same mystery. Organic chemists and biologists in their attempts to make sense of this problem also struggle with the point at which one transforms into the other.

How Concrete Acts of Violence Get Triggered by Energy

The relevance of this conundrum will become clearer as we establish that the two primary energies of conservation versus adaptation lie buried deep in the emergence of life itself. It is interesting to note that in the biblical description (taken as an historical account) two primary themes emerge from the beginning: first, there is Nothing (stasis dominates the state of the universe) before a dramatic burst of energy and creativity, life forces that lead to the creation of the substance and form of the universe and its contents. This culminates in the creation of Adam and Eve and their subsequent procreativity, creating life themselves through their union. This burst of creativity and procreativity, libidinal forces in the universe, nature, and humankind itself appears to represent the first major theme of human history. The second major theme to emerge in the narrative is about humankind's first recorded enactment of aggression, murder in fact, a very concrete act conceived through not-concrete feelings.

The narrative introduces aggression as its second most significant theme of human life. Become created, create, and conserve those creations. However one interprets this narrative, theologically or as a story of creation, it is intriguing that the earliest narrative of the human condition describes the two fundamental drives that Freud noted in his extensive reaches into the human psyche. Eros, libidinally driven, and the death drive governed by aggression dominate the fundamental inner tension of the mental apparatus. The mind serves the function of interfacing between the external environment and its many challenges and impingements and the internal environment and its many complex needs to maintain equilibrium and survive. But this complex emergence of these dynamic tensions appears embedded deeply in the energetics of all organic life, from the simplest to the most complex of organisms.

The relevance of engaging the question of energy, not as some esoteric notion of 'the feels', but as a primary driver in cosmology, physics, biochemistry, and life itself, is that in many senses Freud's great discoveries of mental life rely on energy as their primary drivers. This intangible concept is not about measuring wattage across a wire but the recruitment of energy into the mental and somatic systems to enable subjectivity to form, and the *feelings* this ultimately portends. If we cannot find a viable principle of energetics in life's formation, as a fundamental driver of all organic life, we risk the ruin of some profound observations. Libido and aggression rely on energy to drive them, rely on the intangible force of these primary mental drives to convert energy from one mental state into the concrete and often scalable impact of action. The death drive has the capacity, we observe, to transcend the realm of the intangible energetic to become concrete, creating physical destruction and ironically, in the ultimate form of nuclear destruction, converting matter back into intangible energy. The intangible driving the tangible back into the intangible of energetic destruction. A digression into the biochemistry of energetics makes sense, since as Nick Lane describes biochemically, the origin of life as a procreative trend derives from energy gradients, more specifically proton gradients in alkaline thermal vents that facilitated life's formation. The eventual impact on free energy is that life forming requires itself to self-organise, capturing energy from the random to the organised. This trend can only work forward in time to avoid entropy. Those molecules or life forms that do not self-organise, creating their Markov blanket differentiating self from other, subject themselves, so to speak, to a choice towards entropy and demise albeit over extended periods of time.

Energy and the Driver of Life

As the molecular biologists note, energy is the critical driver of molecular formation, cell formation and division, and life. The concrete organic emerges from Nature's ability to utilise effective energy over time to form systems with internal governance. These microscopic energy sources within cellular structures, such as the mitochondria, are complex and efficient and give rise to increasingly complex cellular structures and organisms for whom biological necessity is driven by energy. In human beings, biology is best served by an emergent mental apparatus that can efficiently register changes to equilibrium through feelings states, primarily through the sensory apparatus. This is also where Freud and molecular biology neatly converge – libidinal energy in higher order systems drives development, this muddle of the entirely intangible and the tangible converging: "It is to this ego that consciousness is attached; the ego controls the approaches to motility – that is, to the discharge of excitations into the external world; it is the mental agency that supervises all its own constituent processes…".[22] Freud's emphasis on the relationship between the somatic and the mental apparatus is important, inseparable, interrelated, mutually influencing. "The ego", said Freud, "is first and foremost a bodily ego; it is not merely a surface entity, but is itself the projection of a surface". Since the ego is ultimately derived from bodily sensations, it may be regarded as a mental projection of the surface of the body.[23] This point of the mind and its relationship to the body implies that the principle drives of energy, both kinds of instinct "would be active in every particle of living substance",[24] though in unequal proportions, since "the instinct of destruction is habitually brought into the service of Eros".[25]

This is a way of suggesting that the life drive carries greater energetic demand since it has to adapt under conditions of threat than conservation by the homeostatic drive. The latter drive utilises resistance, powering up to aggression to achieve such conservancy. Its aim is quietude and restoration, not change. But once again, the challenge of converting energy into the driving forces of the mind-body system remains. Molecular biology assists in the conundrum since the earliest formation of life carries this conversion and tension from the outset and more complex organisms do not escape the gravitational pull of these early and primitive origins. On the contrary, emergent complexity never loses its (epi)genetic foundations, forged in the furnaces of Life's creation. The 'felt-sense', that phrase so popular amongst psychologists, reflects a deeper emergent trend and meaning for human life and the efficiency of the mental apparatus in detection, evaluation, and actioning in the service of homeostasis and adaptation. Energy is a crucial ingredient of all formations of both inorganic and organic life. This is not some esoteric notion or namby-pamby idea. This is central science and forms the foundation of the biochemistry of life and its origins. Disruption to the process of energy in life, such as the ingestion of arsenic, results in a quick death.

As an extension of somatic regulation and functioning, energy also drives the mental apparatus, without which there could be none. Libidinal drives form the thrust of the adaptive mechanism and its various constituent manifestations – including the complex requirements for creative and procreative work. If feelings represent *a measure of the demand made upon the mind for work in consequence of its connection with the body*, and feelings are by definition subjective and must be *felt* in order to have any meaningful role in re-regulation of the body, their employment of energy remains central. The intangible drives the tangible. In so far as energy may be viewed as intangible, physicists would likely have conniptions at this characterisation, since beneath the naked eye lies a world of atomic and sub-atomic particles, from which proton and electron gradients drive power in the macro-universe and the micro-universe. The intangible is only intangible at a surface level, but nonetheless, it is fair to think about psychic characteristics and their felt sense, that is subjective states, as being driven by complex elements that have no obvious concrete observability. This 'hidden spring', to borrow Solms' reference to this source of deep brain-driven feeling states and affects, sources the feelings from which action ultimately is derived.

Energy is essential for the development of living matter from the outset. Electrochemical gradients, whether proton or ion gradients enable biological life and cellular and neuronal activity. Whilst some bacterium has remained stuck in static life forms for millions of years, others have evolved into cellular life of unimaginable complexity. For life to have emerged and evolved at all, the chemo-biological imperative was to evolve under the pressures of the environment. One can imagine that this energetic trend forms the primitive basis for libidinal drives in more complex organisms and humans. Basic principles in nature, physics, and organo-chemistry should retain their character as they permeate through greater complexity in living organisms. Friston's Free Energy Principle, if accepted as a natural character of all systems, should then also find its way into psychic systems of the mental apparatus which emerge from somatic or physiological process. Patrick Connolly[26] in a paper on the subject makes a convincing case for the application of the laws of nature and free energy into the psyche and its character, melding Freud with a language of modern physics. Connolly writes that recent work by scientists such as Friston has framed the selection of action as a gradient descent of expected free energy under different policies of action. From this perspective, "conflict could potentially be formalised as a situation where opposing action policies have similar expected free energy, for example between actions driven by competing basic prototype emotion systems as described by Panksepp (1998)".[27]

Complexity and Survival

The drives of the psyche in their complexity aim to be true to natural laws that suggest the fundamental conservative nature of the free-energy principle, to prompt a self-organising system, in this case biological, to survive. It must conserve itself to avoid entropy – but conservation overwhelmed by impingement demands adaptation in order to survive. In these fundamental energetic drivers are present in the most primitive beginnings of life – stay as you are or evolve to minimise the greater risk of demise through over-conservation. In essence, conservations may enable a primitive organism to maintain itself through eons of time, *provided the conditions of its existence remain unaltered*. But when that environment changes, complexity is triggered because with complexity comes the ability to adapt and evolve, favouring survival over time. Under *conditions* of increasing complexity, in other words, adaptation favours complexity. The more change impinges upon an organism, even one that has remained intact for billions of years through an unaltered environment, the more survival favours the ability to adapt. And as has been argued, the ability to adapt favours complexity because genetic variation, which creates complexity, favours adaptation and survival. At the end of the day, human beings will overtime defeat a bacterium or virus more effectively than a virus or bacterium will beat the human race.

A self-organising system that has greater capacity for adaptation will be able to efficiency minimise free energy whilst preventing loss of its own identity. Adaptability, therefore favours subjectivity, the organism's capacity to maintain its own identity in the face of threat to it. This enables it to emerge slightly changed in the face of its conservation threshold being breached, but nonetheless still with its core identity intact. Anti-entropy versus adaptation to avoid entropy appears to emerge as the core tension within all living systems, the mental apparatus included. A conservative versus a creative drive dominates the tension of the living mind. What Freud termed the Death Drive, since it aims to navigate the mind-body system through its own internal course to restore a state of an earlier condition (from dust to dust) tensions constantly against the Life Drive whose aim is to forge new and greater complexities as a measure of its adaptability and hence survivability.

The conservative drive uses aggression to maintain itself, its identity, its subjectivity in a world of constant challenge and threat. Complex organisms are challenged constantly by the external environment and will tend to respond according to its 'subjective' perception of that threat. Which brings us full circle to scalable aggression as a manifestation of human injury encoded into unconscious memory whose initial aim was that of conservation. The guardian of the peace has become perverted. It begs a fateful question for the human species, wrote Freud, "to be whether and to what extent their cultural development will succeed in mastering the disturbance of their communal life by the human instinct of aggression and self-destruction".[28]

When Cain kills Abel because his feelings are hurt, we find a central tenet of human psychic functioning. Scale the projections of hurt into external objects, under the guidance of the Markov blanket and self-organising pressures, and geopolitical trends can emerge which procure us-them divisions under the umbrella of ideology. Everywhere, we notice that people form identities that preserve that particular self-organising system. On a bicycle, identification with other cyclists against 'inconsiderate' and dangerous motorists represents preservation through a self-organising system premised on this particular identity. Get back into the car after the cycle and the same person's identity might shift, cursing at the peloton whose failure to ride in single file is obstructing their ability to get home speedily! Self-organising systems retain some fluidity, depending on context, which allows for safety through identification, whether ideological, nationalistic, theoretical, gendered, sporting team, or some other variant. Whilst it would seem naive to suggest that context determines the Markov blanket and the nature of self-identity, which seems to make the concept almost void for vagueness as the philosophers might suggest, such fluidity retains the uniquely human capacity for adaptability in the service of greatest survival. The intensely complex interface between the inner and outer worlds, or the intra-psychic versus the inter-psychic environments, has provided humans with an enormous capacity for complex adaptation and a fluid movement between conservation and adaptation. Hence, the observation that people are capable of multiple identities, sometimes even contradictory ones, holds sway. The rapist at college may be a doting son and brother at home, protecting his own to the death. But when desire is triggered to which access may be denied, the resultant feelings of humiliation and frustration may be the trigger for violent enactment against women, or against a woman. Or when a parent smacks their child half to death because of feeling humiliated by the child's non-compliance to their authority, yet will a second later feel like killing someone threatening their child's safety or integrity, we can see the daily moments of shifting identities. This multiplicity of identity enables sophisticated navigation of highly complex emotional and social contexts and their demands. It also assists in noting how fluid the shift from victim to perpetrator and back to victim can be in all areas as diverse as the domestic battlefield and the geopolitical one. Mobility demands a sophisticated ability to adapt and shift to preserve in complex different demands. *If Eros is rooted in the imperative to adapt-or-die, aggression is rooted in the requirement to first minimise free energy through conservation.*

Aims and Effects

We arrive at a point where the function of aggression, its aim rather than its effects, can be noted. From its primitive origins in organismic life, the tension between conservation versus adaptation underlies the psychic drives Freud identified in the mental apparatus. Eros drives the capacity to adapt, a creative drive that aims to forge greater unities in the interests of survival in complex environments that threaten equilibrium constantly. The death drive, as Freud named it, strives to resist entropy through reacting to threats to equilibrium, pushing back as it were, to maintain stasis at all costs. Because this drive relies so heavily on memory to be able to recognise threats to equilibrium, the unconscious becomes a vast reservoir of ideational traces, memories that enable rapid retrieval to indicate when threats are present and to mount an 'immune' response whose aim is simply the restoration of the state that existed prior to the impingement. But often, as we have discussed earlier, aggression is mounted without any objective external provocation or threat. Memory relies on the all-important elements of subjectivity, which implies both interpretation of events and an associative capacity where stimuli that may not be apparent objectively to an outside observer are present to the person themselves. This repetition of earlier experience, often significantly amplified through the lens of the infant's experience which has become fixated psychically in memory, will tend to influence current (adult) responses. Hence, by association, an insignificant trigger can lead to significant enactments of destructive energies. The rapist who is triggered by desire for a woman that he cannot access may invoke deep feelings of humiliation and unworthiness intra-psychically, leading to a violent predatory response (in Panksepp's terms, the rage circuit is activated which may be in cold calculated or hot angry form).

Inevitably, these links in the psychic chain point us to an inescapable conclusion – that from a subjective point of view, aggressive enactments invariably derive from perceptions of injury and threat. It is an uncomfortable conclusion which raises issues of culpability to those who become victims or perpetrate enactments. The science of describing these mechanisms in no way serves to justify violence or destructive enactments at the personal or political level. Rather, science must be invoked to make sense of the often-unfathomable realties of complex life and the demands of living. Perhaps, by understanding why individuals or leaders of countries aggress in often vile and unfathomable ways we might better intervene to reduce such effects of what in essence is a benign drive. But both psychic drives can become perverted. Both can develop a life-of-its-own in split-off and separated ways. This perversion of the sexual drive remains invariably at an individual level. But perversion of the aggressive drive can be scaled and this makes it so dangerous. Separated from its origins in the unconscious, its immense power derives from the proportionality of threat perceived by a helpless infant or child where such threat represents the totality of experience, rather than the partial experience which applies as they mature.

Accordingly, the tendency of a reactivation of old injuries will invariably be disproportionate to the trigger and only makes sense with the perspective of subjectivity in mind. Put in neuroscientific terms, aggression serves the function of protecting the Markov blanket of the self-organising system from entropy. Or a little more strictly, aggression protects the subjectivity of the self-organising system from the perception of threats to equilibrium and entropy. The guardian of equilibrium is essential to the mental apparatus' ability to reregulate both mind and body, but especially the mind's function in the service of the mind-body system. Hence, under the strain of perversion when this mechanism develops a life of its own, separated from its original activation in infancy, this guardian of the peace becomes a weapon of war, the guardian of stasis becomes a tool of retaliation, trading outer destructiveness for inner peace of mind.

At least in theory, this would be its purpose but there is invariably a cost to the perversion of the aggressive drive – internal guilt and evacuation, like a bee that stings and, in the process, eviscerates itself. Or on a grander scale, the loss of life that invariably leads to the aggressors own geopolitical demise. Such is nature's tendency to balance the books in the bigger picture of living life – but this may be little comfort to those who suffer at the hands of aggression whether in the domestic or social space. Understanding the aim of aggression, however, in both the clinical and social space, may edge us closer to entering the unconscious motivators of those who aggress and decode and decipher the underlying unconscious triggers. As we have seen, amidst the myriad of individual complexity and subjectivity, these links are not so mysterious after all, and we may be able to enable healthy aggression in the service of being the guardian of the mind's peace rather than its acceleration into scaled destruction, perverse in its effects and unwanted at the end of the day, by everyone. This exquisite complexity of the mental apparatus is humbling but like many phenomena in science and nature, paradoxes are often evident and counter-intuitive, like the concept of time being relative and space can curve. How strange to think of aggression and destructiveness as originating as the guardian of the peace!

Notes

1 See also the reference to Auret van Heerden, the student leader who sued the Minister of Police for the severe torture he had endured whilst in Security Police detention at around the same time as Dr. Neil Aggett was tortured to death in Security Police custody. In Grant, T. (2022). *The Mandela Brief: Sydney Kentridge and the Trials of Apartheid*, pp. 286–287.

2 Pinker, S. (2011). *The Better Angels of Our Nature: A History of Violence and Humanity*.

3 See https://en.wikipedia.org/wiki/Vladimir_Putin for a more detailed description.

4 See https://en.wikipedia.org/wiki/Vladimir_Putin for a more detailed description and relevant references.

5 "For this other element of the psychical representative the term *quota of affect* has been generally adopted. It corresponds to an instinct in so far as the latter has become

detached from the idea and finds expression, proportionate to its quantity, in processes which are sensed as affects. From this point on, in describing a case of repression, we shall have to follow up separately what, as the result of repression, becomes of the *idea*, and what becomes of the instinctual energy linked to it" (Freud, 1915, Repression, p. 152).

6 Freud, S. (1930). *Civilisation and Its Discontents*, p. 306.

7 Solms, M. (2022). *The Hidden Spring: A Journey to the Source of Consciousness.*

8 Boyce, T. W. (2019). *The Orchid and the Dandelion: Why Some Children Struggle and How All Can Thrive.*

9 As Solms expresses it: "The internal body is not an object of perception unless it is externalised and presented to the classical senses; it is the *subject* of perception. It is the back-ground state of *being* conscious. This is of paramount importance. We may picture this aspect of consciousness as the page upon which external perceptions are inscribed. The relationship between the two aspects of consciousness – the objects and the subject of perception—is also what binds the components of perception together; objects are always perceived by an experiencing subject (cf. the "binding problem")" (Solms, M. (2013). The Conscious Id, p. 12).

10 Nurse, P. (2021). *What Is Life? David Fickling Books*, p. 208.

11 Says Solms, "The internal aspect of consciousness "feels like" something. Above all, the phenomenal states of the body-as-subject are experienced *affectively*. Affects do not emanate from the external sense modalities. They are states *of the subject*. These states are thought to represent the biological value of changing internal conditions (e.g., hunger, sexual arousal). When internal conditions favour survival and reproductive success, they feel "good"; when not, they feel "bad." This is evidently what conscious states are *for*. Conscious feelings tell the subject how well it is doing. At this level of the brain, therefore, consciousness is closely tied to homeostasis."

12 Solms argues: "Emotional or affective representations of experience may be represented to consciousness through higher level cortical structures in the brain, but ultimately, consciousness emerges from internal brain structures that generate sensory experiences of dysregulation. "The classical conception is turned on its head. Consciousness is not generated in the cortex; it is generated in the brainstem. Moreover, consciousness is not inherently perceptual; it is inherently affective. And in its primary manifestations, it has less to do with cognition than with instinct. In terms of the parallels drawn in Section 2, the conclusion is inescapable: *consciousness is generated in the id*, and the ego is fundamentally unconscious. This has massive implications for our conceptualisation of the ego and all that flows from it, such as our theories of psychopathology and clinical technique. It was, after all, the essence of the "talking cure" that words, being ego memory-traces derived from external perception and therefore capable of consciousness, must be attached to the deeper processes of the mind (which are unconscious in themselves) before they can be known by the subject".

13 "The answer to our question, "What does cortex contribute to consciousness?", then, is this: it contributes representational memory space. This enables cortex to *stabilise* the objects of perception, which in turn creates potential for detailed and synchronised processing of perceptual images. This contribution derives from the unrivalled capacity of cortex for *representational* forms of memory (in all of its varieties, both short and long-term). Based on this capacity, cortex transforms the fleeting, wavelike states of brainstem activation into "mental solids." It generates *objects*. Freud called them "object-presentations" (which, ironically, predominate in what he called the "system unconscious")" (Solms, M. (2013). The Conscious Id, p. 12).

14 Solms, M. (2013). The Conscious Id, p. 12.

15 Kandel, E. (2006). *In Search of Memory: The Emergence of a New Science of Mind, Kandel*, (my italics), p. 314.

16 Kandel, E. (2006). *In Search of Memory: The Emergence of a New Science of Mind*, p. 343.
17 Kandel, E. (2006). *In Search of Memory: The Emergence of a New Science of Mind*, p. 344.
18 See https://murderpedia.org/male.B/b/barnett-david.htm for more detail.
19 Hendel, R. "First Murder (Gen 4:1-16)", n.p. [cited 22 April 2022]. Online: https://www.bibleodyssey.org:443/en/passages/main-articles/first-murder.
     (https://www.google.co.za/url?sa=t&rct=j&q=&esrc=s&source=web&cd=&v
     ed=2ahUKEwjPps-9maf3AhVXgFwKHVhfAIUQFnoECCAQAQ&url=https%3
     A%2F%2Fwww.bibleodyssey.org%2Fen%2Fpassages%2Fmain-articles%2Ffirst-
     murder&usg=AOvVaw2l-ONaiamc3LJ2qP8sFwj_).
20 Genesis 4:9.
21 Kandel, E. (2006). *In Search of Memory: The Emergence of a New Science of Mind*, p. 381.
22 Freud, S. (1923). *The Ego and the Id*, p. 355.
23 Freud, S. (1923). *The Ego and the Id*, p. 364.
24 Freud, S. (1923). *The Ego and the Id*, p. 381.
25 Freud, S. (1923). *The Ego and the Id*, p. 382.
26 Connolly, P. (2018). Expected Free Energy Formalises Conflict Underlying Defence in Freudian Psychoanalysis, https://doi.org/10.3389/fpsyg.2018.01264.
27 Connolly, P. (2018). Expected Free Energy Formalises Conflict Underlying Defence in Freudian Psychoanalysis, https://doi.org/10.3389/fpsyg.2018.01264).
28 Freud, S. (1930). *Civilisation and Its Discontents*, pp. 339–340.

Chapter 7

A Unifying Theory – Symptoms and Implications

Unifying the Elements

Einstein made the point that sometimes theoretical development relies on more than a summation of data, like the compilation of a classified catalogue, for this by no means embraces the whole of the actual process; "for it slurs over the important part played by intuition and deductive thought in the development of an exact science".[1] Much of the apparent divergence in scientific thought can often be seen to be different foci explaining the same phenomena from the respective specialisation of that discipline and when examined closely enough there often is no real divergence at all.

Darwin's notion of 'natural selection' reflects on the concept that changes in the conditions of life "give a tendency to increased variability".[2] Where *conditions* have changed, the environment demands adaptation, as this "would manifestly be favourable to natural selection, by affording a better chance of the occurrence of profitable variations".[3] The notion of 'survival of the fittest' (a term used originally not by Darwin but by Herbert Spencer) can create a misconception that evolution appears driven by prowess or strength. But in essence, it describes the balance between conservation and appropriate adaptability – that is, survival reflects the form in which replication is maximised through generations, a strategy of maintaining the Markov blanket that represents a species subjectivity in a vast world. Overzealous organismic adaptability could lead to self-destruction, and over-conservation of the same. Darwin described therefore that under the pressures of environmental change that demands adaptability from the organic, an organism will forgo its conservation priority and adapt in the interests of survival. This is the creative-procreative tendency of all living matter struggling against its own nature to maintain the familiar identity already created, a tension that is never lost through the hierarchy of development and increasing complexity of biological systems. This point is embedded in Darwin's description

> It may metaphorically be said that natural selection is daily and hourly scrutinising, throughout the world, the slightest variations; rejecting those that are bad, preserving those and adding up all those that are good; silently and insensibly

DOI: 10.4324/9781003452522-8

working, *whenever and wherever opportunity offers*, at the improvement of each organic being in relation to its organic and inorganic conditions of life.[4]

Survival of the fittest may therefore be seen as a misnomer, in that brawn is not the determinant of the drive for adaptability in the face of impingements that do not any longer allow for conservation. Rather, the tendency to 'variability' underlies this notion, that when *conditions have changed*, an organism, including primitive ones without any brawn at all, will face the existential dilemma that all living matter faces: conserve your identity against the impingements of life or adapt to them through (creative) change when that fails. The link to Freud's observations of the mental apparatus becomes clearer, that in the complexity of the human mind these two primary drivers of all organic matter, from the most primitive unicellular to the most complex of all, two fundamental drives underpin all existence: the death drive, a conservative drive striving to keep the organisms in a state of constancy and homeostasis, and the life drive (Eros) in which libidinal energy facilitates creative and procreative tendencies that best enable life to survive the endless challenges of living. The paradox of the conservative drive that aims to preserve stasis against the challenges of the environment is that the chief mechanism any organism has for this purpose is its aggressive capability. To the outside observer, aggression is destructive. It causes pain or damage of some sort to another. In humans, this can take emotional or verbal forms but originates from the same source. Aggression is the psyche's immune system, aiming to preserve the subject from dysregulation and entropy through preservation. This is the aim of the aggressive drive. It does not technically seek a fight – it mobilises in response to one perceived as having been already picked.

Freud identified these two fundamental drives underpinning the human psyche – and the tension between these two energetic forces can be seen to underlie organic development from the outset of life. As the biochemists demonstrate, life itself began with these two forces in play, with primitive electron gradients striving to maintain the self-organising system against entropy and under conditions of environmental change and challenge, striving to vary the familiar in order to survive the challenge, "clearly aiming at by every possible means is the coalescence of two germ-cells which are differentiated in a particular way", since if this does not happen, the germ-cell dies along with other elements of the multi-cellular organisms.[5] The two instincts are those which "seek to lead what is living to death, and others, the sexual instincts, which are perpetually attempting to achieve a renewal of life". Freud's *dualistic* model of the instincts, between the life and death instincts, the former seeking the renewal through adaptation or what Darwin termed variability and the latter preservation through the aggressive drive aimed at maintaining stasis.

The Riddle of Life

Freud had argued that his speculations had suggested that Eros appeared as a 'life instinct' in opposition to the 'death instinct' and sought to "solve the riddle of life by supposing that these two instincts were struggling with each other from the very first".[6]

Freud's alluding to his awareness that the complexity of the human brain and its emergent mental apparatus – which neuroscience claims as the adaptably, mechanisms that feelings facilitate in the survival and sustainability of the subject – begins, well, at the very beginning. Even the most primitive of biological systems have in a sense subjectivity, the tendency, nay, the *requirement* to see the world through its own lens, to experience the world through its own senses and do what it can to survive, at both an individual and species level. The individual, of course, increases survival by being a part of a broader collective, biological or ideological. The collective in general prompts an organism into a better state of sustainability – and as Freud points out when germ-cells combine they increase this likelihood: "But the essence of the processes to which sexual life is directed is the coalesce of two cell-bodies. That alone is what guarantees the immortality of the living substance in the higher organisms".[7] The psychoanalytic description of mind contained in Freud's more mature works dovetails well with both Darwinian notions of variability as well as biochemist's such as Lane's mining of the complex origins of life from the primary elements of matter and energy into self-replicating life forms evolving greater and greater unities and complexities, through the passage of immense quanta of time and the challenges of a complex environment demanding adaptation or entropy. These primary notions of duality apply to basic organisms as they do to emergent systems that become infinitely and exquisitely more complex. The human brain, despite being the most complex machine in the universe, does not free itself from these two drivers of life – preservation or entropy, adaptation (or 'variation') or entropy, and the endlessly repetitive cycles of micro- and macro-adjustments required by life for this purpose. The theological account captures these same two tendencies of life, in the form of first nothing (homeostasis), then the creative burst of cosmic development (creation), then the coalescing into self-contained systems requiring self-preservation (aggression) – portending the two most fundamental drivers in cosmic and human history.

The Tapestry of Science and the Mind

The thread that binds different specialised paradigms in science can be observed in both the theory and empirical data. Without attaching any judgement or evaluation to the data, whether sex or aggression is good or bad, we can begin to decode its function in animate matter, life in its simplest forms, and life in its magnificently transcendent complexity. At the pinnacle of this complexity sits the human brain and emergent mental apparatus. Whilst the almost infinite complexity of this body-brain-mind system makes it appear entirely transcendent from the humble origins of electron gradients in deep-water alkaline vents of early cosmic history, the emergence of complexity in higher systems carries inevitably the essential character and energetic trends of these humble origins, which are never entirely lost through

evolution and development. The same applies through human developme·
developmental pressures through the life cycle, where emergent menta!
invariably increasingly complex through time, still retain the essential driving energies that strive to preserve and adapt.

Defensive mechanisms of the mind become recruited as those manoeuvres available to the developing infant-child at the time impingements are experienced and
these may become fixated to give expression to personality as life evolves. Such fixated mechanisms are often adaptive at the time they become dominant, given the
limited options available for both libidinal and aggressive needs, and only become
maladaptive under the influence of the repetition compulsion discussed earlier, plying
their wares, so to speak, in adult life where other healthier options might be available
and prevail. But without the essential instinctual drives within the mental apparatus, life would not be viable. Entropy would ensue without a guardian to conserve
the body-mind system and preserve identity and subjectivity, in terms of physics its
self-organising system identity. It is here that the aims of this aggressive drive often
diverge from its effects, captured in the headline narratives we are plied with daily.

If the origin of aggression could be tracked in a perpetrator's personal history
and subjective experience, we would inevitably see that conservation of the body-
mind system, underpinning later aggressing, and that its aims, if viewed in the
abstract, could be regarded as noble and meritorious. But its perversion in later life
actions leads often to effects that are destructive, damaging, and painful, paradoxically even to the person themselves, to their people, or to humanity. The paradox
that no villain ever takes pride in being the villain in their own story because no
villain sees themselves as the villain in their own story.

How does it possibly serve the interests of infamous Olympic athlete Oscar Pistorius, with the world at his feet in every respect, to shoot his beautiful model girlfriend Reever Forman, knowing full well that spending the next 25 years in a South
African prison cannot be in his interests? The answer is that the part of Pistorius doing the shooting was probably rooted in the primal narcissistic injury of humiliation
and struggle that was likely associated with the amputation of his legs as a young
boy. The re-experiencing of narcissistic injury and consequent rage sprung from
this regressive place psychically, and from this vantage only, the response made
sense. Did Pistorius feel like the villain in his story? Not if his defence in court is
to be believed. Long-term self-harm does not always square with the monumental
heat of the moment in response to perceived injury. Did Germany benefit from their
aggressing during World War II? Or Ted Bundy executed for serial murders? Obviously not – and yet in the service of some perceived injury the individual or the collective end up self-destructing through aggressing, more often than not injuries that
are *felt*. Humiliation, degradation, and frustration often underpin the most heinous
of aggressing, on both the individual and collective geopolitical stage, *feelings* that
have no bearing on physical or even resource threat. It seems so often, that the
most violent of episodes are driven by little other than the subjective feelings of the
perpetrator, perceiving themselves to be the victim in their story.

You and Yours

Think no further than your own relationship. How often do you feel yourself to be the victim and how often the perpetrator in the domestic squabbles and conflicts that pepper every intimate couple? And when you are regretful at having been the perpetrator, how often was that excess driven by feeling hurt and injured?

Cain begins our historical narrative demonstrating these elements of human nature, using the term nature in its most literal sense, for nature must follow the laws it sets for itself across the board including in apparently intangible ways, such as feelings and emotional states. The mental apparatus must be subject to the same laws that governed the origins of life itself and which govern the most primitive of life forms to the present day. The less tangible aspects of higher order functioning – thinking, feeling, perceiving, and the 'hard problem' of consciousness and subjectivity must with enough insight also follow the laws of nature and science, as authors such as Solms point out. In focusing on aggression, this book has aimed to deconstruct in these terms the function of this conservative drive and attempt to make sense of the paradoxical nature of how something so destructive can be driven by something so conservative and preservative. Like many aspects of nature, the deeper we drill, the more paradoxical the findings can be – like time being relative and the fabric of space bendable by gravity.

Subjectivity applies to all living matter, even that which has no transcendent consciousness in the human sense, since all evolution and development must happen, by definition, from the vantage point of the particle or entity doing the perceiving of its place in the environment in which it finds itself. Variability in natural selection, which Darwin described, is supported by the evidence of modern biochemistry which recognises that the ability to be genetically fluid-enabled primitive organisms to invent themselves anew in response to environmental demands early in cosmic evolution, and so procreativity, the extension of cellular systems to combine genetically in order to modify genetic makeup in the service of variability, provides nature's best impetus for survival. The life drive that Freud identified in the human psyche extends this most powerful of drives from the swapping of genetic material to ensure survival of the most basic cellular systems to the infinite and exquisite complexity of the human being. Sexuality extends the early evolutionary imperative to adapt through variation or suffer the real risk of entropy over time as environmental conditions invariably change and challenge the preference all living systems have for homeostasis, as Lane says, "Genes are almost infinitely permissive: anything that can happen will happen".[8]

The energetic trends that Freud identified in the mental apparatus and which so powerfully drives the human spirit, that of Eros and libido, underpin life from the outset, passed from generation to generation through the energetic mitochondria pumps of the cells, from the first stirrings of life four billion years ago in the deep hydrothermal vents of the earth. Lane puts in chemical terms what Freud identified in the death drive that organisms seek to come to rest through their own natural and circuitous path – again, from the outset of life. "If life is nothing but an electron looking for a place to rest, death is nothing but that electron come to rest", says Lane[9] Or, as Freud suggested, "everything living dies for *internal* reasons – becomes inorganic once again – then we shall be compelled to say that '*the aim of all life is death*' and looking backwards, that '*inanimate things existed before living ones*'".[10] In contrast to the life drive and its energetic promptings, are the conservative instincts whose aim is to preserve and assure that any living organisms shall follow its own path to death, and as Freud puts it "to ward off any possible ways of returning to inorganic existence other than those which are immanent in the organism itself".[11]

Humanity and Inhumanity – A Balancing Act

And so we see two grand forces in tension with each other present from the outset of living matter and the transition from the inanimate to the animate. In its most primitive and humble origins of electron gradients driving cellular life differentiating itself through the cell membrane towards the exquisite splendour of multicellular life and the infinite grandeur of the human brain-body-mind system, the underlying energetic tensions remain. Life, even in its grand complexity, never frees itself from these constraints and tensions. Nor does any living thing free itself from the constraints of subjectivity, since without a self-organising system to hold coherent as an identity, entropy would ensue. This too finds its way through life from the earliest and most simple of organisms to the most magnificent and complex. Every living thing must navigate the world though its own lens, protecting its own resource interests, maintaining its identity and internal order, both as an individual and of course as a species whose genetic creativity seems to ensure the best possible chance of achieving a sustained and actualised life path.

The puzzle of human violence and destructiveness appearing to contradict these tenets of science, showing the scalability of genocidal intra-species destructiveness, and that too-worn phrase of 'man's inhumanity to man', as Burns (1787) wrote in his poem, "And man, whose heav'n-erected face, The smiles of love adorn, – Man's inhumanity to man Makes countless thousands mourn!"[12] This is no more prevalent on the geopolitical stage as it is in every domestic context, and especially the marital one. How do we square these contradictions? Human subjectivity works through an emergent mental apparatus that is itself inordinately complex and driven by feeling states which filtered through a capacity to regress, revisit old versions of emotional reality, and amplify reality proportionally to the ability available to combat states of disequilibrium. The infant has few avenues available for remedy, nor experiences their own world through the wisdom of perspective. Rather, any state of discomfort feels total, global, unconstrained, and when these states are prolonged leave the infant mind clinging to memories that are disproportionate – but only from the perspective of the outsider knowing of the remedies available.

For the infant, there is no perspective other than its immediate reality, undifferentiated and intense, prompting an aggressive response that is equally intense and total. When adults revisit such parts of their own minds, a disproportionate response may be triggered, attaching to hot or cold variants of the aggressive system. In this regression, a separation occurs in which a person's destructiveness or hate may seem utterly at odds with objective reality, and likely it is – such perversion underlying and driving it. And left untamed by external reality, such aggressive hubris plays out in both the personal and geopolitical stages to genocidal proportions. But ironically, more often than not, the perpetrator *feels* themselves to be the victim and in accordance with the repetition compulsion principle, often ends up being exactly that: in prison, executed, or a country and culture trashed. Whilst nature, it is said by the evolutionists, abhors a vacuum so too does nature resist imbalance, and cosmic sensibility eventually, it seems, finds a way to restore balance by never allowing any one person or group to expand their dominance beyond a point of endurance. War in both the domestic and geopolitical spaces, perhaps, becomes the mechanism that humans may use to restore balance and prevent one system from enveloping another. The paradox of human destructiveness is how often this drive, in its perverse forms, ends up destroying the perpetrator. The perception of victimhood that drives destructiveness often end up in victimhood, and a self-destructive outcome. Sometimes, this is through self-destructive outcomes, such as suicidality, the internalisation or introjection of the aggressive drive so that instead of the homicidal impulse being expressed, infantile aggression is internalised and channeled against the person's own ego.

Remedy for Destruction

None of this would come as any comfort to anyone who has suffered the effects of aggression's destructive potential. The 'blood that cries out from the soil'[13] cannot be revived and the forward march of time undone. But, on the other hand, if we understand better the deeper generic and personal reasons that make an aggressor aggress, we might be better equipped to shift perceptions of injury when they occur and enable subjectivity to restore itself through the preservative drive in more 'conservative' ways. Perceived threats are often not real threats and this is where the objective and subjective realities diverge. But on the other hand, without understanding the subjective drivers for aggressive enactments, we also fail to remedy them, for perception is everything when subjectivity is the prominent driver.

Sitting as a student with my hands handcuffed behind my back in an interrogation room of the South African Security Police might appear to any objective observer that I was the victim of total control and power, including over my very life and its future. To the subjectivity of my interrogators, neither psychopathic nor truly sadistic I don't believe, they felt they were defending their own existence against severe and sustained existential threat, that I *represented* to them. From *their subjectivity and perspective*, aggressing against me in the service of conservation was not a choice but a requirement to resist cultural and economic entropy. Their identity, their Markov blanket that enabled differentiation of self and other, that which sustains their life drive versus those forces that threaten it, using whatever ideological suppositions were required to do so, pushed the *imperative* to find whatever aggressive means could sustainably be used to prevent entropy of that identity.

I did not like it. It gave me PTSD. And I had many fantasies of finding these men after the Struggle days were over and democracy finally reigned and exacting some revenge for the intimate violence they perpetrated against so many people in their interrogation rooms, an example of how fluid and close the shift from victim to perpetrator invariably is. The State recognised that without adaptation to the intense pressures for change, it would surely perish alongside its identity, culture, and material interests. It was intimate in the interrogation room, close up, breath to breath at times. Body fluids mix in these moments of violent intimacy, sweat, spit, blood, mucous, and yet it is simultaneously so utterly impersonal. A job that requires violence to get done. Ironically, on one drive from my prison cell to their interrogation headquarters we stopped at a traffic light in the middle of Johannesburg at 8 am rush hour. And just for a moment, we three men in a car shared the visual delights of an attractive woman walking across the road, a different identity binding us for a moment before the call of duty and its business divided us once again into different identities – the guardians of the peace against the forces of revolution arraigned against it.

South Africa and Its Revolution: Adapt or Die

When pressures mounted to unsustainable levels from both outside and within the country, Prime Minister PW Botha famously noted, "We must adapt or die". Adapt or die became, in fact, one of the motifs for marketing a new plan of the *verligte* (liberal) shifting from the *verkrampte* (conservative), liberalisation, and power-sharing to prevent revolution. From the humble origins of this imperative faced by the simple bacterium or cell in pre-historic times billions of years before in evolution, these complex demands for a collective of individuals facing the existential dilemma of adapt or die, adaptation became, ultimately, the only sane course to consider. But before this 'evolutionary' imperative took hold, under the intense pressures of the environment, the first port of call was conservation for homeostasis. Maintain homeostasis against the impingements upon their subjectivity, employing more and more aggression for this purpose, both by the individual and State, or eventually adapt to create a new identity in which survival is better enabled. The effects of these processes are that aggression became perverted, as aggression removed from its unconscious sources often does, creating terribly destructive effects in its wake, but which in the wisdom of life's Creator, as Darwin noted, starts out with every good intention: to protect and preserve the individual organism and its collection into what Freud called greater and greater unities, against the threats of entropy or to adapt through natural selection and find new forms to the self-regulating system and its identity.

The Victim Behind the Perpetrator

None of us escape these conflicts, and every intimate relationship struggles with perceptions and experiences of hurt leading to anger and hate against the one that was originally so beloved. Marriage and family life presents a cauldron for these ambivalences and contradictions and every couple I have ever seen in the consulting room experience themselves to be the injured party, and the other the aggressor. No-one truly experiences themselves to be the perpetrator, everyone the victim. Such remain the challenges of living and loving – for as soon as we love we invite into the interpersonal space a cauldron of projections and expectations, readying for failure as the ascendance of the libidinal elements wane over time, as wane they must, and with it feelings of betrayal and dejection, loss, and disappointment. It is perhaps no wonder that no matter what the content of the conflict in marriage, there it will always be, a manifest expression in the complexity of the interpersonal between Eros and conservation, psychic immunity against the pathogenic triggers of the other's slights and hurts. And no wonder with these contradictory and simultaneously complimentary tensions of life people aggress against people – in love, in hate, individual, and in groups. We can mitigate these enactments of aggression by understanding what drives them, and when we are able to tap into the core experience of injury, just perhaps the next conflagration be it in the home or geopolitical stage could be prevented. Perceptions are, after all, subjective experiences held in memory and hence also malleable, amenable to modification and change. This, perhaps, is the lesson of evolution too – that we all can evolve towards better versions of ourselves, adapting, striving for variation, and in working through achieving better outcomes for living. There are those who suggest that what is past has passed, and that the past cannot be changed. One hears this lament often in the treatment rooms of psychotherapists. But the psychological and neurobiological reality is that the past is invariably in the present, and that making it conscious removes those influences that create automatons of behaviour out of us and instead creates agency. For when we resolve these hidden influences, they no longer hijack the present and free us from old constraints to live better lives and make better choices. And maybe also, enactments of personal conflicts and social violence would diminish.

Loss and Aggression

We have hopefully done the theoretical heavy lifting above and in heading towards the ending of this book, I wish to allow the reader to cruise to the finish line by pointing out some of the implications of these insights. In psychotherapeutic treatment, as in life more generally, two great themes appear to distill much of what psychologists deal with: namely, *loss* and *longing*. Distilling to the essence so much of what ails us in living brings us to these two themes. The trauma of actual lost objects, attachments that have had meaning in a person's life, or their potential. Lost promises of a future, breakups representing lost potential, loss of meaning and control over one's life and destiny. Loss, also, of a sense of self, esteem, purpose.

There are the longings, unmet needs that persist as needs must, rooted in the libidinal drive that prompts for fulfilment, the unrequited love, loneliness, sense of purpose, and belonging. All promptings to serve the life drive and enable survival and sustenance through having biological needs met, surviving the natural course of the life cycle in as pain-free way as possible. These two themes of many presenting problems and many interventions are only half of the story, despite often occupying the lion's share of the psychotherapeutic work. Behind loss and longings are invariably frustrations and states of disequilibrium – and technically, as now hopefully recognised – states of disequilibrium will invariably prompt the aggressive drive to mobilise in the service of restoration of homeostasis.

But this aspect of the human psychic response is often under-recognised in treatment. That aggression and its pathway will inevitably also require attention. Psychopathology and psychological symptoms are usually driven not by the pain of loss and longing but by the aggressive response triggered by these failures of stasis, and the defensive manoeuvres each individual mounts against this response. Understanding aggressive promptings in the unconscious and where these get stuck remains a key imperative for treating the presenting difficulties in the mental health space. The emphasis on empathy, or what some clinicians refer unkindly to the 'nod and cluck' approaches to dealing with patient's feelings, does not always get to the heart of the matter. Invariably in treatment the initial positive relationship with the clinician changes, and noted Freud, "such fine weather cannot last forever. One day it clouds over",[14] a recognition of the emergence of the resistances and aggressions that underlie unconscious process and which emerges in the transference of the therapeutic relationship. Since when we register pain and loss, or the frustrations of longings unmet, we get resentful and angry and feel hate towards objects, both familiar and unfamiliar. If a stranger stimulates desire in someone, just because they are noticed as attractive, but they are simultaneously unavailable, a state of desire and simultaneous frustration may trigger feelings of anger. Loss and longing are never held in a vacuum since these failures invariably are triggers for states of psychic disequilibrium, some minor and fleeting and some persistent and embedded. Loss and longing invariably lead to some underlying, albeit aggressive response aimed at psychic restoration. Most psychopathology can be understood as disorders of this response mechanism, aggression inadequately metabolised through different developmental stages, fixed there, and to which the individual mind returns repeatedly in its attempts to restore stasis and survive another moment. Sometimes, surviving that other (psychological) moment leads to self-immolation in the real world. The restorative drive improperly metabolised invariably leads to some sort of psychological, physiological, interpersonal, or group consequence – a form of entropy that reflects the improper balancing of the conservative drive tensions against the life drive.

Why Symptoms

In my view, Freud's emphasis on sexuality may have missed some of the implications of his own formidable discoveries – and the evidence that seems to foreground the conservative drive in the genesis of psychopathology and psychological symptoms. The fulfilment of frustration of the sexual adaptive drive leads to psychopathology because its frustration activates the aggressive drive aimed at recognizing deviations from, and restoring stasis. This secondary effect is where psychological symptoms become manifest, not by the sexual drive itself but the unconscious associations that are triggered – loss, rage, frustrated oedipal longings, and debasement of the object as a defence against these feelings. People do not develop symptoms because they have longings – they develop them because those longings get frustrated and trigger the aggressive response that cannot always manifest in a way that enables its metabolising. The impairment of this metabolic function for developmental and defensive reasons underpins the emergence of symptoms, which we end up treating in consulting rooms. Where we treat depression, for example, as the patient being the victim, we neglect the internal mechanisms that depression is a result of introjected aggression, anger and hate turned in, the perpetrator struggling to own feelings of hostility and hate. Trevor Lubbe, a psychoanalytical clinician and theorist, makes the point in his work on depression that what he terms the "conflict of ambivalence – the clash of the opposing attitudes of love and hate towards the same object"[15] leads to impoverishment of the ego, via a self-attacking process which Freud identified as an effect of loss, or what Freud described as the ego divided, "fallen apart into two pieces, one of which rages against the second".[16] This loss is only felt as strongly because there is first and foremost an over-investment in the love object before loss of that object can be felt. The problem in treating depression is not only the loss – it's the rage response and hate triggered by the loss that takes on etiological significance in the dynamic of depression.

States of anxiety are another example. Anxiety is not a primary diagnosis – it is what Freud considered a 'signal state',[17] much like being pyrexial is not a primary diagnosis but a reflection of some deeper state of infection or illness. Or pain is not a diagnosis in itself, but a signal of some deeper pathology or physiological disruption. When the aggressive drive is mobilised but cannot manifest in an effective way, sometimes for internal albeit unconscious reasons (what we may call 'neurotic anxiety') and sometimes due to external threat (what we may call 'objective anxiety') it comes to represent a threat to the ego functioning effectively.[18] When the individual defences start to fail under the pressures of psychological life, and the aggressive elements threaten to 'break through' into consciousness, panic disorder or other forms of anxiety may manifest. Or another example being PTSD which represents the simultaneous massive mobilisation and immobilisation of a powerful aggressive drive in response to existential threat being unable to manifest. Under conditions of such severe threat against which mobilisation of an aggressive response is impossible, for example being hijacked at gunpoint, induces a later cascade of symptoms consistent with a massive upsurge in an aggressive response entirely paralysed by the initial situation. The difference in perception of the gun being real or being a toy would significantly impact the capacity to mobilise a response and hence mitigate future sequelae.

These are merely a few conceptual examples and the topic for another book – but same applies across most psychopathology and its symptoms presenting for treatment, from eating disorders to depression and anxiety to sexual dysfunction.

Symptoms are representations of the form and pathways in which the aggressive drive can mobilise or remain immobilised through the various individual defensive layers from early development. Treatment that does not address the 'perpetrator within', and stays on the track of empathic collusions with the victim in the patient, will often tend to be prolonged and sometimes ineffective for positive outcomes.

Stress and the Agent Provocateur

We use the term 'stress' liberally to cover all manner of malady. The term is broad and descriptive – but does little to explain the pathways that manifest in an individual when stress is present. Stress really refers to states of disequilibrium, a felt sense of un-ease and heightened arousal. Impingements in life's demands and frustrations induce a stress response, the cascade of which can be experienced in the form of psychological or often physical symptoms. Perceptions of heightened arousal captures the underlying state of disequilibrium being induced by feelings of helplessness and activation that require remedy, an internalising of a locus of control to mediate the arousal response. Filtered through the individual's defensive system, these states of disequilibrium, if prolonged and unmanaged, can lead to a cascade of stress hormones and physiological arousal, turning over time into mental symptoms that trigger anxiety, depression, burnout, insomnia, and so on. In turn, such mental arousal triggers a neurophysiological cascade of arousal which can lead to psychological and somatic symptoms. A person's history in relation to how they manage this response of the aggressive drive will influence the path these responses take and the effects they have. But the stress is merely a trigger for these cascade effects, an *agent provocateur* that aims to induce a restorative response, a return to stasis. Problems to not emerge from the stress itself, they emerge from the response within the individual's personal psychology and how this drive is manifest.

Couple Relations and the Uninvited Guest

These individual pathways scale up in relation to others. In couples and couple treatment, this applies in a form we can all recognise since we all universally struggle in relationships, particularly intimate ones. Disequilibrium and conflict is intrinsic to the nature and structure of coupling. The problems we encounter in relationships and relationship treatments are not the failures of loss and longing per se, but the hurt-anger response these trigger and the difficulties many people have then with how to metabolise these feels of anger, hate, and resentment. It is a principle of coupling that what initially attracts later repels. Couples come to grief because the gradual withdrawal of positive projections and the increase in negative ones lead to relationship trouble that cannot be avoided – it can only be managed and processed to the best possible outcome. This may sound pessimistic as a view of relationships, but it is no more so than the challenges of life more generally, that we constantly struggle against its impingements and challenges, deftly balancing the demands of familiarity and stasis with the energetic push of creative adaptability and engagement.

There is, fortunately or not, no end-state of happiness, no matter what the self-help articles in magazines promise. Life remains always a struggle, because outside the alkaline vents that might have been home for 2 billion years if the evolutionists and biochemists are to be believed, nothing remains static in the environment. Introducing mobility into life adds enormous complexity for an ability to adapt. It is like flying an aeroplane rather than driving a car. A car operates in two dimensions but an aeroplane in three dimensions. The moment the mechanical body becomes airborne, so increases exponentially the complexity of motion. Mobility in life makes enormous demands to be able to read and respond, resist, and evolve *in balance*. Biological and psychological mobility makes for an ever-changing environment and adds complexity to the capacity humans ultimately need to navigate the intricate complexity of an ever-changing biological and emotional environment. Being part of a couple invites significant emotional complexity too, a relationship being more than the sum of its parts. The emergent properties of coupling create complexity that is exponential and which develops a life of its own.

Couples come to grief because the failures of expectation, hope, projective withdrawal, and disappointment lead to hurt and frustration of course, but the anger this triggers is where relationship failure occurs. As the well-known psychoanalytic couple therapist from the United Kingdom, James Fisher[19] reminds the reader in his book *The Uninvited Guest*, the conundrum of relatedness is that marriage is a state of relating that can tolerate the tensions of the oscillation between oneness and separation, and the narcissistic injury that results when this fusion and de-fusion of oneness leads to pain and grief. Or, more accurately, the failure of the metabolic function for an evoked aggressive response when there is injury, loss, and hurt is what threatens the couple with developmental entropy. As Freud wrote in 1930, "It is that we are never so defenceless against suffering as when we love, never so helplessly unhappy as when we have lost our loved object or its love".[20] Since disappointment is endemic in relationships, not only when there are failures of attunement and the consequent hurts but also because as the libidinal ascendance of the early flushes of romance bump up again the reality of another person and their limitations, developmental disillusionment itself leads to a challenge to stasis and equilibrium. And with these experiences over time, all manner of positive projection that characterising the beginning stages of love are exchanged for all manner of negative projections as hate seeds itself like weeds in a beautiful garden and begins to outgrow the flowers and suffocate them. As Fisher described it, the "shared defence against the agony of the beauty that was found originally in the loved one"[21] and the intolerability of the loss of the original love object and its projection in the adult other. Loss and disillusionment are endemic to meaningful relationships and so weeds invariably grow where nothing but beauty seemed to be in the early flushes of romance. Where the garden is regularly weeded, the emotional metabolic function is utilised healthily, then equilibrium can limp along throughout the life cycle and retain enough of the good stuff to keep love alive and buoyant.

Where Psychotherapy Can Fail

Whilst as mentioned, these issues are topics for another book and require a much more thorough treatment – the psychology of relationships and couples and the function of aggression in the genesis of psychopathology and symptoms is often under-represented by clinicians. It is important I think to mention how traditional psychology has tended to emphasise the issues of loss and longing without paying adequate attention to the central function the aggressive drive plays in most psychopathology and relationship failures. Empathic attunement is the hallmark of almost all therapeutic work, but many simultaneously suffer from technical limitations in their tendency towards 'empathic collusions' with the suffering of patients in their life experience, particularly their childhood injuries that are so central to their adult problems. Empathic collusion means inadequately addressing the drive mobilisation patients have to parental and sibling failures and hurts in childhood, for these must invariably also be accompanied by an activation of the aggressive drive for the reasons we have traversed above. This suggests that where there are injuries there *must* be mobilisation of the conservative drive to these subjective and perceived injuries and this response requires therapeutic focus. These fixations and diversions of this drive lie at the (real) root of psychological symptoms and psychopathology. Freud's emphasis on sexuality is not always sufficiently recognised by clinicians as only being a problem in the genesis of mental symptoms because of the *frustration* of these urges and longings, and where there is frustration, there is a challenge to equilibrium. This will invariably activate the aggressive 'immune' response in the mental apparatus – and what happens to this response is what determines whether and in what form symptoms may occur. Treatment often focuses on the victim within and misses often the 'perpetrator' within.

Where the aggressive drive goes, so therein lies the solution to many of the psychological problems that present to us in life. Of course, where these 'blockages' occur, and why they do, is no simple matter. Developmental pathways determine where fixations occur and why this drive has become stuck in some or other form that over time no longer benefits the psychic functioning of that individual. The details of this I hope to deal with elsewhere – but suffice to consider that our subjective experiences of navigating life's demands and complexities are never free of these two great themes – and our feelings represent to us when these are present or frustrated, fulfilled or failed. We get angry because we get frustrated and hurt and mostly, we manage to metabolise the anger that results. But sometimes, in minor and major ways, this response becomes separated from its underlying reasons for being activated and instead are turned into perversions of the drive, always beginning in infancy and the foundational mental experiences of psychic life.

What begins as a protective mechanism to maintain psychic homeostasis ends up in a perverse loop, aggression at others that are perceived through projection to be the source of risk to one's own subjectivity, the internal self-identity that creates a sense of cohesion in the world. The guardian of the self now becomes a perverted guardian, and in its wake all manner of psychopathology and interpersonal strife can manifest.

Symptoms are messengers, signalling deeper challenges to stasis and longevity. When we are pressed beyond healthy parameters particular to each individual, the aggressive drive is activated and how this manifests will determine whether it achieves its aim of restoration or tilts over into symptoms or enactments. There is no end-state for stasis or happiness nor any 12 rules to fulfil such a wish, at least not whilst we yet live. For as surely as we meet one need another manifests and makes its presence felt. Feelings are exquisite and complex and delicately balanced and often pull in diverging directions but they are also pesky visitors that come and go at their own initiative, seeking neither invite nor permission to enter the mind. And so, as humans we are doomed to grapple with the gyrations of living and the oscillations of life's gains and losses throughout the life cycle, each moment of fulfilment bringing in its wake its opposite, finding consistent rest and quietude only once our last breath is breathed.

Notes

1   Einstein, A. (1995). *Relativity*, p. 123.
2   Darwin, C. (2003). *The Origin of Species*, p. 90.
3   Darwin, C. (2003). *The Origin of Species*, p. 90.
4   Darwin, C. (2003). *The Origin of Species*, pp. 91–92.
5   Freud, S. (1920). *Beyond the Pleasure Principle*, p. 316.
6   "Our speculations have suggested that Eros operates from the beginning of life and appears as a 'life instinct' in opposition to the 'death instinct' which was brought into being by the coming to life of inorganic substance. These speculations seek to solve the riddle of life by supposing that these two instincts were struggling with each other from the very first" (p. 334).
7   Freud, S. (1920). *Beyond the Pleasure Principle*, p. 329.
8   Lane, N. (2016). *The Vital Question: Why Is Life the Way It Is?*, p. 289.
9   Lane, N. (2016). *The Vital Question: Why Is Life the Way It Is?*, p. 290.
10 Freud, S. (1920). *Beyond the Pleasure Principle*, p. 311.
11 Freud, S. (1920). *Beyond the Pleasure Principle*, p. 311.
12 Burns, R (1786). *Poems, Chiefly in the Scottish Dialect* (First ed.). Kilmarnock. Retrieved from internet archive, see https://en.wikipedia.org/wiki/Poems,_Chiefly_in_the_Scottish_Dialect#cite_note-1
13 Genesis 4:10
14 Freud, S. (1917). *Introductory Lectures*, p. 440.
15 Lubbe, T. (2011). *Object Relations in Depression: A Return to Theory*, p. 14.
16 Freud, S. (1921). *Group Psychology and the Analysis of the Ego*, p. 139.
17 See Freud's writings on anxiety, such as Freud, S. (1917). Anxiety, pp. 440–461; Freud, S. (1926). Inhibitions, Symptoms and Anxiety, pp. 82–83; Freud, S. (1933). Anxiety and Instinctual Life, pp. 113–144.
18 Incidentally, Freud noted that there was not one root to anxiety – anxiety may manifest in response to real threat ('objective anxiety'), anxiety die to the threat of individual unconscious material breaking through the defences ('neurotic anxiety'), and anxiety derived from internal superego attacks ('super-ego anxiety'). See Freud (1926), Inhibitions, Symptoms and Anxiety and also his (1933) *New Introductory Lectures on Psychoanalysis* for discussions on the subject.
19 Fisher, J. (1999). *The Uninvited Guest*.
20 Freud, S. (1930). *Civilisation and Its Discontents*, p. 82.
21 Fisher, J. (1999). *The Uninvited Guest*, p. 187.

Chapter 8

Concluding Comments

Healthy for
Freud practitioners

We need not shy away from recognising and understanding the positive and essential role the conservative drive, the death drive, plays in psychic life. Some of the discoveries we make in science are not pretty or good or desired. But if we fail to understand them, so much worse off our treatment of individual patients with symptoms, or of humanity as a whole becomes, and if we privilege denial, ignorance, or disavowal of the unpalatable, we denude our ability to trend towards the betterment of life on our little blue marble.

Aggression is not nice, any more than is polio or sepsis. But without the germ theory of disease, we cure nothing and suffer that much more. In its technical and pure form, the conservative drive is the guardian of the psyche, its immune system, and of the mind-body system also, and relies on being addressed for the treatment of symptoms or of systems to be effective. For often, it is this drive that leads to symptoms and enactments when improperly metabolised. And inadequately metabolised, perversions of this aggressive drive arise in the many awful manifestations we experience or read about every day or through our own individual symptoms and suffering or relationship conflicts and failures, these invariably led by the hurts and perceptions of injury that our subjectivity dictates, based on our history and our expectations and projections. But through a proper technical understanding of these mechanisms, we may yet be able to mitigate the destructive effects of the drive and instead enable its protective aims to foreground. Then it does us well, like our immune systems do us well when properly in balance, and we can reduce the individual's mental suffering that arise through symptoms, syndromes, and interpersonal conflict and strife. But also, it can mitigate the carnage of relationship conflicts and failures, family breakups and breakdowns, and intergroup conflicts, whether local and small or international and geopolitical, through putting in perspective the perceptions of victimhood behind the violence of the aggressor.

There are those who consider human life to be insignificant in the broader context of the cosmos. Or at best, regard an individual life after this fashion. Stephen Hawking, the famous cosmologist and physicist, debilitated by motor neurone disease, apparently expressed this view:

> The human race is just a chemical scum on a moderate-sized planet, orbiting around a very average star in the outer suburb of one among a hundred billion

DOI: 10.4324/9781003452522-9

galaxies. We are so insignificant that I can't believe the whole universe exists for our benefit. That would be like saying that you would disappear if I closed my eyes.[1]

But then again, Hawking may have missed the paradox of his own statement, his own particular contribution to knowledge, and in fact his own uniqueness as an unusual and distinct human like no other. This debate as to the significance and value of individual life depends on how one defines value. If value is a measure of rarity or scarcity, then Hawking is not correct, and our little blue planet may be argued, as many cosmologists do, to be exceedingly rare and finely tuned like no other for the genesis of living matter. But even more importantly, if the science and neuroscience of *subjectivity* is correct, then we can also note that there simply is not anywhere in the explored universe, and never can be, any individual subjectivity in duplicate. One subjectivity, that is, each individual human, is thus perfectly unique in all the matter of the universe, perfectly rare we might say, and thus may be regarded as holding infinite value and being infinitely precious.

So whilst we live, and as long as we choose life, then it behooves us to lend an ear to the philosophers and theologians that as life and death has been set before us, the blessings and the curses, we might choose life so that humanity proceeds through the generations.[2] Hence, in choosing life we choose the bitter-sweet of loves and losses, longings and disappointments, and the aggressive responses that are activated, and the angry feelings we get; so long as we process them, we grow, using it like fertiliser in the garden, and find fulfilment that is good enough without becoming struck by perversions that damage and destroy and denude the richness of living life, then we choose well. The tension between adaptation and conservation cannot end, since life is premised on this struggle. But in balance, and navigated fluidly, fixations from one's past resolved, life remains intricate, exquisitely complex, and a beautiful journey whose ultimate purpose only the philosophers and theologians can determine.

Notes

1 From an interview with Ken Campbell on Reality on the Rocks: Beyond Our Ken, 1995.
2 As mentioned in Deuteronomy: "I call heaven and earth to record this day against you, that I have set before you life and death, blessing and cursing: therefore choose life, that both thou and thy seed may live."

Appendix A

Minutes of the Wannsee Conference 1942

"Under proper guidance the Jews are now to be allocated for labor to the East in the course of the final solution. Able-bodied Jews will be taken in large labor columns to these districts for work on roads, separated according to sexes, in the course of which action a great part will undoubtedly be eliminated by natural causes.

The possible final remnant will, as it must undoubtedly consist of the toughest, have to be treated accordingly, as it is the product of natural selection, and would, if liberated, act as a bud cell of a Jewish reconstruction (see historical experience).

In the course of the practical execution of this final settlement of the problem, Europe will be cleaned up from the West to the East. Germany proper, including the protectorate Bohemia and Moravia, will have to be handled first because of reasons of housing and other social-political necessities.

The evacuated Jews will first be sent, group by group, into so-called transit-ghettos from which they will be taken to the East.

SS-Obergruppenfuehrer HEYDRICH went on to say that an important provision for the evacuation as such is the exact definition of the group of persons concerned in the matter.

It is intended not to evacuate Jews of more than 65 years of age but to send them to an old-age-ghetto – Theresienstadt is being considered for this purpose.

Next to these age-groups – of the 280,000 Jews still in Germany proper and Austria on 31 October 1941, approximately 30% are over 65; Jews disabled on active duty and Jews with war decorations (Iron Cross I) will be accepted in the Jewish old-age-ghettos.

Through such expedient solution the numerous interventions will be eliminated with one blow.

The carrying out of each single evacuation project of a larger extent will start at a time to be determined chiefly by the military development. Regarding the handling of the final solution in the European territories occupied and influenced by us it was suggested that the competent officials of the Foreign Office working on these questions confer with the competent "Referenten" from the Security Police and the SD.

In Slovakia and Croatia the difficulties arising from this question have been considerably reduced, as the most essential problems in this field have already been brought near to a solution. In Rumania the Government in the meantime has also appointed a commissioner for Jewish questions. In order to settle the question in Hungary it is imperative that an <u>adviser in Jewish questions be pressed upon the Hungarian government without too much delay.</u>

As regards the taking of preparatory steps to settle the question in Italy SS-Obergruppenfuehrer HEYDRICH considers it opportune to contact the chief of the police with a view to these problems.

In the occupied and unoccupied parts of France the registration of the Jews for evacuation can in all probability be expected to take place without great difficulties.

Assistant Under Secretary of State LUTHER in this connection calls attention to the fact that in some countries, such as the Scandinavian states, difficulties will arise if these problems are dealt with thoroughly and that it will be therefore advisable to defer action in these countries. Besides, considering the small numbers of Jews to be evacuated from these countries this deferment means not essential limitation.

On the other hand, the Foreign Office anticipates no great difficulties as far as the South-East and the West of Europe are concerned.

SS-Gruppenfuehrer HOFMANN intends to send an official from the Main Race and Settlement Office to Hungary for general orientation at the time when the first active steps to bring up the question in this country will be taken by the Chief of the Security Police and the SD. It was determined officially to detail this official, who is not supposed to work actively, temporarily from the Main Race and Settlement Office as assistant to the police attache."

1) Treatment of Persons of Mixed Blood of the first Degree.

Persons of mixed blood of the first degree will, as regards the final solution of the Jewish question, be treated as Jews.

From this treatment the following persons will be exempt:

a Persons of mixed blood of the first degree married to persons of German blood if their marriage has resulted in children (persons of mixed blood of the second degree). Such persons of mixed blood of the second degree are to be treated essentially as Germans.

b Persons of mixed blood of the first degree to whom up till now in any sphere of life whatsoever exemption licenses have been issued by the highest Party or State authorities.

Each individual case must be examined, in which process it will still be possible that a decision unfavorable to the persons of mixed blood can be passed.

In any such case only <u>personal</u> essential merit of the person of mixed blood must be deemed a ground justifying the granting of an exemption. (Net merits of the parent or of the partner of German blood.)

Any person of mixed blood of the first degree to whom exemption from the evacuation is granted will be sterilised – in order to eliminate the possibility of offspring and to secure a final solution of the problem presented by the persons of mixed blood. The sterilisation will take place on a voluntary basis. But it will be conditional to a permission to stay in the Reich. Following the sterilisations the "person of mixed blood" will be liberated from all restrictive regulations which have so far been imposed upon him.

2) Treatment of Persons of Mixed Blood of the Second Degree.

Persons of mixed blood of the second degree will fundamentally be treated as persons of German blood, with exception of the following cases in which persons of mixed blood of the second degree will be treated as Jews:

a   The person of mixed blood of the second degree is the result of a marriage where both parents are persons of mixed blood.
b   The general appearance of the person of mixed blood of the second degree is racially particularly objectionable so that he already outwardly must be included among the Jews.
c   The person of mixed blood of the second degree has a particularly bad police and political record sufficient to reveal that he feels and behaves like a Jew.

But also in these cases exceptions are not to be made if the person of mixed blood of the second degree is married to a person of German blood..."

"6) Marriages between Persons of Mixed Blood of the First Degree and Persons of Mixed Blood of the Second Degree.

Both partners will be evacuated, regardless of whether or not they have children, or committed to a ghetto for old Jews, since as a rule these children will racially reveal the ad-mixture of Jewish blood more strongly than persons of mixed blood of the second degree.

SS-Gruppenfuehrer HOFMANN advocates the opinion that sterilisation must be applied on a large scale; in particular as the person of mixed blood placed before the alternative as whether to be evacuated or to be sterilised, would rather submit to the sterilisation.

Under Secretary of State Dr. STUCKART maintains that the possible solutions enumerated above for a clarification of the problems presented by mixed marriages and by persons of mixed blood when translated into practice in this form would involve endless administrative work. In the second place, as the biological facts cannot be disregarded in any case, it was suggested by Dr. STUCKART to proceed to forced sterilisation..."

Under Secretary of State Dr. BUEHLER stated that it would be welcomed by the Government General if the implementation of the final solution of this question could start in the Government General, because the transportation problem there was of no predominant importance and the progress of this action would not be hampered by considerations connected with the supply of labor. The Jews had to be removed as quickly as possible from the territory of the Government General because especially there the Jews represented an immense danger as a carrier of epidemics, and on the other hand were permanently contributing to the disorganisation of the economic system of the country through black market operations. Moreover, out of the two and a half million Jews to be affected, the majority of cases was <u>unfit for work</u>.

Under Secretary of State BUEHLER further stated that the solution of the Jewish question in the Government General as far as the issuing of orders was concerned was dependent upon the chief of the Security Police and the SD, his work being supported by the administrative authorities of the Government General. He had this one request only, namely that the Jewish question in this territory be solved as quickly as possible.

Towards the end of the conference the various types of possible solutions were discussed; in the course of this discussion Gauleiter Dr. MEYER as well as Under Secretary of State Dr. BUEHLER advocated the view that certain preparatory measures incidental to the carrying out of the final solution ought to be initiated immediately in the very territories under discussion, in which process, however, alarming the population must be avoided.

With the request to the persons present from the Chief of the Security Police and the SD that they lend him appropriate assistance in the carrying out of the tasks involved in the solution, the conference was adjourned."

Appendix B

President Vladimir Putin's Speech to His People 2022 – (with Commentary Added through the Text)

Citizens of Russia, friends,
I consider it necessary today to speak again about the tragic events in Donbass and the key aspects of ensuring the security of Russia.

I will begin with what I said in my address on February 21, 2022. I spoke about our biggest concerns and worries, and about the fundamental threats which irresponsible Western politicians created for Russia consistently, rudely and unceremoniously from year to year. I am referring to the eastward expansion of NATO, which is moving its military infrastructure ever closer to the Russian border.

It is a fact that over the past 30 years we have been patiently trying to come to an agreement with the leading NATO countries regarding the principles of equal and indivisible security in Europe. In response to our proposals, we invariably faced either cynical deception and lies or attempts at pressure and blackmail, while the North Atlantic alliance continued to expand despite our protests and concerns. Its military machine is moving and, as I said, is approaching our very border.

Ukraine is not under threat from Russia – Russia is under threat from Ukraine. Russia has 146 million citizens and a massive military capacity, including a wide arsenal of nuclear weapons that it is now threatening to use. Ukraine has 41 million citizens, no nuclear weapons or any military even remotely close to that of Russia.

Putin continues:

Why is this happening? Where did this insolent manner of talking down from the height of their exceptionalism, infallibility and all-permissiveness come from? What is the explanation for this contemptuous and disdainful attitude to our interests and absolutely legitimate demands?

The answer is simple. Everything is clear and obvious. In the late 1980s, the Soviet Union grew weaker and subsequently broke apart. That experience should serve as a good lesson for us, because it has shown us that the paralysis of power and will is the first step towards complete degradation and oblivion.

We lost confidence for only one moment, but it was enough to disrupt the balance of forces in the world.

Interestingly – the Soviet Union became weak and in its degradation of power, says Putin, the former glorious strength and dignity of this superpower has become lost and it is a country and a proud people *threatened with extinction!*

As a result, the old treaties and agreements are no longer effective. Entreaties and requests do not help. Anything that does not suit the dominant state, the powers that be, is denounced as archaic, obsolete and useless. At the same time, everything it regards as useful is presented as the ultimate truth and forced on others regardless of the cost, abusively and by any means available. Those who refuse to comply are subjected to strong-arm tactics.

Russia is being bullied geopolitically. Is being subjugated. Forced increasingly into a state of vulnerability. The weak victim has to fight back to restore its geopolitical pride of place or it will perish. Putin goes on to substantiate his existential apprehension with the 'evidence' at hand:

What I am saying now does not concerns only Russia, and Russia is not the only country that is worried about this. This has to do with the entire system of international relations, and sometimes even US allies. The collapse of the Soviet Union led to a redivision of the world, and the norms of international law that developed by that time – and the most important of them, the fundamental norms that were adopted following WWII and largely formalised its outcome – came in the way of those who declared themselves the winners of the Cold War.
Of course, practice, international relations and the rules regulating them had to take into account the changes that took place in the world and in the balance of forces. However, this should have been done professionally, smoothly, patiently, and with due regard and respect for the interests of all states and one's own responsibility. Instead, we saw a state of euphoria created by the feeling of absolute superiority, a kind of modern absolutism, coupled with the low cultural standards and arrogance of those who formulated and pushed through decisions that suited only themselves. The situation took a different turn.

Perception of a conspiracy of hegemonic imperialism, unrestrained by international norms and laws, indicates for Putin that this trend is imperilling the Motherland too. Many different examples of apparently imperialist war, each one with their own complexity and reasons, are lumped together in a shopping list of one single concept – there is a Them and there is an Us. This binary polarisation is present in many examples of individual and geopolitical aggression, and enables the aggressor to position themselves as warding off a threat to its existence. The Goliath is now the David, surrounded by enemies bent on existential challenge to the threatened entity. Note that like when the ancient Cain killed Abel because of his *feelings*, Putin refers repeatedly to pride, dignity, and feelings of humiliation. *Feelings!* Feelings justifying the escalation of a world war. Lumping many diverse and distinct historical events and conflicts, Putin goes on:

> There are many examples of this. First a bloody military operation was waged against Belgrade, without the UN Security Council's sanction but with combat aircraft and missiles used in the heart of Europe. The bombing of peaceful cities and vital infrastructure went on for several weeks. I have to recall these facts, because some Western colleagues prefer to forget them, and when we mentioned the event, they prefer to avoid speaking about international law, instead emphasising the circumstances which they interpret as they think necessary.
>
> Then came the turn of Iraq, Libya and Syria. The illegal use of military power against Libya and the distortion of all the UN Security Council decisions on Libya ruined the state, created a huge seat of international terrorism, and pushed the country towards a humanitarian catastrophe, into the vortex of a civil war, which has continued there for years. The tragedy, which was created for hundreds of thousands and even millions of people not only in Libya but in the whole region, has led to a large-scale exodus from the Middle East and North Africa to Europe.
>
> A similar fate was also prepared for Syria. The combat operations conducted by the Western coalition in that country without the Syrian government's approval or UN Security Council's sanction can only be defined as aggression and intervention.
>
> But the example that stands apart from the above events is, of course, the invasion of Iraq without any legal grounds. They used the pretext of allegedly reliable information available in the United States about the presence of weapons of mass destruction in Iraq. To prove that allegation, the US Secretary of State held up a vial with white power, publicly, for the whole world to see, assuring the international community that it was a chemical warfare agent created in Iraq. It later turned out that all of that was a fake and a sham, and that Iraq did not have any chemical weapons. Incredible and shocking but true. We witnessed lies made at the highest state level and voiced from the high UN rostrum. As a result we see a tremendous loss in human life, damage, destruction, and a colossal upsurge of terrorism.

No context, no deconstructing of the unique elements in the build up to these conflicts, no references to who the aggressors were in these conflicts, as for example, when Iraq under a ruthless dictator invaded a sovereign country. The 'vulnerable under threat' narrative develops the polarisation of us and them, in psychological terms self and other. This differentiation, an ideological Markov Blanket, if you will, creates the imperative, a no-choice reaction, to this perceived threat. From Putin's point of view, the external world threatens to breach the skin, and hence an immune reaction is warranted – mobilising the system uniquely enabled to defend against threat. Physical, mental, cultural, geopolitical. The emergent qualities give rise to systems that require defence – aggression in the service of defence, even if nuclear war is the outcome. In other words, sometimes this 'immune' response will activate even if it leads to a form of suicide, or in the Cold War lingo, Mutually Assured Destruction (MAD).

Overall, it appears that nearly everywhere, in many regions of the world where the United States brought its law and order, this created bloody, non-healing wounds and the curse of international terrorism and extremism. I have only mentioned the most glaring but far from only examples of disregard for inter-national law. This array includes promises not to expand NATO eastwards even by an inch. To reiterate: they have deceived us, or, to put it simply, they have played us.

Inch by inch, all over the world, are forces arraigned against the Russians. *They have played us.* Note the humiliation embedded in the narrative. We have been hu-miliated by the West, in their expansionist designs to annihilate the Russian entity and reduce it to a subservient and humiliated pawn of the West, spearheaded by what the Iranian's refer to as 'the Great Satan', the USA.

Sure, one often hears that politics is a dirty business. It could be, but it shouldn't be as dirty as it is now, not to such an extent. This type of con-artist behaviour is contrary not only to the principles of international relations but also and above all to the generally accepted norms of morality and ethics. Where is justice and truth here? Just lies and hypocrisy all around. Incidentally, US politicians, polit-ical scientists, and journalists write and say that a veritable "empire of lies" has been created inside the United States in recent years. It is hard to disagree with this – it is really so. But one should not be modest about it: the United States is still a great country and a system-forming power. All its satellites not only hum-bly and obediently say yes to and parrot it at the slightest pretext but also imitate its behaviour and enthusiastically accept the rules it is offering them. Therefore, one can say with good reason and confidence that the whole so-called Western bloc formed by the United States in its own image and likeness is, in its entirety, the very same "empire of lies."

The Empire of some Great Conspiracy, one might frame it. Whatever merit there is, the cherry picking of detail to support a preconceived narrative of subjective perception and positioning those details into a clustering of themes, provides the authentic foundation from the vantage of the perceived victim, to respond and pro-tect itself. To conserve what it can in the face of grave danger.

As for our country, after the disintegration of the USSR, given the entire un-precedented openness of the new, modern Russia, its readiness to work honestly with the United States and other Western partners, and its practically unilateral disarmament, they immediately tried to put the final squeeze on us, finish us off, and utterly destroy us.

Immediately tried to utterly destroy us. Fascinating inversion of the vast majority of countries around the world seeing Russia as the aggressor, the perpetrator in the Ukrainian invasion. Not so for Putin.

This is how it was in the 1990s and the early 2000s, when the so-called collective West was actively supporting separatism and gangs of mercenaries in southern Russia. What victims, what losses we had to sustain and what trials we had to go through at that time before we broke the back of international terrorism in the Caucasus! We remember this and will never forget.

Properly speaking, the attempts to use us in their own interests never ceased until quite recently: they sought to destroy our traditional values and force on us their false values that would erode us, our people from within, the attitudes they have been aggressively imposing on their countries, attitudes that are directly leading to degradation and degeneration, because they are contrary to human nature. This is not going to happen. No one has ever succeeded in doing this, nor will they succeed now.

Destroy our traditional values and force on us their false values that would erode us, our people from within...Nor will they succeed now!

Despite all that, in December 2021, we made yet another attempt to reach agreement with the United States and its allies on the principles of European security and NATO's non-expansion. Our efforts were in vain. The United States has not changed its position. It does not believe it necessary to agree with Russia on a matter that is critical for us. The United States is pursuing its own objectives, while neglecting our interests. Of course, this situation begs a question: what next, what are we to expect? If history is any guide, we know that in 1940 and early 1941 the Soviet Union went to great lengths to prevent war or at least delay its outbreak. To this end, the USSR sought not to provoke the potential aggressor until the very end by refraining or postponing the most urgent and obvious preparations it had to make to defend itself from an imminent attack. When it finally acted, it was too late.

As a result, the country was not prepared to counter the invasion by Nazi Germany, which attacked our Motherland on June 22, 1941, without declaring war.

An interesting rendering of memory – memory has a critical function related to preservation. When memory fails, so too does survival. *Memory is the unconscious store of subjective perception* (of events), that creates the store against which reality can be checked and navigated. Last time I ate this poison berry, I became sick. Better not do that again. In order to accomplish this task, the mind has to 'go back', that is, to place itself in an old scenario in which ideational stores, ideas are accessed, which can be used to configure current experience. As such, regression in the service of the ego, as Freud put it, becomes the normal method of psychic maintenance. Regression to the old, because in accessing old ideational stores in this timeless mechanism old affects are also triggered, as if they were in the present. Since memories are subjective, individual reactivity to those memories, forged through the subjectivity that is embedded in all living matter, can never be accessed in any objective sense. We can never peer into your 'mind's eye' no matter the technology we may develop in any futuristic scenario. The mind hides her secrets behind a veil inaccessible to any outside observation, except through inference. Says Lane,

> Our life experience is written into synaptic networks, each neurone forming as many as 10,000 different synapses. If the neurone dies by apoptosis. those synaptic connections are lost forever, along with all the experience and personality that might have been written into them. That neurone is irreplaceable.
>
> (p. 256)

This tragic effect for the individual suffering any form of brain insult or degeneration is also the determining factor for the exquisite beauty of subjective experience and its infinite variability that makes people so eternally interesting, novel, and, in an analytic sense, object-seeking. Human love attachments, especially those that are relatively novel, because subjectivity enhances experience through the mosaic of difference, or as the French might suggest, "Viva la difference!". But, and it is a significant reservation, difference also promotes threat in the competition for resources and survival and the drive for preservation can counter this SEEKING system in neuroscience, as Panksepp calls it, with violent effect.

> The country stopped the enemy and went on to defeat it, but this came at a tremendous cost. The attempt to appease the aggressor ahead of the Great Patriotic War proved to be a mistake which came at a high cost for our people. In the first months after the hostilities broke out, we lost vast territories of strategic importance, as well as millions of lives. We will not make this mistake the second time. We have no right to do so.
>
> Those who aspire to global dominance have publicly designated Russia as their enemy. They did so with impunity. Make no mistake, they had no reason to act this way. It is true that they have considerable financial, scientific, technological, and military capabilities. We are aware of this and have an objective view of the economic threats we have been hearing, just as our ability to counter this brash and never-ending blackmail. Let me reiterate that we have no illusions in this regard and are extremely realistic in our assessments.

As for military affairs, even after the dissolution of the USSR and losing a considerable part of its capabilities, today's Russia remains one of the most powerful nuclear states. Moreover, it has a certain advantage in several cutting-edge weapons. In this context, there should be no doubt for anyone that any potential aggressor will face defeat and ominous consequences should it directly attack our country.

Ominous consequences – an implied threat of nuclear retaliation. If we are going to die at the hand of your sword, we will take you down with us.

At the same time, technology, including in the defence sector, is changing rapidly. One day there is one leader, and tomorrow another, but a military presence in territories bordering on Russia, if we permit it to go ahead, will stay for decades to come or maybe forever, creating an ever mounting and totally unacceptable threat for Russia.

Even now, with NATO's eastward expansion the situation for Russia has been becoming worse and more dangerous by the year. Moreover, these past days NATO leadership has been blunt in its statements that they need to accelerate and step up efforts to bring the alliance's infrastructure closer to Russia's borders. In other words, they have been toughening their position. We cannot stay idle and passively observe these developments. This would be an absolutely irresponsible thing to do for us.

Any further expansion of the North Atlantic alliance's infrastructure or the ongoing efforts to gain a military foothold of the Ukrainian territory are unacceptable for us. Of course, the question is not about NATO itself. It merely serves as a tool of US foreign policy. The problem is that in territories adjacent to Russia, which I have to note is our historical land, a hostile "anti-Russia" is taking shape. Fully controlled from the outside, it is doing everything to attract NATO armed forces and obtain cutting-edge weapons.

For the United States and its allies, it is a policy of containing Russia, with obvious geopolitical dividends. For our country, it is a matter of life and death, a matter of our historical future as a nation. This is not an exaggeration; this is a fact. It is not only a very real threat to our interests but to the very existence of our state and to its sovereignty.

We face a mortal threat says Putin. A matter of life or death.

It is the red line which we have spoken about on numerous occasions. They have crossed it.

This brings me to the situation in Donbass. We can see that the forces that staged the coup in Ukraine in 2014 have seized power, are keeping it with the help of ornamental election procedures and have abandoned the path of a peaceful conflict settlement. For eight years, for eight endless years we have been doing everything possible to settle the situation by peaceful political means. Everything was in vain.

As I said in my previous address, you cannot look without compassion at what is happening there. It became impossible to tolerate it. We had to stop that atrocity, that genocide of the millions of people who live there and who pinned their hopes on Russia, on all of us. It is their aspirations, the feelings and pain of these people that were the main motivating force behind our decision to recognise the independence of the Donbass people's republics.

I would like to additionally emphasise the following. Focused on their own goals, the leading NATO countries are supporting the far-right nationalists and neo-Nazis in Ukraine, those who will never forgive the people of Crimea and Sevastopol for freely making a choice to reunite with Russia.

They will undoubtedly try to bring war to Crimea just as they have done in Donbass, to kill innocent people just as members of the punitive units of Ukrainian nationalists and Hitler's accomplices did during the Great Patriotic War. They have also openly laid claim to several other Russian regions.

Interesting that the President of Ukraine in this invasion is himself Jewish – but for Putin the head of "neo-Nazi thuggery" openly imperialistic in their designs and ambitions just like Hitler.

If we look at the sequence of events and the incoming reports, the showdown between Russia and these forces cannot be avoided. It is only a matter of time. They are getting ready and waiting for the right moment. Moreover, they went as far as aspire to acquire nuclear weapons. We will not let this happen.

I have already said that Russia accepted the new geopolitical reality after the dissolution of the USSR. We have been treating all new post-Soviet states with respect and will continue to act this way. We respect and will respect their sovereignty, as proven by the assistance we provided to Kazakhstan when it faced tragic events and a challenge in terms of its statehood and integrity. However, Russia cannot feel safe, develop, and exist while facing a permanent threat from the territory of today's Ukraine.

Let me remind you that in 2000–2005 we used our military to push back against terrorists in the Caucasus and stood up for the integrity of our state. We preserved Russia. In 2014, we supported the people of Crimea and Sevastopol. In 2015, we used our Armed Forces to create a reliable shield that prevented terrorists from Syria from penetrating Russia. This was a matter of defending ourselves. We had no other choice.

The same is happening today. They did not leave us any other option for defending Russia and our people, other than the one we are forced to use today. In these circumstances, we have to take bold and immediate action. The people's republics of Donbass have asked Russia for help.

In this context, in accordance with Article 51 (Chapter VII) of the UN Charter, with permission of Russia's Federation Council, and in execution of the treaties of friendship and mutual assistance with the Donetsk People's Republic and the Lugansk People's Republic, ratified by the Federal Assembly on February 22, I made a decision to carry out a special military operation.

The purpose of this operation is to protect people who, for eight years now, have been facing humiliation and genocide perpetrated by the Kiev regime. To this end, we will seek to demilitarise and denazify Ukraine, as well as bring to trial those who perpetrated numerous bloody crimes against civilians, including against citizens of the Russian Federation.

It is not our plan to occupy the Ukrainian territory. We do not intend to impose anything on anyone by force. At the same time, we have been hearing an increasing number of statements coming from the West that there is no need any more to abide by the documents setting forth the outcomes of World War II, as signed by the totalitarian Soviet regime. How can we respond to that?

The outcomes of World War II and the sacrifices our people had to make to defeat Nazism are sacred. This does not contradict the high values of human rights and freedoms in the reality that emerged over the post-war decades. This does not mean that nations cannot enjoy the right to self-determination, which is enshrined in Article 1 of the UN Charter.

Let me remind you that the people living in territories which are part of today's Ukraine were not asked how they want to build their lives when the USSR was created or after World War II. Freedom guides our policy, the freedom to choose independently our future and the future of our children. We believe that all the peoples living in today's Ukraine, anyone who want to do this, must be able to enjoy this right to make a free choice.

In this context I would like to address the citizens of Ukraine. In 2014, Russia was obliged to protect the people of Crimea and Sevastopol from those who you yourself call "nats". The people of Crimea and Sevastopol made their choice in favour of being with their historical homeland, Russia, and we supported their choice. As I said, we could not act otherwise.

The current events have nothing to do with a desire to infringe on the interests of Ukraine and the Ukrainian people. They are connected with the defending Russia from those who have taken Ukraine hostage and are trying to use it against our country and our people.

I reiterate: we are acting to defend ourselves from the threats created for us and from a worse peril than what is happening now. I am asking you, however hard this may be, to understand this and to work together with us so as to turn this tragic page as soon as possible and to move forward together, without allowing anyone to interfere in our affairs and our relations but developing them independently, so as to create favourable conditions for overcoming all these problems and to strengthen us from within as a single whole, despite the existence of state borders. I believe in this, in our common future.

I would also like to address the military personnel of the Ukrainian Armed Forces.

Comrade officers,

Your fathers, grandfathers and great-grandfathers did not fight the Nazi occupiers and did not defend our common Motherland to allow today's neo-Nazis to seize power in Ukraine. You swore the oath of allegiance to the Ukrainian people and not to the junta, the people's adversary which is plundering Ukraine and humiliating the Ukrainian people.

I urge you to refuse to carry out their criminal orders. I urge you to immediately lay down arms and go home. I will explain what this means: the military personnel of the Ukrainian army who do this will be able to freely leave the zone of hostilities and return to their families.

I want to emphasise again that all responsibility for the possible bloodshed will lie fully and wholly with the ruling Ukrainian regime.

I would now like to say something very important for those who may be tempted to interfere in these developments from the outside. No matter who tries to stand in our way or all the more so create threats for our country and our people, they must know that Russia will respond immediately, and the consequences will be such as you have never seen in your entire history. No matter how the events unfold, we are ready. All the necessary decisions in this regard have been taken. I hope that my words will be heard.

Citizens of Russia,

The culture and values, experience, and traditions of our ancestors invariably provided a powerful underpinning for the well-being and the very existence of entire states and nations, their success and viability. Of course, this directly depends on the ability to quickly adapt to constant change, maintain social cohesion, and readiness to consolidate and summon all the available forces in order to move forward.

We always need to be strong, but this strength can take on different forms. The "empire of lies," which I mentioned in the beginning of my speech, proceeds in its policy primarily from rough, direct force. This is when our saying on being "all brawn and no brains" applies.

We all know that having justice and truth on our side is what makes us truly strong. If this is the case, it would be hard to disagree with the fact that it is our strength and our readiness to fight that are the bedrock of independence and sovereignty and provide the necessary foundation for building a reliable future for your home, your family, and your Motherland.

Dear compatriots,

I am certain that devoted soldiers and officers of Russia's Armed Forces will perform their duty with professionalism and courage. I have no doubt that the government institutions at all levels and specialists will work effectively to guarantee the stability of our economy, financial system and social wellbeing, and the same applies to corporate executives and the entire business community. I hope that all parliamentary parties and civil society take a consolidated, patriotic position.

At the end of the day, the future of Russia is in the hands of its multi-ethnic people, as has always been the case in our history. This means that the decisions that I made will be executed, that we will achieve the goals we have set, and reliably guarantee the security of our Motherland.

I believe in your support and the invincible force rooted in the love for our Fatherland.

Appendix C

Hitler's Speech

Back in the 20th century, Hitler in his (similar) narrative opined:

Don't misunderstand me however. If this revolution was bloodless that was not because we were not manly enough to look at blood. I was a soldier for more than four years in a war where more blood was shed than ever before throughout human history. I never lost my nerve, no matter what the situation was and no matter what sights I had to face. The same holds good for my party colleagues. But we did not consider it as part of the program of the National Socialist Revolution to destroy human life or material goods, but rather to build up a new and better life. And it is the greatest source of pride to us that we have been able to carry through this revolution, which is certainly the greatest revolution ever experienced in the history of our people, with a minimum of loss and sacrifice. Only in those cases where the murderous lust of the Bolsheviks, even after the 30th of January 1933, led them to think that by the use of brute force they could prevent the success and realisation of the National Socialist ideal–only then did we answer violence with violence, and naturally we did it promptly. Certain other individuals of a naturally undisciplined temperament, and who had no political consciousness whatsoever, had to be taken into protective custody; but, generally speaking, these individuals were given their freedom after a short period. Beyond this there was a small number who took part in politics only for the purpose of establishing an alibi for their criminal activities, which were proved by the numerous sentences to prison and penal servitude that had been passed upon them previously. We prevented such individuals from pursuing their destructive careers, inasmuch as we set them to do some useful work, probably for the first time in their lives.

And thus it happens that for the first time it is now possible for men to use their God-given faculties of perception and insight in the understanding of those problems which are of more momentous importance for the preservation of human existence than all the victories that may be won on the battlefield or the successes that may be obtained through economic efforts. The greatest revolution which National Socialism has brought about is that it has rent asunder the veil which hid from us the knowledge that all human failures and mistakes are due to the conditions of the time and therefore can be remedied, but that there is one error which cannot be remedied once men have made it, namely the failure to recognise the importance of conserving the blood and the race free from intermixture and thereby the racial aspect and character which are God's gift and God's handiwork. It is not for men to discuss the question of why Providence created different races, but rather to recognise the fact that it punishes those who disregard its work of creation.

Unspeakable suffering and misery have come upon mankind because they lost this instinct which was grounded in a profound intuition; and this loss was caused by a wrong and lopsided education of the intellect. Among our people there are millions and millions of persons living today for whom this law has become clear and intelligible. What individual seers and the still unspoiled natures of our forefathers saw by direct perception has now become a subject of scientific research in Germany. And I can prophesy here that, just as the knowledge that the earth moves around the sun led to a revolutionary alternation in the general world-picture, so the blood-and-race doctrine of the National Socialist Movement will bring about a revolutionary change in our knowledge and therewith a radical reconstruction of the picture which human history gives us of the past and will also change the course of that history in the future.

The answer which I then gave may be stated under the following headings: The elements of confusion and dissolution which are making themselves felt in German life, in the concept of life itself and the will to national self-preservation, cannot be eradicated by a mere change of government. More than enough of those changes have already taken place without bringing about any essential betterment of the distress that exists in Germany.

How much blood flowed around this destination in vain! How many millions of German men, consciously or unconsciously in the service of this purpose, have gone the bitter road of rapid or painful death for more than a thousand years! How many others were condemned to end life behind fortress and dungeon walls, that they wanted to give to Greater Germany! How many hundreds of thousands have flowed into the wide world as an endless stream of German emigration, driven by distress and anxiety! For decades thinking of the unfortunate homeland, after generations forgetting it. And now, in one year, the realisation of this dream has succeeded. Not without a fight, as thoughtless citizens may believe it.

Before this year of German unification, there are almost two decades of the fanatical struggle of a political idea.

Hitler's narrative continues:

When the rest of the world took away the foreign capital of the German people, when they took all the colonial possessions, the philanthropic considerations of the democratic statesmen apparently had no decisive influence.

Today, I can only assure these gentlemen that, thanks to the brutal education that the democracies have bestowed upon us for fifteen years, we are completely hardened to all sentimental tendencies.

We have seen that, after more than 800,000 children died of hunger and food shortages at the end of the war, almost a million pieces of dairy cows were driven away after the cruel paragraphs of a dictate imposed by the democratic, humane world apostles impose us as a peace treaty.

We have seen that one year after the end of the war, more than one million German prisoners of war were detained without any reason in captivity. We had to endure that far more than one and a half million Germans from their frontier areas were being wrenched from their belongings and whipped almost exclusively with what they carried on their bodies.

We have endured the loss of millions of our fellow citizens without hearing them, or giving them even the slightest chance of further preserving their lives.

I could add dozens of the most gruesome examples to those examples. So stay tuned with humanity. The German people do not want their interests to be determined and governed by a foreign people. France to the French, England to the English, America to the Americans and Germany to the Germans!

Today I want to be a prophet again: If international financial Jewry in and outside Europe should succeed in plunging the peoples once again into a world war, then the result will not be the Bolshevisation of the earth and thus the victory of Judaism, but annihilation the Jewish race in Europe.

For the time of the propagandistic defencelessness of non-Jewish peoples is over. National Socialist Germany and Fascist Italy possess those institutions which, if necessary, may enlighten the world of the nature of a question which is instinctively conscious to many peoples and only scientifically unclear.

At present, Judaism may, in certain states, conduct its incitement under the protection of a press, film, radio propaganda, the theatre, literature, etc., which it holds in its possession. But if this people succeeds again, the masses of millions of peoples should be united To rush for this completely meaningless and only Jewish interests fight, then the effectiveness of an enlightenment will express itself, which is completely succumbed to the Judaism in Germany already in few years.

The peoples no longer want to die on the battlefields to earn this rootless international race in the business of war and satisfy their Old Testament vengeance. On the Jewish slogan 'proletarians of all countries, unite' will win a higher realisation, namely: creating members of all nations, recognise your common enemy!

I've been a prophet in my life very often and was mostly laughed at. At the time of my struggle for power, it was primarily the Jewish people who only accepted my prophecies with laughter. Once in Germany I would take over the leadership of the state and thus of the entire people and then, among many others, the Jewish problem Bring solution. I believe that this laudable laughter, meanwhile, has stifled Judaism in Germany already in the throat.

At that time England was the principal initiator of this struggle, England, which over a period of 300 years, through a continuous succession of bloody wars, subjugated roughly a quarter of the globe. Because at that time it wasn't as if one day a few Indian princes or Indian localities or Indian representatives proceeded to London with the request "Britishers, come to India, reign over us or lead us," but it was the English who went to India and the Indian people did not want the British and tried to get rid of them by force. They forced their way in and could not be gotten rid of through more force. Through the use of force they subjugated this continent of over 380 million people, and kept them subjugated.

Only through force did they make one state after another pay them tribute and taxes. Behind this force, of course, stood the other one, which scents business everywhere where a state of disturbance exists: our international Jewish acquaintances. In this manner England, over a period of a few hundred years, has subjugated the world; and, to make secure this conquest of the world, this subjugation of the people, England endeavours to maintain the so-called balance of power in Europe.

This means in reality that it endeavours to make sure that no European state is able to gain over a certain measure of power and perhaps in this way rise to a leading-role in Europe. What they wanted was a disunited, disintegrated Europe, a Europe all of whose forces completely offset one another.

To reach this goal, England conducted one war after another in Europe. She has seen first its powerful position menaced by Spain. When they had finally conquered Spain, they turned their attentions to the Netherlanders. When Holland seemed to represent no further danger, British hate concentrated itself against France. And when finally France was crushed with the help of all Europe, to be sure, they then imagined that Germany must be, of necessity, the one factor which might possibly be able to unify Europe.

Then it was that the struggle against Germany began, not out of love for the nations or their people, but only in their own most selfish, rational interests, behind which, as previously said, stands the eternal Jewry, which, in every struggle between nations, is capable of making profits and winning wherever there is confusion and wrangling. It is well-known that they have always been the instigators of unrest among the nations…

Acknowledgements

Knowledge, creativity, and discovery, like all things in Nature, grow in a medium that nourishes guides, and facilitates. But like all things in Nature, reality prunes the wild speculations, excesses, and fantasies. We evolve because others have evolved before us, we discover because others have discovered before us, and with a little luck, we create a little more or limp a few steps further. The work and dedication of many *adventurers* of knowledge have invariably cleared the paths and made things so much easier. Wrote Freud, "I am by temperament nothing but a *conquistador* — an adventurer…" who himself built on the hard work of others and whose giant leaps of insight form the foundation of this work. But this book owes a great deal more to a great many on a much more personal level, some of whom have had a direct bearing on what is written here, and some of whom may not even know the part they played in the genesis of these ideas. It certainly takes a village to open the doors to life and I wish to thank those that did so along the way.

Many of those I have encountered along the *trek* have given of their time and knowledge with a great deal of gracious generosity and to all of them I remain professionally indebted. Noleen Loubser and Mike Saling, originally from the University of the Witwatersrand, and the wonderful crew of the University of Natal (Pietermaritzburg), Graham Lindegger, Doug Wassenaar, Bev Killian, Terri Broll, Stuart Anderson, and Vernon Solomon. I also thank the team from the Department of Psychology of the University of the Western Cape, all of whom contributed in their own ways, often without even knowing it. My family of colleagues in the analytic and psychological community in South Africa and abroad who have shared without restraint their ideas and insights across countless meetings, conferences, and reading and peer supervision groups over many decades. I remain particularly indebted to my many colleagues from the various professional groups I have worked with, including the Association of Couple Psychoanalytic Psychotherapists (ACPP), the South African Psychoanalytic Confederation (SAPC), the South African Psychoanalytic Initiative (SAPI) and, in particular, the SAPI Instinct Group (a wonderful incubator of ideas), the South African Psychoanalytic (SAPI) College, the Cape Town Society for Psychoanalytic Psychotherapy (CTSPP), the Mind-body Behavioural Medicine Group, the International Journal Couple and Family Psychoanalysis, and my colleagues on the editorial boards of the Psychoanalytic

Psychotherapy in South Africa journal, the Journal Couple and Family Psychoanalysis, the Bellevue Therapy Centre Peer Supervision Group, and also the band of philosophising gentlemen of the WIMP club, all of whom have contributed to a world of ideas, thinking, shared stories, and the rich challenges that go with rigorous engagement of theory and practice over so many decades.

I also remember Barry Stein, the most perceptive and insightful anti-psychology and anti-psychologist I ever met, whose infectious can-do approach to life kept me endlessly entertained and refuelled, and who taught me the value of not taking oneself too seriously. And so too Simon Nkodi, who survived the torture by men but not by nature.

I have had the privilege of working with some enormously talented colleagues over the years and of having their works both directly and indirectly at hand as stepping stones to greater insights. Occasionally, along the journey of professional life, there are those who stand out significantly and one gets invited to feast at a table of abundant and groundbreaking thinking, ideas, and selfless facilitation. In this case, it was not once-off or even occasional; at the end of a 'long and dusty road' down on the Southern tip of Africa in our own little Garden of Eden, it was over many years that Professor Mark Solms, a world-class academic and *conquistador* in his own right, brought his unfailing generosity of spirit, time, and knowledge to enliven and nourish both the professional community and me personally. Seldom have I encountered someone of his stature willing to give of himself without limits, and never requiring anything at all, literally, in return. To Mark for his generous sharing of knowledge over the years and, on a personal note, his wise counsel in helping this book find a home, my gratitude.

Thanks also to the reviewers of the earlier draft of this manuscript. And a special word of gratitude to the prolific Dr Barnaby Barratt and Dr Amita Sehgal for their support, useful comments on an earlier draft of the manuscript, and encouragement.

The genesis of ideas and writing is seldom smooth sailing. Einstein wrote in the preface to his Theory of Relativity that he had "spared himself no pains in his endeavour to present the main ideas (of his Theory of Relativity) in the simplest and most intelligible form…", and following the theoretical physicist Boltzmann, suggested that "matters of elegance ought to be left to the tailor and to the cobbler".[1] Unfortunately, this gift of simplicity has always escaped my writing. Many years ago, I had an editor of a Psychoanalytic journal take the trouble to come to meet with me to tell me that my writing "went down like lumpy porridge", as he put it. He was right of course. So, to smooth the ingestion and digestion of the complex material of this book, I leaned on my trusted best critic whose talent for simplifying complex theory and research and presenting it to the reader in beautifully digestible ways remains the stuff of personal envy. My journey through life has been immeasurably enriched by my wife Jenny, who is a published author in her own right and so her case is not one of 'the best coaches are in the stands'. Her deft hand has smoothed the way in simplifying the work in this book and hopefully making it so much more accessible to a wider readership than it was in its earlier drafts.

To the Jester and the Butterfly, from whom it all began. And to our Little Mouse, who knows how to roar and has already begun to dent the universe in her own way, my deep gratitude for her endlessly enriching presence. You have made the journey infinitely worthwhile, beyond riches, and perfectly lovely. One day I hope to figure out who raised who.

I am also indebted to Routledge for believing in this project and in particular to Zoë Meyer and Priya Sharma, the Editors of Psychoanalysis and Mental Health Division, whose gracious and complimentary support for this work has been simply wonderful from the outset. Also, many thanks to Sashivadana and her excellent production team for their skilful, and professional copyediting.

Whilst so many people have had a direct or indirect hand in the genesis of the ideas contained in this book, if I were to list them it would prove longer than the book itself. Nonetheless, responsibility for what is written in these pages remains entirely my own. I trust I have captured the essence of others' ideas fairly, wisely, and with appropriate acknowledgement but for any omissions or errors of authors or individuals who I have left out in the text or these acknowledgements, and I suspect there are some, these were not intentional.

Note

1 Einstein, A. (1995). *Relativity*, p. ix.

Bibliography

Barratt, B. (2013). *What Is Psychoanalysis: 100 Years after Freud's 'Secret Committee'*. London: Routledge.

Bion, W.R. (1959). Attacks on linking, *International Journal of Psychoanalysis, 40,* 308–315.

——— (1962). *Learning from Experience*. London: Jason Aronson.

——— (1963). *Elements of Psychoanalysis*, 4: i–iv. William Heinemann Medical Books Ltd., reprinted 1989. London: Karnac.

Boyce, T.W. (2019). *The Orchid and the Dandelion: Why Some Children Struggle and How All Can Thrive*. London: Allen Lane.

Burns, R (1786). *Poems, Chiefly in the Scottish Dialect* (First ed.). Kilmarnock. Retrieved from internet archive, see https://en.wikipedia.org/wiki/Poems,_Chiefly_in_the_Scottish_Dialect#cite_note-1

Cohen, D. (2009). *The Escape of Sigmund Freud*. London: JR Books.

Connolly, P. (2018). Expected free energy formalises conflict underlying defence in Freudian psychoanalysis. *Frontiers in Psychology, 19.* https://doi.org/10.3389/fpsyg.2018.01264.

Darwin, C. (2003). *The Origin of Species: By Means of Natural Selection of the Preservation of Favoured Races in the Struggle for Life*. New York: Signet Classic.

Einstein, A. (1995). *Relativity*. New York: Prometheus Books.

Fisher, J. (1999). *The Uninvited Guest*. London: Karnac.

Fonagy, P., Gergely, G., Jurist, E., & Target, M. (2002). *Affect Regulation, Mentalisation, and the Development of the Self*. New York: Other Press.

Freud, S. (1900). *Letter from Freud to Fleiss, February 1, 1900. The Complete Letters of Sigmund Freud to Wilhelm Fleiss, 1887-1904,* 42: 397–398. Cambridge: Belknap Press.

——— (1911). Formulations on the two principles of mental functioning. In J. Strachey & A. Richards (Eds), *On Metapsychology: The Theory of Psychoanalysis*. London: Penguin.

——— (1914). On narcissism. In J. Strachey & A. Richards (Eds), *On Metapsychology: The Theory of Psychoanalysis*. London: Penguin.

——— (1915a). The unconscious. In J. Strachey & A. Richards (Eds), *On Metapsychology: The Theory of Psychoanalysis*. London: Penguin.

——— (1915b). Instincts & their vicissitudes. In J. Strachey & A. Richards (Eds), *On Metapsychology: The Theory of Psychoanalysis*. London: Penguin.

——— (1915c). Repression. In J. Strachey & A. Richards (Eds), *On Metapsychology: The Theory of Psychoanalysis*. London: Penguin.

————— (1915d). Thoughts for the times on war and death. In J. Strachey & A. D (Eds), *Civilisation, Society and Religion*. London: Penguin.

————— (1917a). Anxiety. In J. Strachey & A. Richards (Eds), *Introductory Lec*.... .. *Psychoanalysis*. London: Penguin.

————— (1917b). Psychoanalysis and psychiatry. In J. Strachey & A. Richards (Eds), *Introductory Lectures on Psychoanalysis*. London: Penguin.

————— (1917c). The paths to the formation of symptoms. In J. Strachey & A. Richards (Eds), *Introductory Lectures on Psychoanalysis*. London: Penguin.

————— (1920). Beyond the pleasure principle. In J. Strachey & A. Richards (Eds), *On Metapsychology: The Theory of Psychoanalysis*. London: Penguin.

————— (1921). Group psychology and the analysis of the ego. In J. Strachey & A. Dickinson (Eds), *Civilisation, Society and Religion: Group Psychology, Civilisation and Its Discontents and Other Works*. London: Penguin.

————— (1923). The ego and the id. In J. Strachey & A. Richards (Eds), *On Metapsychology: The Theory of Psychoanalysis*. London: Penguin.

————— (1924). The economic problem of masochism. In J. Strachey & A. Richards (Eds), *On Metapsychology: The Theory of Psychoanalysis*. London: Penguin.

————— (1926). Inhibitions, symptoms and anxiety. In J. Strachey & A. Richards (Eds), *On Psychopathology*. London: Penguin.

————— (1930). Civilisation and its discontents. In J. Strachey & A. Dickinson (Eds), *Civilisation, Society and Religion: Group Psychology, Civilisation and Its Discontents and Other Works*. London: Penguin.

————— (1933a). Anxiety and instinctual life. In J. Strachey & A. Richards (Eds), *New Introductory Lectures on Psychoanalysis*. London: Penguin.

————— (1933b). Why war? In J. Strachey & A. Dickinson (Eds), *Civilisation, Society and Religion*. London: Penguin.

Grant, T. (2022). *The Mandela Brief: Sydney Kentridge and the Trials of Apartheid*. London: John Murray.

Hopkins, J. (2004). Conscience and conflict: Darwin, Freud, and the origins of human aggression. In D. Evans & P. Cruse (Eds), *Emotion, Evolution and Rationality*. London: Oxford University Press.

Kandel, E. (2006). *In Search of Memory: The Emergence of a New Science of Mind*. New York: WW Norton & Co.

Kershaw, I. (2000a). *Hitler 1889 - 1936: Hubris Volume 1*. London: Penguin Books.

————— (2000b). *Hitler 1936-1945: Nemesis Volume 2*. London: Penguin Books.

Kirchhoff, M., Parr, T., Palacios, E., Friston, K., & Kiverstein, J. (2018). The Markov blankets of life: autonomy, active inference and the free energy principle. *Journal of the Royal Society Interface, 15*(138), 1–11.

Lane, N. (2016). *The Vital Question: Why Is Life the Way It Is?* London: Profile Books.

Lindenfors, P. & Tullberg, B.S. (2011). Evolutionary aspects of aggression the importance of sexual selection. *Advances in Genetics, 75*, 7–22.

Lubbe, T. (2011). *Object Relations in Depression: A Return to Theory*. London: Routledge.

Mandela, N.R. (1994). *Long Walk to Freedom: The Autobiography of Nelson Mandela*. Boston, MA: Little, Brown & Co.

Margaret, M.S. & Gosliner B.J. (1955). On symbiotic child psychosis: genetic, dynamic, and restitutive aspects. *Psychoanalytic Study of the Child, 10*, 195–212.

Mahler, M.S. (1967). On human symbiosis and the vicissitudes of individuation. *Journal of the American Psychoanalytic Association, 15*, 740–763.

Mahler, M., Pine, F. & Bergman, A. (1975). *The Psychological Birth of the Human Infant: Symbiosis and Individuation.* New York: Basic Books.

Mills, J. (2006). Reflections on the death drive. *Psychoanalytic Psychology, 23*(2), 373–382.

Nurse, P. (2020). *What Is Life?* Oxford: David Fickling Books.

Panksepp, J. & Biven, L. (2012). *The Archaeology of Mind: Neuroevolutionary Origins of Human Emotions.* New York: Norton.

Perkel, A. (2004). The first seduction: exploring resistance to the acknowledgement of maternal sexual abuse. *Psycho-analytic Psychotherapy in South Africa, 12*(2), 52–71.

———— (2006). The phallic container in the couple: splitting and diversion of maternal hate as protection of the infant. *Psycho-analytic Psychotherapy in South Africa, 12*(2), 13–38.

———— (2007a). Fusion, diffusion, de-fusion, confusion: exploring the anatomy of the couple psyche. In M. Ludlam & V. Nyberg (Eds), *Couple Attachments: Theoretical and Clinical Studies.* London: Karnac.

———— (2007b). Hate in the phallic container: a reply to long. *Psycho-analytic Psychotherapy in South Africa, 15*(1), 31–38.

———— (2007c). The couple and its instincts. *Psycho-analytic Psychotherapy in South Africa, 15*(2), 38–59.

———— (2008). The phallic container in the post-partum couple: splitting and diversion of maternal hate as protection of the infant. In Sasha Brookes & Andrea Hill (Eds), *Psychoanalytic Perspectives on Couple Work 2008: An International Publication.* London: Society of Couple Psychoanalytic Psychotherapists.

———— (2013a). The immunising function of aggression in the couple. *New Therapist, 91,* 6–13.

———— (2013b). Till death-drive us apart: associating injury and aggression in the couple. *Psychoanalytic Psychotherapy in South Africa, 21*(2), 7–38.

———— (2017). Psychoanalytic couple and family therapy. In J.L. Lebow et al. (Eds), *Encyclopaedia of Couple and Family Therapy.* Springer International Publishing. https://doi.org/10.1007/978-3-319-15877-8_36-1.

Pinker, S. (2011). *The Better Angels of Our Nature: A History of Violence and Humanity.* New York: Penguin.

Rank, O. (1929). *The Trauma of Birth.* London: Routledge.

Schlapobersky, J. (2021). *When They Came for Me: The Hidden Diary of an Apartheid Prisoner.* Cape Town: Jonathan Ball.

Schroeder, G. (1997). *The Science of God: The Convergence of Scientific and Biblical Wisdom.* New York: The Free Press.

Schwab, V.E. (2014). *Vicious.* London: Titan Books.

Shelly, M. (1891, 1918, 1934). *Frankenstein.* London: George Routledge.

Solan, R. (1999). The interaction between self and others: a different perspective on narcissism. *Psychoanalytic Study of the Child, 54,* 193–215.

Solms, M. (2013). The conscious id. *Neuropsychoanalysis, 15,* 5–19.

———— (2017). What is "the unconscious", and where is it located in the brain? A neuropsychoanalytic perspective. *Annals of the New York Academy of Sciences, 1406*(1), 90–97.

———— (2019). The hard Issue on consciousness and the free energy principle. *Frontiers of Psychology, 9.* https://doi.org/10.3389/fpsyg.2018.02714.

——— (2021). *The Hidden Spring: A Journey into the Source of Consciousness*. London: Profile Books.

Winnicott, D.W. (1949). Hate in the counter-transference. *International Journal of Psycho-Analysis, 30*, 69–74.

——— (1975). *Through Paediatrics to Psychoanalysis, Collected Papers*. London: Hogarth Press.

van Wyk, C. (1979). *It Is Time to Go Home*. Johannesburg: AD Donker.

Index

Note: Page numbers followed by "n" denote endnotes.

abstract thinking 21
adaptation and variation 9, 19, 31, 58, 62, 63, 65, 68–71, 100, 144, 150, 152
African National Congress (ANC) 121
Aggett, N. 121
aggression 8, 58–60, 73, 74, 172–174; aims of 11–13; annihilatory threats 79; biology and neuroscience 69; cold predatory 46–48, 83; death drive 141; dynamics of 19, 138; effects of 156, 157; faces of 44–46; feelings and retaliatory 137; function 146, 163; hierarchical 116–117; homeostasis 157; immunity 39–41, 60; infantile 156; innate 11; introjected 160; and loss 158–159; mate selection 11; memory and 28, 35–37, 90, 91; mental and physical systems 91; nature of 6, 8; perversion 31, 113–116, 163; psychic 15, 61, 151; representation 49; restoration 88, 89; scalability of 14, 30, 63, 124, 126, 128, 145; self-destruction 145; self-organising system 147; sexuality 140, 152; theory of 9; unconscious identification 92; and violence 10, 30, 34, 83, 117
aggression-as-conservation theory 72
alpha elements 103–104, 119n38
alpha-function 103, 119n38
Angelou, Maya 15
annihilation 2, 14, 74, 77–79, 124
anxiety 23, 25, 36, 43, 110–112, 160, 161, 164n18
Apartheid 14, 117, 121, 122

Apgar, Virginia 32n5
APGAR score 23, 32n5
Aplysia 21, 98–100
artistic villain 41–44
Atta, Mohamed 5–6, 19

Barnett, David Michael 136
Barratt, B. 50–52
Beer Hall Putsch 1
behaviour therapy 94
beta elements 103, 105, 119n38
Beyond the Pleasure Principle (Freud) 16, 60, 114; aggression, faces of 44–46; aggression is immunity 39–41; artistic villain 41–44; death drive 60; dialectical tension 60; dualistic view 53–55; embodiment and emergent mind 49–51; first drive 51–53; genocide 48–49; homeostasis and quiescence 34; internal perception 35; life and death instincts 34; memory and aggression 35–37; rage and predation 46–48; reality impingements 33; resilience/sensitivity 33–34; the Unconscious 37–39
Big Bang 52, 97, 101
biochemistry 53, 57, 87, 102, 141–143, 154
biological intelligence 12
biology: and neuroscience 69; subjectivity 22, 26, 27, 38, 39, 47, 63, 64, 68–70, 130, 133, 140, 141, 152
Bion, W.R. 103–104, 107–109
body-brain-mind system 152, 155
Botha, P.W. 117, 121–123, 157

Boyce, T. 129
Bundy, Theodore Robert 3–4
Burns, R. 155

Cold War 74, 172, 174
Connolly, P. 144
consciousness 37–38, 64
conservatism mechanism 113
conservative drive 102, 154
conservative instinct 70, 115, 155
cosmological constant 9
counter-cathexis 13
counter-intuitive concept 15
couple conflict 6, 53, 81, 154, 158
cultural identity 31

Darwin, C. 9–11, 18, 30, 31, 61–65,
   67–70, 84n11, 85n17, 87, 100,
   101, 110, 116, 128, 150–152,
   154, 157
death-drive 11, 46, 62, 142, 146,
   154; aggressive response 66;
   conservative template 68, 151,
   165; Eros 141; extrapolation 67;
   Friston's Law 65; function 60;
   homeostasis 67; and life 16–19, 34,
   52, 58, 65, 81, 101, 103; Markov
   blanket 66; mind-body
   system 144
death instinct 17–18, 34, 35, 53, 55n24, 60,
   65, 83, 110, 151–152
defence mechanisms 50, 116
depression 4, 26, 37, 64, 88, 132,
   160, 161
destructiveness 8–10, 14–16, 39–40, 50,
   114, 128, 156
disavowal defence 112
domestic violence 8, 155
drives 11, 17, 25, 58, 79–83, 127–128, 131,
   139–140, 142–144, 158; dialectical
   tension 60; disavowal 112; Eros
   146; feeling states 104; innate 44,
   47, 115; instincts 70, 114, 153;
   levels 41; organic 6; primary 105,
   128, 140, 142; psychic 146, 151,
   154; reality principle vs. pleasure
   principle 101; restoration 89;
   thermo-regulation 59; unconscious
   94; victimhood 156; violent 19; see
   also death-drive
dual-drive theory 81
dualistic view, psychic function 53
Dylan, Bob 63, 115

economics of life 70
ego 25, 42, 50, 53–54, 57, 74–75, 82–83,
   87–90, 93–96, 107, 132, 139, 142,
   148n12, 160
Einstein, A. 7, 9, 97, 98, 110, 114, 115,
   120n51, 140, 150, 186
electrochemical gradients 143
Ellis, Havelock 86
emotional valence 105
empathic collusions 163
energy harvesting 18
entropy 10, 52, 103, 116, 123, 130,
   131, 142, 144, 155–157, 159,
   162; adaptation 152; body-mind
   system 153; chaos 57, 58; and
   dysregulation 151; Friston's
   Free Energy Principle 54, 59; vs.
   homeostasis 98; premature 18, 132;
   prevention 57; risk of 74, 154; self-
   organising principle 57, 86, 124,
   147; vs. synaptic circuits
   27–28
environmental stimulation 27
Eros 10, 33, 34, 54, 60, 61, 65, 68, 87,
   101, 123, 141, 143, 146, 151–152,
   154, 158
evolutionary theory 49, 61, 80
explicit memory 22

feedforward process 93, 109, 110
Filho, Pedro Rodrigues 4–5
First World War 80, 81, 116
fixation psychology 39–41, 44, 89, 113,
   163, 166
Fonagy, P. 103
Frankenstein 2–5
Freud, S. 3, 6, 7, 86, 96–103, 106, 110,
   111, 114–116, 151, 155, 185;
   aggression 8, 9, 11–13, 114;
   Beyond the Pleasure Principle
   33–55; contemporary neuroscience
   93; death drive 16–19, 60;
   destructiveness 8–9, 14–16,
   114; ego 88, 90; empathy 159;
   geopolitics 121–147; human psyche
   57–84, 151; ideology and ideas
   11; libidinal energy 28; life drive
   16–19, 154; life instinct 151–152;
   narcissism 87; polymorphous
   perversity 25–27; proliferation and
   preservation 9–11; psychosexual
   89; regression 176; repetition
   compulsion 24, 92, 107; self-same

mechanism 8; sexual drive 112, 163; stasis and equilibrium 162; symptoms 159–161; thinking process 105; *The Trauma of Birth* 23; the Unconscious 21, 28, 37–39, 92, 93, 108

Friston, K. 144; Free Energy Principle 54, 57, 97, 102, 144

fudge factor 9

genetics and epigenetics 7, 10, 17–18, 31, 52, 64, 65, 68–71, 100, 102, 143, 144, 145, 155

genetic variation 17, 18

genocide 29, 48–49, 178

geo-political data 79, 80, 83, 133, 134

geo-political violence 8, 79, 83, 115, 145–147, 153, 155, 165; concrete acts of 141–142; crime 136–138; personal and political 121–124; scalability 127–128; victimhood 124; victim to perpetrator 124–126

geopolitics: aims and effects 146–147; ANC 121–122; annihilation 124; complexity and survival 144–146; concrete acts of violence 141–142; conscious Id 130–132; conserve attack 132–134; energy of feelings 140–141; first homicide 138–140; Friston's Free Energy Principle 144; ideological surrogates 134–136; internal psychic tensions 128; libidinal energy 142; mental disequilibrium 128–129; mind-body system 143; National Party government 121; orchids and dandelions 129–130; overdetermined 127; scalability of 126–127; somatic regulation and functioning 143; UDF 121; victimhood and narratives 124; victim to perpetrator 124–126; violent crime 136–138; vulnerability perception 123

Grant, T. 14

Great Patriotic War 75, 76, 176, 178

group identity 30, 115–118, 130

Hawking, Stephen 165, 166

hegemonic imperialism 172

Hendel, R. 139

heteronormativity 112

Heydrich, Reinhard 29

Hitler, A. 1, 2, 29, 43, 44, 76–79, 89, 90, 104, 107, 116, 124, 127, 134, 136, 178, 181–184; Stalingrad Speech 2

homeostasis 13, 16, 26, 28, 36, 38, 99, 157; adaptation 143; conservative drive 102; death drive 65–67; defence of 133–134; emergent 54; *vs.* energy 70, 98; entropy prevention 57; equilibrium 12; life drive 151; organismic 17; psychic 58, 59, 163; quiescence 34; restoration 51, 97, 159; self-organising systems 98, 100–101; violation 64; violent disruption 127

homeostatic regulation 131, 140

homicide and suicide 6, 9–10, 14, 31, 74, 79, 117, 138–140, 174

humanity and inhumanity 155–156

human psyche 8–9, 11, 12, 17, 24, 25, 34, 35, 43, 48, 50, 53, 63, 97, 98, 103, 110–112, 133, 141, 151, 159

humiliation 14, 43, 129–130, 173

Id 99–100, 130–133, 140

ideation 28, 82–83, 91–94, 105–108, 127, 130, 135, 176

ideological narratives 73, 124–125, 173

"I" development: abstract thinking 21; explicit memory 22; neurotransmission 21; polymorphous perversity 25–27; preservation 29–31; pure subjectivity 22; symbolic thinking 21; synaptic circuits *vs.* entropy 27–28; trauma 22–25

immune system 16, 39, 40, 48, 51, 59–61, 65, 83, 84, 87, 90, 91, 105, 106, 151, 165

implicit subjectivity 63

infancy and oceanic bliss 87–90

innate instinct 31

inner guardian: aggression 113–116; alpha elements 103–104; *Aplysia* 98–100; despots and dictators 104–105; ego and memory 90; feedforward process 109, 110; Friston's Free Energy Principle 102; group identity and war 116–118; human psyche 110; infancy and oceanic bliss 87–90; Initial Singularity 101; linking 108–109; love and hate 94–96; narcissistic injuries and attacks 86–87; perversity/perversion

105–107, 111–112; primordial soup 96–98; psychic meaninglessness 96–98; regression 107, 108; repetition compulsion and memory 90–94; self-organising systems 100–101; sex 112–113; thinking process 105–107; trauma 108
instinct 16, 115, 120n52, 127, 142–143, 182; conservative 70, 115, 155; death 17–18, 34, 35, 53, 55n24, 60, 65, 83, 110, 151–152; ego 53, 55n24, 87; innate 31; self-preservatory 6, 10; sexual 53, 55n24, 70, 100, 151; symbolisation and diversion 47; unconscious 94; violence 30, 82
intra-psychic symbolic representation 47
intra-species aggression 11

Jewish reconstruction 167–168
Judaism 183

Kandel, E. 21, 22, 27, 28, 38, 68, 91, 93, 98, 99, 134, 135, 140
Kentridge, Sydney 14
Kirchhoff, Michael 53–54, 56n27

Lane, N. 13, 18, 22, 35, 39, 69, 71, 75, 100–102, 104, 112, 142, 152, 154, 155, 176
libidinal 8, 53, 54, 60, 67, 68, 71, 75, 81, 87–89, 94–98, 100–102, 106–108, 126, 141–143, 162
life-drive 6, 11, 16–19, 33, 53, 54, 61–64, 69, 81, 103, 151, 154–157, 159
love and hate 3, 8, 15, 83, 94–96, 114, 160, 162, 184

Mahler, M.S. 35–36, 51, 88, 95
Mandela, N.R. 15
Markov blanket 54–55, 56n27, 65–66, 79, 84, 87, 108, 130, 142, 145, 147, 150, 156–157, 173
meaninglessness 96–98, 103, 104, 107, 109
memory 21–22, 24–28, 64–65, 67–69, 74–77, 87–90, 98–99, 108–110, 148n13, 175–176; and aggression 35–37; consciousness 105; cultural 78; and ego 90; emotional 131; ideation 127; immune system 40, 59, 83; long-term 134, 135; neurological and psychological data 38; primitive 39; psychic

14, 40, 60; regression 107–108; and repetition compulsion 90–94; sexual abuse 134; short-term 134; unconscious 84, 108, 129, 140, 145, 146; undifferentiated and differentiated experience 104
mental disequilibrium 128–129
Mills, J. 52, 60–61, 87
moral emotions 11
mortality and morbidity 36, 59
Mutually Assured Destruction (MAD) 74, 174

narcissism 42, 60–61, 86–89, 93, 95, 96, 107, 132; injuries and attacks 86–87, 89
National Socialism 181–182
natural selection 62–63, 100
neo-Nazi thuggery 76
neural circuits, memory 27
neural memory 25
neuroplasticity 106
neuropsychoanalysis 9, 24, 46, 51, 66–67, 134
neuroscience 9, 46, 47, 49–50, 59, 89, 93, 94, 131, 133–135, 140, 152, 166, 176
neurotransmission 21
Nurse, P. 66, 99–100, 103, 106, 130

Oedipus Rex 3
orchids and dandelions 129–130
organismic distress 36

Panksepp, J. 33, 46, 47, 54, 77, 80, 82–84, 93, 144, 176
perpetrators 161; aggression 77, 153, 154; human destructiveness 156; Ukrainian invasion 74, 175; victim 2, 4–5, 72, 116–118, 122, 124–126, 128, 137, 145–146, 157, 163
perversion 60, 127, 128, 156, 163, 166; of aggression 31, 113–116, 124, 126, 130, 146, 147, 165; of inner guardian (see inner guardian); of sexuality 124, 146; strain of 147
physical injuries 14
polymorphous perversity 25–27
pornography 3
post-partum depression 88
Post-traumatic Stress Disorder (PTSD) 64, 66–67, 108, 157, 160

preservation 181; *vs.* adaptation 63–64; "I" development 29–31; mind-body system 27; and proliferation 9–11; service of 29–31; war of 79
primordial soup 98
projection as defence 81–84
psychic disequilibrium 88
psychic immunity 40, 58–60, 91, 158
psychic meaninglessness 96–98
psychic superfluousity 13
psychoanalysis 9, 41, 60, 87, 94, 95, 98, 107–108, 120n52, 133, 139, 185–186
psychological attitude 86
psychological distortions 4
psychopathology 7, 9, 36, 50, 86, 91, 148n12, 159, 160, 163
Putin, Vladimir 72–77, 79, 83, 89, 90, 104, 114, 116, 124–126, 171–180
puzzling phenomenon 2

rage and predation 46–48
RAGE system 46–47
Rank, O. 23–24
reaction-formations 115, 120n52, 132
realpolitik 80
Red Army 1
regression 39, 41, 44, 75, 83, 98, 126, 156, 176; conscious Id 130; feedforward process 109–110; linking 108–109; in psychoanalysis 107–108
repetition compulsion 24, 35, 39, 90–94, 107, 153, 156
resilience/sensitivity 33–34
resource acquisition 11
Russia 72–76, 125, 171, 172, 174–180

scalable aggression and specicide 10, 30, 31, 145
Schroeder, G. 67–69
Schwab, V.E. 5
Second World War 43, 125
SEEKING system 46–47, 54, 83, 176
self-governing system 26
self-organising 26, 48, 62, 65, 97, 98, 100–102, 106, 107, 116, 130, 131, 139, 140, 144, 145, 151, 153, 155; cells 49; complexity levels 54; entity 57, 86; entropy 147; group/collectives 123
self-preservation 6, 61, 77; egoism 87
self-replicating organisms 17
self-same mechanism 8

serial killers 2, 4, 128, 129, 137
sex 18, 70–71, 111–113, 135, 152
sexual drive 18, 40, 112, 113, 160, 163
Shelly, M. 2, 3
social anxiety 120n49
Solms, M. 25, 26, 37, 54, 57, 58, 63, 65, 67, 82, 86, 90, 93, 99, 100, 102–104, 107, 109, 129–133, 135, 139, 140, 143, 148n12, 154, 186
somatic immunity 40, 50
South Africa: history of 123, 153, 156; and revolution 157
Stalingrad Speech (Hitler) 2
stress 54, 129, 161
subjectivity biology 22, 26, 27, 38, 39, 47, 63, 64, 68–70, 130, 133, 140, 141, 152
sucking reflex 50
superego 164n18
symbolic thinking 21
symptoms 8, 9, 26, 50, 66–67, 165; enactments 165; unifying theory 150–164
synaptic circuits 27–28
systemic conflicts 53, 67, 81, 103, 144, 165
system unconscious 90, 93, 129, 140

temperament 33–34, 93, 97–98, 110, 129, 130, 181, 185
theological narratives 139
Third Reich 1

the Unconscious 21, 37–39, 92, 93, 108
unifying theory: aggressive system 156; body-brain-mind system 152, 155; conservative drive 154; couple relations 161–163; death instinct 151–152; defensive mechanisms 153; destruction 156–157; empathic collusions 163; entropy 153; humanity and inhumanity 155–156; loss and aggression 158–159; Markov blanket 150; natural selection 150; psychotherapy failure 163–164; self-preservation 152; South Africa and revolution 157; stress and the agent provocateur 161; subjectivity 154; symptoms 159–161; *The Uninvited Guest* 162; victim, behind perpetrator 158
United Democratic Front (UDF) 121

victimhood: aggression perceptions 116; destructiveness 156; and narratives 124; Nazis and perceptions 77–81, 83; oppression 1; perverse projections 114; violence 126, 165
victims and villains 2, 5, 6, 43, 124, 153
violent offenders 4

Wannsee Conference 29, 30, 44–45, 49, 167–170
war 1, 2, 6, 29–30, 78, 179, 181, 183, 184; Cold 74, 90, 172, 174; Europe 72; First World War 80, 81, 116; German 49; Great Patriotic 75, 76, 176, 178; group identity 116–118; group psychology 81; imperialist 73, 172; Nazi regime 31; nuclear 74, 174; preservation 79–80; prevention 175; prosecution of 126; resource hungry system 71; Second World War 43, 125; South African civil 123; violent aggression 83, 115; wage 79–80
Winnicott, D. 8, 36, 88, 95, 104, 107, 118n24